ADVANCED PROGRAMMING

COMPUTER SCIENCE SERIES

COMPUTER SCIENCE SERIES

ADVANCED PROGRAMMING

Programming and Operating Systems

Harry Katzan, Jr.
Pratt Institute

VAN NOSTRAND REINHOLD COMPANY
New York   Cincinnati   Toronto   London   Melbourne

Van Nostrand Reinhold Company Regional Offices:
New York   Cincinnati   Chicago   Millbrae   Dallas

Van Nostrand Reinhold Company Foreign Offices:
London   Toronto   Melbourne

Library of Congress Catalog Card Number: 78-108648

Manufactured in the United States of America

Published by Van Nostrand Reinhold Company
450 West 33rd Street, New York, N.Y. 10001

Published simultaneously in Canada by
D. Van Nostrand Company (Canada), Ltd.

15 14 13 12 11 10 9 8 7 6 5 4 3 2

To Margaret, Kathy, and Karen

PREFACE

This book presents an introduction to advanced concepts in computer programming. The reader is assumed to be familiar with the field of programming and to have had experience with at least one higher-level programming language, such as FORTRAN or ALGOL. He should have been exposed to an assembler language of some kind and possess a reasonable amount of mathematical maturity; however, a formal background in mathematics or science is certainly not required.

The book is an outgrowth of a series of first-year graduate courses on the same subject, given at Pratt Institute in Brooklyn, New York. Most of the students were employed in computer technology while taking the course; this has given the material an "industrial flavor" and has preserved the practicality of the topics covered. The book is intended to be used in the following situations:

1. In an advanced undergraduate course in Computer Science for students who have completed a first course in basic programming. When used for this purpose, the course should include a practical programming project, and the text should be supplemented by manuals for the particular computer used.

2. As an introduction to Computer Science at the graduate level. Used in this way, the book provides a valuable introduction to the remainder of the graduate Computer Science curriculum. In this context, it is recommended that less emphasis be placed on a programming project and more on an in-depth paper, investigating some topic in the field.

3. As a professional developmental text for programmers, analysts, and managers employed in the field of computers and data processing. The objective here is to provide a background and frame of reference from which the current literature can be read and understood.

The text is composed of two major sections as follows:

Part I, entitled "Programming Systems," is the core of the material. It covers assembler programs and symbol tables; string manipulation and the SNOBOL language; basic compiler methods; grammars, syntax representation, syntax encoding and recognition, and syntax-checking algorithms; list processing concepts, the LISP language, and list processing in PL/I; the structure of computer languages, macros, and the compile-time facilities in PL/I; advanced concepts in compiler design; and decision-logic tables.

It is recognized that all of the topics will not be new to every reader; however, the wide variety of topics covered should compensate for individual differences in background, which occur when a field such as computer science draws people from other disciplines. *No topic is completely exhausted by this treatment.* It is expected that some topics will be supplemented by references to the literature or from the experience of the participants, and others will be omitted as required.

Part II, entitled "Operating Systems," supplements and provides background material for Part I. It contains two chapters: an introduction to the structure of operating systems covering basic functions, the user environment, and the structure and operation of control programs; and time-sharing systems design philosophy, including a discussion of the various types of systems, virtual memory and paging, and the sharing of programs and data.

Although the material on the structure of operating systems is not new, it has not been previously presented as a unified topic. The chapter on time-sharing systems is included because of its current popularity and because it provides a setting for the chapter on advanced compiler design contained in Part I.

Obviously, each of these topics is a field in itself. A brief exposure to them early in one's career, however, is of great benefit in cultivating an interest in the fundamentals of programming theory. Each of the chapters is self-contained and easily accessible to the advanced undergraduate.

The text draws heavily from examples written in the "popular" programming languages. FORTRAN is used throughout; ALGOL is used with the study of algorithmic languages; COBOL is used with syntactical methods; and PL/I is used in discussing list processing and compile-time facilities. As a consequence, four appendices are included, each of which is devoted to a presentation of one of the above languages. It is hoped that these appendices would serve as an added benefit and as a source of reference for the reader.

The material in this book supports the Computer Science curriculum recommended in the March, 1968 issue of the *Communications of the ACM*. On the other hand, the method of organization and presentation has been left to the freedom of the instructor to draw from his background as desired.

I am indebted to: my students in CS 501 at Pratt; Professor Tamas I.

Bartha, director of the computer education and research center at Pratt, for the opportunity to teach 501 the necessary number of times; Professor John A. N. Lee of the University of Massachusetts for valuable comments and suggestions; and my wife Margaret for typing and retyping the manuscript.

White Plains, New York   Harry Katzan, Jr.
January 1, 1970

CONTENTS

ADVANCED PROGRAMMING

PART ONE:
PROGRAMMING SYSTEMS

1 | INTRODUCTION

The essence of computer programming is the encoding of algorithms for subsequent execution on automatic computing machines. The notion of an algorithm is one of the basic ideas in mathematics and has been known and used since antiquity.

> An *algorithm* is a list of instructions specifying a sequence of operations which will give the answer to any problem of a given type.

Algorithms have several properties of interest: 1. In general, the number of operations which must be performed in solving a particular problem is not known beforehand; it depends on the particular problem and is discovered only during the course of computation; 2. The procedure specified by an algorithm is a deterministic process which can be repeated successfully at any time and by anyone; it must be given in the form of a finite list of instructions giving the exact operation to be performed at each stage of the calculations; and 3. The instructions comprising an algorithm define calculations which may be carried out on any appropriate set of initial data and which, in each case, give the correct result. In other words, an algorithm tells how to solve not just one particular problem, but a whole class of similar problems.

The design of modern computing machines parallels the algorithmic nature of most practical applications. The computer operates under control of a series of instructions which reside in internal storage and are interpreted and executed by the circuitry of the arithmetic and control parts of the machine. The instructions are usually primitive in nature, each being composed basically of an operation and one or more operands or modifiers, and exist in a form chosen for the internal representation of data. Machine instructions which exist in this form are said to be in *machine language*, since they are numerically coded and directly executable by a specific computer.

Similar to both an algorithm and a sequence of machine language instructions is the concept of a computer program (usually referred to as a program), which can be defined as follows:

> A *program* is a meaningful sequence of statements, possessing an implicit or explicit order of execution, and specifying a computer-oriented representation of an algorithmic process.

Statements, in turn, are strings of symbols from a given alphabet, composed of letters, digits, and special characters. The form of each statement obeys a set of rules (*syntax*) and possesses an operational meaning (*semantics*). Collectively, the alphabet, syntax, and semantics are termed a *language*. Clearly, a machine language has an alphabet of internal machine codes, a primitive syntax of operations, operands, and modifiers, and semantic rules determined by the circuitry of the machine. Although machine languages provide for economy of construction, they are usually inconvenient for direct human use for a variety of reasons. The set of basic operations provided is not, in general, directly suited to the execution of commonly needed procedures, and the representation of operands, i.e., numeric addresses, affords little mnemonic advantage. The mechanics of constructing programs are also cumbersome in that all constituents of the program must be written in some numeric code, and all addresses written in this code must be absolutely defined. This poses problems in transforming the coded instructions into a machine-readable form, in reading a program into the computer for execution, and finally in modifying programs and in combining separate programs.

As a result of these inherent difficulties, *programming languages* and *operating systems* have been developed which significantly reduce the inconveniences involved with the programming of computers.

1.1 PROGRAMMING LANGUAGES

It is entirely possible, on the other hand, to define languages for computer programming with the following advantages: 1. They are more suitable for human use than machine languages; 2. They tend to be associated in some sense with the problems under consideration; and 3. They are designed to facilitate computer programming. As in ordinary mathematical notation, rules are required for representing data, for naming and referencing data (*variables*), and for specifying operations (*operators*). Moreover, these program constituents are referred to symbolically, rather than in a form more closely related to machine language. For this reason, programming languages are often called *symbolic languages*, although this terminology is usually reserved for assembler languages which will be discussed shortly. One of the features that promulgated the widespread acceptance of programming languages is the fact that computer programs written in this more convenient form could be translated to machine language or to a form closely akin to machine language by another computer program running on the same or possibly a different machine. One of the significant aspects of the philosophy behind the use of programming languages and translation programs is the fact that the same machine may process programs written in many different languages, provided that a translator program is available for each language.

Assembler Language

The most primitive type of programming language is known as *assembler language*, which provides commands or operations that are very similar to the machine language of the computer being programmed. Operation codes, which are expressed numerically in machine language, may be represented by symbolic equivalents (often called mnemonics); similarly, symbols are also used to represent locations in main storage. It follows, therefore, that storage locations and modifiers which are used in computer instructions may also be denoted symbolically. An assembler language also contains facilities for establishing constants and storage areas, for communicating with the assembler program itself, and possibly for incorporating sets of standard instruction sequences into the machine language text. A very basic syntax is used with assembler languages with each line of coding being composed of two basic fields: the statement field and the identification-sequence field. It follows that a statement in assembler language consists of one to four entries in the statement field. As described in chapter 2, they are, from left to right: location, operation, operand, and comments; the coding form for assembler language programming is designed accordingly.

If the assembler language is used in conjunction with a one-address computer, then the operand field tends to reflect this design. This is also true for multiple address machines and machines with many accumulators. Because of the close correspondence between assembler language and actual machine language, the translation process is not considered to be a major task.

Procedure-Oriented Languages

Just as assembler languages tend to parallel the computer for which they are developed, *procedure-oriented languages* are usually related to a class of problem types.* FORTRAN, for example, has become a widely accepted programming language for the coding of mathematical applications. A similar but more sophisticated programming language is ALGOL, which has received recognition as a means of expressing computational algorithms without ambiguity. Both of the above languages are mathematical in nature and are intended for use by the scientific community. The commercially-oriented language COBOL, on the other hand, was developed for the business community as a subset of normal English and facilitates the programming of record keeping and file processing applications.

The above examples are characteristic of a class of programming languages which are more suitable for human use than assembler or machine language but are not similar in syntax to that accepted by the circuitry of the computer on which the programs are to be run. In fact, the syntax and semantics of these languages are inclined to be very sophisticated, making the translation to machine language a complex process.

A Comparison of Assembler and Procedure-Oriented Languages

Although locations, operations, and operands are, for the most part, referenced symbolically, assembler languages in general have the overwhelming characteristic that one machine instruction is generated for each line of coding. For each statement written in a procedure-oriented language, many machine instructions are usually generated. Syntax is another major difference, as indicated in the preceding paragraphs. The most significant difference, however, is the complexity of the translator needed to convert programs written in source language† to a suitable machine language form. This translation process is covered in more detail in the next section and in the chapters that follow.

Problem-Oriented Languages

Although procedure-oriented languages may be viewed as problem-oriented in that they tend to be used for certain classes of applications, the term *problem-oriented* is usually reserved for languages restricted to the description of specialized problems. These languages often adopt specific phrases and keywords from the standard vocabulary of the prospec-

---

*The most noteworthy exception to this is IBM's newest language PL/I which is proposed to be a general programming language (see Appendix D).

†The term *source language* is used collectively to refer to programs not written in machine language and which require translation to machine language or require interpretation and immediate execution by specially prepared program. A *source program*, therefore, is a program as it exists in a source language.

tive user and, as a result, are commonly interpretively translated and executed. Some familiar examples are COGO, STRESS, and ECAP. The subject of interpreters is covered in the following section on metaprograms.

1.2   METAPROGRAMS

Any given algorithm may be programmed in a number of programming languages. In many cases, a specific language may be appropriate for the description of a given application but inappropriate for execution on a computer or even for the optimization of subsequent execution-time. The process of translating from one language form to another is of interest, therefore, particularly when it involves translation programs from source language to machine language.

Translators and Interpreters

A computer program which operates on programs as data is termed a *metaprogram.** An element of the set of inputs to the metaprogram is termed an *argument program*. If the set of outputs of a metaprogram is also comprised of programs, then the metaprogram is called a *translator*, and an element of the output set is termed a *function program*. Thus, a translator accepts argument programs as data and produces function programs as output.

Three main types of translators are identified: compilers, assemblers, and interpreters. A *compiler* accepts programs expressed in a given language, i.e., the *argument language*, and produces corresponding programs expressed in a second language, i.e., the *function language*.

An *assembler* is a special case of a compiler where: 1. the statements of the argument program are relatively independent; and 2. the statements of the argument program are primitive, in that they need not be analyzed into component statements. Since a fixed correspondence usually exists between symbolic instructions and actual machine instructions and between symbolic locations and addresses, translation essentially consists of a substitution of numeric values for symbolic operations or operands.

An *interpreter* is a special case of a translator where no function program is produced. The function program is normally generated only as an intermediate result and is discarded after it has been executed by the interpreter. The execution of an interpreter usually proceeds as follows: each statement in the argument language is first translated to an intermediate function language, is then *interpreted* in that language, and is

---

*A more common name is *language translator*, which has been adopted by several computer manufacturers and applications groups.

finally executed. Only the results of the executed statement are retained. It follows that statements from the argument program are selected for processing by the interpreter in a sequence determined by the execution of preceding statements.

Clearly, the objective of an assembler metaprogram is to produce machine language function programs. Although the majority of compiler metaprograms also produce machine language function programs, they are not so restricted by definition. In fact, many compilers do produce assembler language function programs. The question tends to be one of economics rather than one of basic philosophy.

Metaprogramming Languages

Most computer applications require mainly a combination of mathematical, file processing, and retrieval techniques. Accordingly, these facilities are well ingrained in most procedure-oriented languages. Metaprograms, however, tend to involve character manipulation, table construction and searching, and various types of error analysis. For this purpose, most procedure-oriented languages are either inconvenient or inefficient for programming metaprograms. Therefore, most metaprograms are coded in assembler language. Several problem-oriented languages, more suitable to the requirements of metaprogramming, have been developed and are generally available. Two of them: SNOBOL, a character manipulation language, and LISP, a list-processing language, are particularly attractive to our needs from both educational and practical points of view and are covered in later chapters.

1.3   OPERATING SYSTEMS

An *operating system* is an integrated set of control programs and processing programs designed to maximize the overall operating effectiveness of a computer system. The first operating systems increased system performance by simplifying the operations side of the system. Current operating systems additionally attempt to maximize the use of hardware resources as well as provide a multitude of programmer services.

The operating system operates under the direction of user-prepared control cards, which enable it to call any required program or language translator and to pass automatically from job to job with minimum delay and operator intervention. This is accomplished by designing the system so that it can stack jobs for continuous processing, thereby reducing the setup time between jobs. User communication with the computer is via the operating system, instead of directly, as was previously the case.

The design of modern computers also permits certain hardware devices to be operated simultaneously. An obvious example of this is the input/output-compute overlap available on most computers. Operating systems are designed to utilize this capability for scheduling tasks so as to maximize system throughput. When used in an optimum manner, direct-access storage devices also provide a data management capability previously unrecognized. Most data management systems are available only with a comprehensive operating system.

Control Programs

Control programs monitor the operation of the entire system, supervise the execution of the processing programs, control the location and storage of data, and select jobs for continuous processing. The set of functions performed by the control programs are separated into three categories: 1. System Management functions, 2. Data Management functions, and 3. Job Management functions. *System Management* handles all actual input/output operations, interrupt conditions, and requests for the allocation of system resources. It also controls the stacking of jobs for continuous processing and maintains sequential and priority job schedules which control the execution of the processing programs. *Data Management* handles the cataloging of data sets,* the allocation of space on external storage devices, the building of program libraries, and the coordination of input/output activity between problem programs and the necessary system management functions. *Job Management* reads and interprets user control cards, readies programs for execution, monitors the execution of processing programs, and provides a variety of system services.

Collectively, it is the control programs which tie the rest of the system together and permit the maximum use of a central computer facility capable of servicing many users.

Processing Programs

Processing programs consist of language translators, system service programs, and user-written problem programs. The programmer uses these programs to specify the work that the computing system is to perform and to aid in program preparation. *Language translators* were discussed previously as metaprograms and are defined as routines which accept statements in a programming language and produce equivalent programs in a target language.† *System service programs* include the utility programs‡

---

*The term *data set* refers to a collection of data on external storage, such as tape or disk, regardless of whether the information is organized sequentially or in some "random" fashion.

†It should be recognized that not all language translators produce machine language programs. For example, many compilers for higher level languages produce assembler language programs.

‡Utility programs differ widely in scope and complexity. Some common examples are stand-alone storage print, tape copy, and direct-access storage device initialization.

available with any system, as well as standard applications packages such as Sort/Merge and Mathematical Programming. A comprehensive operating system also supports the generation, storing, and sharing of *user-written programs*, especially those in which well-defined programming standards were employed. Computer users develop many programs to solve specific problems; some of these routines are useful to others with similar problems. Therefore, programming conventions are desirable if programs are to be interchanged among several users, especially on a dynamic basis using program library facilities of an operating system.

PROBLEMS

1.1 Many different types of programs exist: urban development programs, traffic safety programs, computer programs, etc. Distinguish between computer programs and the others.

1.2 Consider the higher level programming language facilities required by a particular application, along with the facilities usually available in a general programming language. In what way can the language be extended so as to be more appropriate for that application?

1.3 Survey the operating environment in your installation. In what way can the operating system be modified so that it meets your needs more precisely?

REFERENCES

1. Brooks, F. P., and K. E. Iverson, *Automatic Data Processing*, New York, John Wiley and Sons, Inc., 1963. Introduces computing fundamentals, machine language programming, and system organization.

2. Hellerman, H., *Digital Computer System Principles*, New York, McGraw-Hill Book Co., 1967. Relates software fundamentals and programming concepts to hardware systems and devices.

3. Lee, J. A. N., *The Anatomy of a Compiler*, New York, Reinhold Publishing Corp., 1967. Presents an introduction to programming systems and languages from the point of view of the compiler writer.

2 | ASSEMBLER PROGRAMS AND SYMBOL TABLES

The principal objective of an assembler program is to translate programs written in a symbolic machine language* into the more precise numeric language of the computer. In addition to being able to specify machine operation codes symbolically, the programmer is permitted to represent numerically addressed storage locations in the computer by alphameric symbols of his own choosing, to define constants and data areas, and to control the operation of the assembler program itself. The assembler program translates symbolic instructions into machine instructions, assigns storage locations, and performs the auxiliary functions necessary to generate an executable machine language program.

In translating a symbolic program into a machine language program, it is necessary that the assembler† construct and use tables of symbols defined by the programmer. This tends to be an important topic in the development of language translators and contributes to the execution-time efficiency of the translator program itself. Since "The Construction and Use of Symbol Tables" is of more general interest, it is included as a special section in this chapter, recognizing that the methods apply to compilers as well.

---

*Called assembler language (see chapter 1).
†The word *assembler* is an accepted abbreviation for the words *assembler program*.

2.1   TYPES OF INSTRUCTIONS

Basic to the assembly process is a determination of the instructions to be assembled. They are generally divided into three categories: machine instructions, assembler instructions, and macro instructions.

Machine Instructions

Actual machine instructions are represented symbolically as assembler language statements. The symbolic format of a machine instruction is similar to, but not identical to, its actual format, which has been built into the circuitry of the machine. Most machine instructions require one or more entries in the operand field, and these operands differ depending upon the functioning of the hardware. Many assembler languages also provide extended operation codes for the convenience of the programmer. An *extended operation code* specifies a special case of a standard machine instruction; use of an extended code permits the operand field to be simplified during assembler language programming. For example, the family of branch instructions, i.e., branch, branch on plus, branch on minus, branch on equal, etc., often corresponds to a single machine instruction which uses mask bits for decision making.

Assembler Instructions

Similar to the manner in which machine instructions request the computer to perform a sequence of operations during the execution of a program, assembler instructions request that the assembler perform certain operations during assembly. Statements containing assembler instructions, in contradistinction to those containing machine instruction codes, do not always cause actual machine instructions to be generated in the assembled code. Modern assemblers have very sophisticated *assembler instruction* repertoires. They relate not only to the assembler program but also to the operating system and the computer configuration. From a general point of view, four classes of assembler instructions are of interest: 1. symbol definition instructions; 2. data definition instructions; 3. listing control instructions; and 4. program control instructions.

   Symbol definition instructions allow symbols to be assigned specific values or to be made equivalent to existent symbols. *Data definition* instructions are used to introduce data into the program in any one of a variety of formats and to define storage areas for later use. These facilities are also used in combination to generate tables of data. *Listing control* instructions are used to prepare the printout of the program itself. These instructions may be used to identify the assembly listing, to provide blank lines in the listing, and to designate how much detail is to be included. *Program control* instructions are used to control the manner in which the program is assembled by the assembler. More specifically, this group of instructions deals with specifying the end of assembly, modifying the location counter,* inserting previously written code in the program, specifying the placement of literals in storage, sequence checking of statements, and indicating the statement format.

Macro Instructions

Many assembler languages provide macro capabilities for simplifying the programming process and for insuring that standard sequences of instructions are used when required. A *macro instruction* is the invocation of a predefined sequence of source statements through use of a mnemonic operation code that has been declared for that purpose. The macro operation code may be determined by the programmer, along with the sequence of statements that the operation represents, or it may be from a library of macros maintained by the installation and stored as part of the operating system.

2.2   THE ASSEMBLY PROCESS

In translating a program from assembler language to machine language, the assembler must perform some well-defined functions. They are listed as follows: syntax analysis, macro instruction processing, maintenance of the location counter, and the synthesis of machine instructions. These functions exist, irrespective of the overall logic of the assembler, and are described in general terms below.

Syntax Analysis

In writing an assembler language statement, the programmer is required to follow certain rules with regard to separation of fields, placement of symbols and delimiters, and the choice of operation codes. These rules relate to the statement field of a line of coding which is divided into four entries: location, operation, operand, and comments. The mechanical inspection of the source statement to determine whether the rules have been observed is called *syntax analysis* and is the first operation performed by the assembler on each statement. This analysis tends to be time consuming, since the statement is usually scanned on a character-by-character basis. Therefore, many assemblers extract the pertinent information from a statement and convert it into a convenient internal form during this process.

The *value* of a symbol, i.e., that which is found in the location field of an assembler statement, must be known before the assembler can construct a

---

*To be discussed in subsequent sections.

machine instruction which utilizes it. If the statements are analyzed in a linear fashion, reference may be made to a symbol before it is defined. As a result, the assembler must postpone construction of a machine instruction until the entire program has been syntactically analyzed and all symbols have been defined and entered into a symbol table. Usually, the symbol table is built during the syntax-analysis process.

Macro Instruction Processing

The assembler's symbol table cannot be considered complete until the sequence of statements represented by macro instructions has been syntactically analyzed. Macro instruction sequences may be processed in one of three ways: 1. prior to analyzing the user's statements, i.e., by searching the program for macro instructions only and merging their instructions with the user's statements; 2. concurrently with the user's statements, i.e., expand the macros as they are encountered; and 3. after the user's statements have been analyzed. Usually a choice of the three alternatives is based on facilities available with the operating system. Macro expansion also involves the recognition of macro parameters, which are known from the macro definition. Since these are only temporary symbols, it is advantageous to record them in a separate symbol table. Macros may also be nested, requiring levels of symbol tables; however, these can often be maintained by using push-down-stack logic.

Maintenance of the Location Counter

One of the major advantages of symbolic programming is the capability of addressing other statements symbolically, i.e., by name instead of by numeric address. Before actual machine language instructions can be synthesized, however, symbolic operands must be replaced by physical storage addresses. The substitution of values for symbols is made practicable with a programming concept termed a location counter, which is introduced in the following paragraphs.

The categorization of instructions must again be considered. Clearly, all macros eventually expand into machine or assembler instructions. Conceptually, they may be viewed in this manner, regardless of when the macros are expanded by the macro instruction processor. Of particular interest are the instructions which generate actual machine instructions, define constants, or reserve storage. Machine instructions and data definition instructions, as defined previously, do so and are termed *generative instructions*. Other instructions are called *nongenerative instructions* and do not occupy physical locations in the resultant machine language program.

Before actual machine language instructions and constant areas can be constructed, the storage address which each location symbol represents must be determined. This is achieved by maintaining a *location counter* for the assembly. The counter is simply a storage area within the assembler which is set to zero initially and is increased by the amount of machine storage required by each generative instruction, as the source program is processed linearly. Whenever appropriate, a machine address is entered into a symbol table so as to correspond with its associated program symbol.

The Synthesis of Machine Instructions

Machine instruction synthesis is achieved by scanning the program, whether it be in statement format or tabular form, and by replacing operation codes and programmer-defined symbols with their respective numeric values. Programmer symbols can be found in the symbol table built by the assembler; similarly, operation codes are predefined and exist in a table internal to the assembler.

2.3   OPERATION OF THE ASSEMBLER

The translation from assembler language to machine language is performed, conveniently, in two passes over the entire program. Assemblers incorporating more than two passes do exist; however, the basic elements of the process seem to be most clearly exhibited in two passes.

Assembler Pass One

The major function of pass one of the assembler is to build a *symbol table* containing programmer-defined symbols and corresponding addresses which have been determined by the assembler. In so doing, it maintains a location counter, which is incremented by the length attribute of each generative instruction as it is processed. Whenever a symbol is recognized in the location field of a generative instruction, it is assigned the current value of the location counter. In the example of an assembler, which follows, a word machine is used, and each instruction occupies one word of storage. It should be recognized that other machines may have variable-length instructions and that the location counter should be maintained accordingly. During pass one, the source program is copied onto an intermediate storage device or entabled in preparation for pass two. The functions performed during pass one are summarized as follows:

1. Read source program from system input stream;
2. Recognize and store macro definitions;
3. Expand macro instructions;
4. Recognize generative and symbol-defining instructions;
5. Maintain location counter;

6. Build the symbol table;
7. Perform syntactic error analysis; and
8. Copy program onto an intermediate device or build a corresponding table of pertinent information.

A sample program showing the relationship of some of the above concepts is given in Table 2.1. In the table, ORG is a program control instruction which initializes the location counter, whereas EQU is a symbol defining instruction which establishes the address 1000 for the symbol X. The remainder of the instructions are of the generative type, as defined.

TABLE 2.1   RELATIONSHIP OF SOURCE PROGRAM, LOCATION COUNTER, AND SYMBOL TABLE DURING ASSEMBLER PASS ONE

Source Program		Location* Counter		Tables	
	ORG	100	100	Symbol Table	
LOOP	ADD	A	100	Symbol	Address
	SUB	B	101		
	MULT	C	102	LOOP	100
	.			X	1000
	.			A	130
	B	LOOP	120	B	131
	.		.	C	132
	.		.		
X	EQU	1000	——	.	
	.		.	.	
	.		.	.	
	.		.		
A	DEC	25	130		
B	DEC	110	131		
C	DEC	1	132		
	END				

*Note that ORG and EQU are nongenerative instructions.

Assembler Pass Two

Pass two of the assembler produces the machine language code and a listing of the program. The program listing may also contain a description of the generated code in a form representing the internal structure of the computer. The machine language program is deposited on punched cards or on a temporary storage device. Pass two uses the symbol table that was built during pass one and a table of operation codes to fill in the operand and operation fields, respectively. The functions performed during the pass two are summarized as follows:

1. Read program from intermediate storage device or fetch it, as required, from an appropriate table;
2. Process the operation and operand fields by looking up necessary symbols in tables;
3. Perform global error analysis, i.e., errors that involve the interrelationship of statements;
4. Punch the machine language program into cards or store it on a temporary storage device; and
5. Prepare the program listing.

A sample program showing the relationship of the source program, program listing, symbol table, and operation table is shown in Table 2.2.

TABLE 2.2   RELATIONSHIP OF SOURCE PROGRAM, PROGRAM LISTING, SYMBOL TABLE, AND OPERATION TABLE.

Program Listing				Tables

LOC	OBJ CODE	SOURCE PROGRAM		Symbol Table

LOC	OBJ CODE				
0100			ORG	100	
0100	E0130	LOOP	ADD	A	
0101	D0131		SUB	B	
0102	G0132		MULT	C	
⋮			⋮		
⋮			⋮		
0120	H0100		B	LOOP	
⋮			⋮		
⋮			⋮		
1000		X	EQU	1000	
⋮			⋮		
⋮			⋮		
0130	00025	A	DEC	25	
0131	00010	B	DEC	10	
0132	00001	C	DEC	1	
			END		

Symbol Table

Symbol	Address
LOOP	100
X	1000
A	130
B	131
C	132
⋮	⋮

Operation Table

Symbol	Code
READ	A
PRINT	B
LOAD	C
SUB	D
ADD	E
DIV	F
MULT	G
B	H
⋮	⋮

Several points should be mentioned regarding the example. First, not all instructions are generative instructions, as evidenced by the ORG and EQU instructions. Second, a program control instruction, i.e., END, was used to indicate the last card in the source program. Lastly, no listing control instructions were shown. These topics are clarified in the sample assembler program which follows.

An Example of a Simple Assembler Program

A basic assembler language for a hypothetical machine is introduced, so that the operation of such an assembler can be described on a realistic basis. The computer is indeed trivial, as is the assembler language itself; however, the methods are clearly exhibited in such an environment.

The computer is a one-address word machine. Each instruction word is composed of a one character op-code followed by a four character address as follows:

op	address

Similarly, a data word occupies the full five characters of a word.

The source document is formatted as follows:

Location field—columns one through four

Operation field—columns six through ten

Operand field—columns twelve on

An asterisk in column one indicates that the source record is a comments card.

The *machine instructions* require a symbolic operand and for obvious reasons do not form an exhaustive set. The symbolic operation codes and internal operation codes are now listed:

Symbolic Operation Codes	Internal Operation Codes
READ	A
PRINT	B
LOAD	C
SUB	D
ADD	E
DIV	F
MULT	G
B	H

Machine instructions are written as follows:

1	4	6	10	12	
Location		Operation		Operand	
(Optional)		Symbolic operation code		Symbolic address	

There exists one *symbol definition* instruction. The EQU instruction defines a symbol by assigning to it the value of the symbol or number in the operand field. The format of the EQU instruction is:

1	4	6	10	12	
Location		Operation		Operand	
Symbol		EQU		A symbol or a number	

If a symbol appears in the operand field, it must have been previously defined.

The *data definition* instruction, DEC, is used to introduce data into the program. It is written as follows:

1	4	6	10	12	
Location		Operation		Operand	
Symbol		DEC		Decimal number	

Two *program control* instructions exist. The ORG instruction initializes the location counter to a specified value. The END instruction indicates end of assembly.

1	4	6	10	12	
Location		Operation		Operand	
		ORG END		Number	

The *listing control* instructions, TITLE, SPACE, and EJECT are used to control the printout of the program being assembled. TITLE prints a title

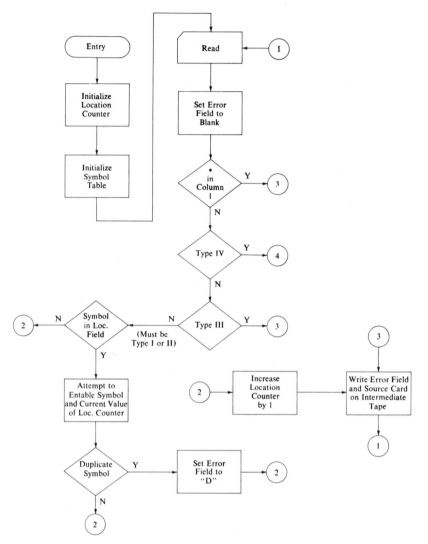

Fig. 2.1   Pass one of the sample assembler program.

on each page of assembler output; SPACE prints a blank line; and EJECT indicates that the next line is to begin on a new page.

1	4	6	10	12
Location		Operation		Operand
		TITLE		A title
		SPACE		
		EJECT		

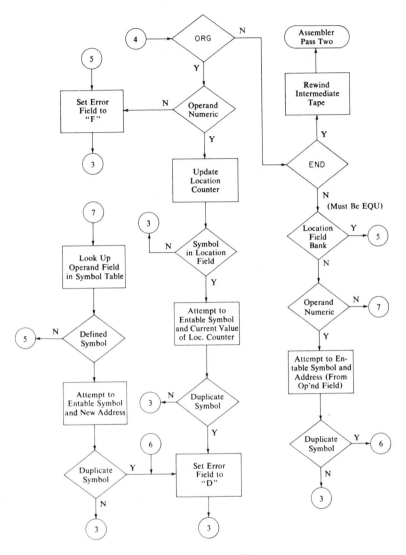

Fig. 2.1 (continued)

The assembly process is described in two passes. In order to facilitate development of the assembler program, the instructions are classified into four types:

Type I		Type II	Type III	Type IV
READ	ADD	DEC	TITLE	EQU
PRINT	DIV		EJECT	ORG
LOAD	MULT		SPACE	END
SUB	B			

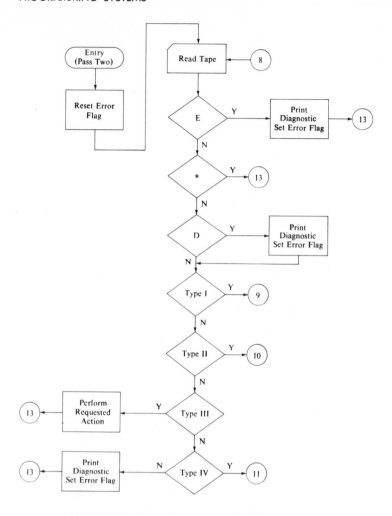

Fig. 2.2   Pass two of the sample assembler program.

The source record is copied onto an intermediate tape in preparation for pass two. Before copying, however, the record is prefixed with a one character error field. This facilitates error checking during pass two.

A flow chart of pass one of the example is given in Fig. 2.1. Similarly, pass two is depicted in Fig. 2.2. Clearly, the flow charts do not define a generalized assembler, but rather they should be viewed as being representative of the processes that are actually performed. In an assembler for an actual machine, considerably more detail is involved. However,

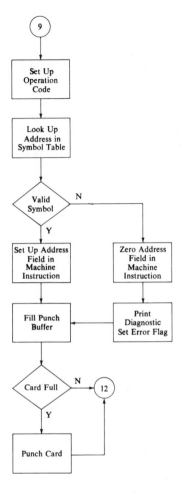

Fig. 2.2 (continued)

there is a potential disadvantage in presenting unnecessary detail; it can, unless extreme care is taken, easily obscure important concepts.

2.4   THE CONSTRUCTION AND USE OF SYMBOL TABLES

An important consideration in advanced programming is the construction and use of symbol tables. After a formal introduction, three methods are described.

A symbol table is a list of ordered pairs (s_i, v_i) with unique first components s_i. The entry v_i is said to be the value associated with the symbol

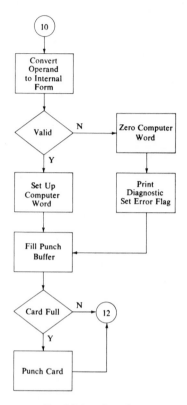

Fig. 2.2 (continued)

s_i. The problem of table lookup involves determining, for a symbol s', the symbol table entry (s_i, v_i) where

$$s' = s_i$$

This process makes available the required value, v_i.

Linear Accumulation and Searching

The most straightforward method of posting and retrieving symbol table entries is *linear accumulation and searching*. The method is essentially one of entabling source and value symbols as they are encountered. Table lookup then involves a linear search of entries. Fig. 2.3 describes this process. The example of Fig. 2.3 implies a table allocated sequentially in storage. Another effective method is to organize the table as a linked-list structure,* in which ordering is achieved by using pointers to preceding

*List structures are considered in chapter 6.

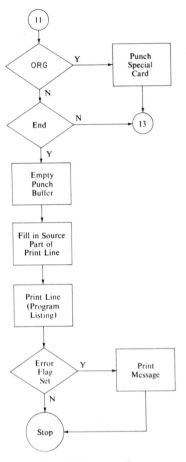

Fig. 2.2 (continued) .

and succeeding entries. Each entry is defined as follows:

p_1	p_2
s	
v	

where:

p_1 = pointer to the address of the preceding entry.
p_2 = pointer to the address of the succeeding entry.
s = source symbol.
v = value symbol.

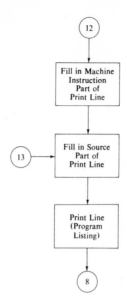

Fig. 2.2 (continued)

By arranging the respective pointers, symbol pairs can be maintained in an ordered sequence. Table lookup involves a linear search of the list structure in either a forward or backward direction, depending upon the current symbol's position in the collating sequence with respect to the first symbol entered. Figure 2.4 depicts this method. Methods exist for rearranging the pointers in the linear linked-list structure to increase the efficiency of the retrieval process; however, they are outside the scope of this chapter.

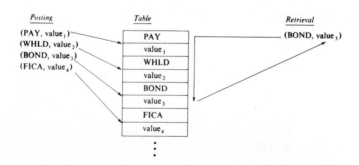

Fig. 2.3   Linear assumulation and searching.

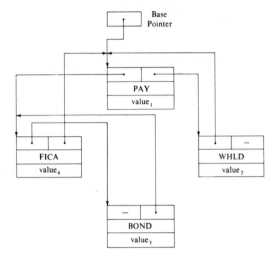

Fig. 2.4   Symbol table constructed as a linear linked list.

The Tree Method

The *tree method* is similar to the linear linked-list structure of the preceding section. Instead of a linear list, the symbol table forms a binary tree. A search of the table is then, by definition, a *binary search*. The structure of each table entry is identical to the entry for a linear linked list.

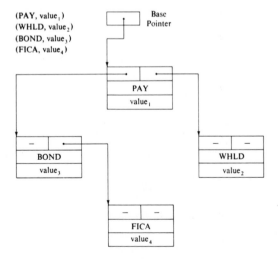

Fig. 2.5   The tree method.

Logically, however, pointers P_1 and P_2 are interpreted in a different manner. P_1 points to the leftmost entry, and P_2 points to the rightmost entry. Again, entries are maintained in order by symbol, or in collating sequence, so that the P_1 pointer may be interpreted as pointing to entries lower in sequence, and the P_2 pointer may be interpreted as pointing to entries higher in sequence. The method is shown best by example, and the symbols of Figure 2.4 are entabled using the tree method in Figure 2.5.

Hashing

A frequently used method for constructing and searching symbol tables is called *hashing*. The principal advantage to this method is the speed with which items can be posted and retrieved. The hashing methodology partitions the set of source symbols into one with a restricted range. The hashing function is chosen so that:

1. The mapping from source symbol to hash code can be computed rapidly; and
2. The mapping of all source symbols to hash codes tends to be evenly distributed over the hash codes.

More specifically, the *hashing function* partitions the set of all source symbols into equivalence classes, such that two source symbols are in the same equivalence class if and only if they hash to the same value.

A hash table satisfies the previous definition of a symbol table with entries of the form (s_i, v_i). However, the "value" entry can be a data value, or it can be the address of a linearly constructed symbol table or a linked-list structure, as described under the tree method. Therein lies the basis for the two ways in which the hashing technique is generally used.

When the "value" entry in the hash table has been established as a data value (termed *linear hashing*), the posting operation involves the following procedures:

1. The hashing function establishes a pointer to a position in the hash table.
2. If the s_i field in the table is zero, then the (s, v) pair is inserted at this position.
3. If the s_i field in the table is the same as the symbol being posted, then a duplicate symbol exists.
4. If the s_i field in the table is different from the symbol being posted, then the value of the pointer is increased by one entry, and steps 2 through 4 are repeated. If it is determined that the table is full, then an error return is appropriate.

The retrieval operation, when the "value" entry has been established as a data value, operates in a similar fashion:

1. The hashing function establishes a pointer to a position in the hash table.
2. If the s_i field in the table is zero, then the symbol is undefined.
3. If the s_i field in the table is the same as the symbol being retrieved, then the v_i field in the table is extracted.
4. If the s_i field in the table is different from the symbol being retrieved, then the value of the pointer is increased by one entry and steps 2 through 4 are repeated. If it is determined that the symbol does not exist in the table, i.e., by an exhaustive search, then an error return is appropriate.

When the "value" entry in the hash table has been established as the address of a linearly constructed symbol table or a linked-list structure, then the procedures for the posting and retrieval operations are as follows:

1. The hashing function established a pointer to a position in the hash table.
2. The v_i field in the table is extracted as the address of the first entry in a linear symbol table or the base address of a linked-list structure.
3. The required operation is then performed on the linear symbol table or linked-list structure, as described in previous sections.

This latter method is termed *nonlinear hashing*. With this method, the symbol field s_i of a hash table entry is unused and is often omitted. The hash table then exists as a linear list of addresses.

Several comments on these methods are pertinent. First, *linear accumulation and search* is efficient for limited-entry tables, since overhead processing is minimal. Second, linear hashing is most useful for dense tables in an operating system with static storage properties. Lastly, the combination of nonlinear hashing and the tree method tend to be efficient for dense tables in a system with dynamic storage* facilities.

PROBLEMS

2.1 List the *assembler instructions* for a particular assembler language, distinguishing between the four classes: symbol definition, data definition, listing control, and program control.

---

*Some operating systems permit main storage to be allocated on a dynamic basis. A job, which determines during execution that additional storage over its primary allocation is required, may request it from an appropriate control program.

2.2   The use of *extended operation codes* facilitates programming. The concept is analogous to that of macros. Develop a set of general purpose macros for a given class of applications.

2.3   Consider how macros could be expanded. Draw a flow diagram of this process.

2.4   Draw flow diagrams for the posting and retrieving of entries from the three general types of symbol tables mentioned in the chapter.

REFERENCES

1. Brooks, F. P., and K. E. Iverson, *Automatic Data Processing*, New York, John Wiley and Sons, Inc., 1963. Presents an introduction to assembler language and assembler programs.
2. Knuth, D. E., *The Art of Computer Programming*, Vol. I., *Fundamental Algorithms*, Reading, Massachusetts, Addison-Wesley Publishing Company, Inc., 1968. Contains a complete description of the various types of list structures and discusses methods for using them.
3. Lee, J. A. N., *The Anatomy of a Compiler*, New York, Reinhold Publishing Corp., 1967. Discusses assembler language and symbol table methods.

3 | STRING MANIPULATION

Early applications of the computer dealt with scientific computations and business data processing. The problems were essentially numerical in that a high percentage of the input symbols were interpreted as numerical values and that most of the internal calculations involved mathematical operations. As computer applications expanded into new areas, such as translators and compilers, applied linguistics, symbolic mathematics, theorem proving, cryptanalysis, and the construction of bibliographies and indexes, a new class of problems arose. These problems accepted strings of characters as input data, and the internal calculations performed operations on the character strings, instead of interpreting them as character equivalents of numerical values.

3.1 DEFINITIONS

A *string* is a sequence of characters. When designating a string explicitly, it is customarily enclosed in quotation marks. For example, the following lines are strings:

'ALL COWS EAT GRASS'
'A BCT'

The word *literal* is used to describe a string written in this manner. More formally, a literal is a quantity which denotes itself or the class of strings similar to itself. The basic property of a string is its *length*. For example, the string

'ABC'

has a length of three. A string with a length of zero is termed a *null string*.

A string can have a name as well as a character value. The following statement assigns the name JOE to the string 'ABCD':

JOE = 'ABCD'

When appropriate, strings may be referred to by their names, instead of by their contents.

Two basic manipulations can be performed on strings: *juxtaposition* and *concatenation*. Juxtaposition means placing the strings together without loss of identity. Strings may be juxtaposed on the left or on the right. For example, the right juxtaposition of 'X' with 'Y' is written 'Y' 'X'; each of the strings is enclosed in quotation marks to preserve its identity. Clearly, the result of juxtaposition is dejuxtaposable. Juxtaposition is neither associative nor commutative.

Similarly, strings may be concatenated on the left or on the right. After the concatenation operation, however, individual strings have lost their identity. For example, the left concatenation of 'XY' and 'Z' is written 'XYZ'. A significant rule may now be stated: *Any concatenation of strings is a string.*

3.2   BASIC STRING OPERATIONS

In general, basic string operations have a certain amount of intuitive appeal. Most people immediately think of concatenation or of character-by-character replacement. Other operations are just as obvious. They are presented here in preparation for the study of higher level languages, which were designed for applications involving these operations.

The operations fall rather naturally into three classes: decomposition, pattern matching, and alteration. *Decomposition* operations separate a string into two or more components. *Pattern matching* operations include matching a sequence of characters, in addition to either a decomposition or alteration operation. *Alteration* operations modify a string without decomposing it.

In the sections which follow, basic string operations are introduced as hypothetical procedures. They are introduced for pedagogical purposes, presupposing that something concrete is more instructional than pure definitions. No claims are made as to the completeness of the set of operations.

Decomposition Operations

Decomposition operations are basic to string manipulation and enable strings to be divided into component parts for more detailed analysis. Decomposition operations are particularly useful in compiler writing, where it is often desired to divide a statement into constituent tokens,* such as variables, literals, operators, and punctuation characters. Five primitive operations are identified:†

1. *Decatenation.*

   DECAT (a,b,c,d)

   DECAT decomposes string a into strings c and d. The first character of d is the leftmost character of a that is also found in string b.

   Example: If SAREA = 'A = 2.*X**2+ 3.*X + 9,' and EQU = '=\$', then DECAT (SAREA, EQU, C1, C2) => C1 = 'A' and C2 = '=2.*X**2 + 3.*X + 9'

2. *Prefixing.*

   PREFIX (a,b,c,d)

   PREFIX decomposes string a into strings c and d. The first character of d is the leftmost character of a that is not found in string b.

   Example: If ABC = 'ƀƀƀƀƀƀ DO 10 I = 1, 100' and BLANK = 'ƀ', then PREFIX(ABC,BLANK,L,R) => L = 'ƀƀƀƀƀƀ' and R = 'DO 10 I = 1,100'

3. *Suffixing.*

   SUFFIX (a,b,c,d)

   SUFFIX decomposes string a into strings c and d. The last character of c is the rightmost character of a that is not found in string b.

   Example: If ABC = 'READ(5,9000) (A(I), I = 1,9)ƀƀƀƀƀƀƀƀƀ' and BLANK = 'ƀ'. then SUFFIX(ABC,BLANK,ABC,R) => ABC = 'READ-(5,9000) (A(I), I = 1,9)' and R = 'ƀƀƀƀƀƀƀƀƀ'

4. *Picking.*

   PICK (a,c,d)

   PICK places the leftmost character of string a in string c. The remainder of the characters of a are placed in string d.

   Example: If STRING = '+1234.5' then PICK(STRING,TOKEN,STRING) => TOKEN = '+' and STRING = '1234.5'

Tokens are elements of a language, i.e., operators, symbolic names, punctuation characters, etc., each with a separate identity.

†The symbol = > should be interpreted to read "yields."

The character ƀ denotes the blank character and is used interchangeably with the character ' '. The special character is used when at least one blank is required or when the explicit occurrence of one or more blank characters should be brought to the attention of the reader.

5. *Peeling.*

PEEL (a,c,d)

PEEL places the rightmost character of string a in string d. The remainder of the characters of a are placed in string c.

Example: If SENT = 'ALL DOGS BITE.' then PEEL(SENT,SX,PCT) => SX = 'ALL DOGS BITE' and PCT = '.'

Pattern Matching Operations

Pattern matching operations provide the facility for matching strings of consecutive characters and then performing a replacement or decomposition operation, accordingly. There are four pattern matching operations, and they are particularly useful for applications like symbolic mathematics and theorem proving.

1. *Matching.*

MATCH (a,b,c,d)

MATCH searches string a for the leftmost occurrence of string b; the characters of a thusly matched are replaced by the string c, and the result is placed in d.

Example: If E1 = '(A + B) * X', E2 = '(A + B)', and E3 = 'C', then MATCH (E1,E2,E3,R) => R = 'C*X'

2. *Prevariable.*

PREVAR (a,b,c)

PREVAR searches the string a for the leftmost occurrence of string b; the characters preceding b in string a are placed in string c.

Example: If S = 'ABCDEFG' and T = 'CDE', then PREVAR (S,T,U) => U = 'AB'

3. *Postvariable.*

POSTVAR (a,b,d)

POSTVAR searches the string a for the leftmost occurrence of string b; the characters following b in string a are placed in string d.

Example: If S = 'ABCDEFG' and T = 'CDE', then POSTVAR(S,T,V) => V = 'FG'

4. *Invariable.*

INVAR (a,b,c,d)

INVAR searches the string a for the character sequence $b \ldots c$; the characters separating b and c are placed in d.

Example: If A = 'A GREAT DAY' and B = 'b̸', then INVAR (A,B,B,C) => C = 'GREAT'

Alteration Operations

Alteration operations permit a string to be modified without actually decomposing it. These operations tend to be particularly useful for text editing applications.

1. *Concatenation.*

   CONCAT (a,b,c)

   CONCAT concatenates strings a and b and places the result in string c.

   Example: If A = 'GOOD' and B = 'GREAT', then CONCAT(A,B,C) = >
   C = 'GOODGREAT'

2. *Replacement.*

   REPLACE (a,b,c,d)

   b and c are two ordered sequences of characters of the same size. The characters of string a, which are also found in string b, are replaced with their respective character from string c. The result is placed in string d.

   Example: S1 = 'APPLE PIE', B = 'ABCDEF', and C = '+ − * / .,', then
   REPPLACE(S1,B,C,S2) = > S2 = '+PPL. PI.'

3. *Deletion.*

   DELETE (a,b,c)

   DELETE deletes the characters of string a, which are also found in string b. The result is placed in string c.

   Example: S1 = 'APPLE PIE' and B = 'PE', then DELETE(S1,B,C) = >
   C = 'AL I'

4. *Squeeze.*

   SQUEEZE (a,b,c)

   String a is searched for characters also found in string b that appear more than once in succession. Each sequence is replaced by a single occurrence of the same character.

   Example: N = 'TENNESSEE' and MSK = 'TPMNER', then SQUEEZE
   (N,MSK,N) = > N = 'TENESSE'

For computer applications requiring a limited amount of string manipulation, a package of basic operations written in subroutine form is perhaps sufficient. If combined with a procedure-oriented language, such as FORTRAN, which compiles into machine language code, subroutine packages provide an efficient method of getting the job done. If the applications, however, require a large amount of string manipulation and support research or experimental work, then an appropriate problem-oriented language, permitting at least the same basic operations and which runs interpretively, is probably more economical of programmer time. One of these languages is SNOBOL, a string manipulation language which has received a great amount of interest in the field of computing.

3.3   AN INTRODUCTION TO THE SNOBOL LANGUAGE

SNOBOL is a problem-oriented language developed to facilitate string manipulation on a computer. The references contain complete descriptions of the language, which has been developed in several versions. A useful subset is described here. The elements of the language are listed in Table 3.1 and are introduced in subsequent paragraphs.

Basic Definitions

A SNOBOL program is an ordered set of statements, each statement involving a rule. A set of rules provides the means for manipulating strings of characters.

A SNOBOL statement has three basic parts. Written from left to right they are: <label>, <rule>, and <goto>.* Each part is optional. The <rule> part may be further divided into a string reference, a pattern, and a replacement portion. The *string reference* is mandatory and indicates the entity upon which operations are to be performed. It may be a string literal only if no replacement operation is specified. A string specified in a pattern or as a replacement string may be written as a string literal or denoted by its name.

String Replacement

The replacement statement is composed of a string reference, a replacement operator, and a replacement string written as follows:

$$\text{<string name>} \not b = \not b \text{<string>}$$

or

$$\text{<string name>} \not b = \not b \text{<string name>}$$

e.g.,

$$\text{STR1} = \text{'HELP'}$$
$$\text{STR2} = \text{STR1}$$
$$\text{STR3} = \text{STR2}$$

---

*The characters < > indicate that the enclosed characters specify the name of a constituent part of the language. The special characters help distinguish these names from something that the user might write. When interpreting statements written in this notation, any characters not enclosed in angular brackets must be included by the user.

TABLE 3.1   BASIC SNOBOL

Character set: 48 symbols: ABC...Z 012...9 + −/ *.,$()'ϸ =

String name: any combination of letters, digits, and periods.

Literal string: any combination of the full character set except quote; the beginning and end are marked with a quote.

Label: any combination of the full character set except blank; the first symbol must be a letter or digit.

String variable: any string name enclosed in asterisks.

   arbitrary: *X*

   fixed-length: *X/N* where N contains a positive integer or is a numeric literal.

   nameless: **

   nameless-of fixed length: */N*

First character of a statement:

   ϸ blank for an unlabelled statement.

   letter or digit for the beginning of a label.

   . for continuation of the preceding statement.

   * for a comment.

System defined strings:

   SYSPOT: causes one line to be written out for printing.

   SYSPIT: causes one card image to be read from SYSIN for *each* reference to SYSPIT.

   QUOTE: this string initially contains a quote and can be used in a program to introduce quotes in a string.

Statement format: parenthesis will be used to indicate optional parts of a statement, which has three basic parts:

   (label)   rule   (goto)

The format for a rule is:

   string-reference   (pattern)   (replacement)

Basic built-in functions:

EQUALS(X,Y)	Test if X and Y contain identical strings.
SIZE(X)	Number of characters in X.
TRIM(X)	Remove trailing blanks from X.
UNEQL(X,Y)	Test if X and Y are not identical.
.EQ(X,Y)	Test if X = Y(X and Y numeric).
.GE(X,Y)	Test if ≥ (X and Y numeric).
.GT(X,Y)	Test if > (X and Y numeric).
.LE(X,Y)	Test if ≤ (X and Y numeric).
.LT(X,Y)	Test if < (X and Y numeric).
.NE(X,Y)	Test if ≠ (X and Y numeric).
.NUM(X)	Test if X is numeric.
.REMDR(X,Y)	Remainder of X/Y.

where STR3 would contain 'HELP', if the statements were executed in sequence. The replacement statement should be interpreted as the replacement of the contents of the string named on the left by the string specified on the right, without disturbing the string on the right. If the string on the right has not been assigned a value, is null, or does not exist, e.g.,

$$STR4 =$$

then the string on the left is said to have the value *null*. The latter operation is often referred to as *deletion*.

Concatenation

Since a string is a finite ordered sequence, any two strings may be combined by concatenation to form a third string. Any finite number of strings may be so combined. Thus, the concatenation

$$Y = X 'AB' X$$

is equivalent to 'ABABAB', if X has the value 'AB'. The simple concatenation operation is written

$$<string> \not{b} <string>$$

where the intervening blank character is required. When used, the concatenation operation is most often present in the replacement string. The concept is also extended to involve pattern matching and string variables, as described later.

Blank Characters

As elements of strings, all blank characters are significant. Otherwise, any number of consecutive blanks is equivalent to a single blank. Spaces are always required between constituents of the language; e.g., the statements

$$A = B C$$

and

$$A = BC$$

are not equivalent. In the first statement, the contents of A are replaced by the concatenation of the string named B with the string named C. In the second statement, the contents of A are replaced by the contents of the string named BC.

Pattern Matching and Replacement

It is often desirable to scan a given string to test for the occurrence of a particular sequence of characters. This is regarded as pattern matching, defined as follows:

<string reference> ♭ <pattern string>

and interpreted as: "Scan the string reference to find the first sequence of characters which match the pattern string." A pattern matching operation may either succeed or fail; the success or failure of the scan may be used to control subsequent operations within the same rule, as well as controlling which statement will be executed next. When a match succeeds, the *success exit* is taken. In the following example,

STR1 = 'MEN, WOMEN, AND CHILDREN'
STR2 = 'AND'   *replacement statements*
STR3 = 'WOMEN AND CHILDREN'

STR1   STR2
                                       pattern matching statements
STR1   STR3

the first match succeeds and the second fails.

The matching operation always proceeds from left to right in a given string reference and terminates with the first occurrence of the specified pattern. The pattern may be given as a string name, a string literal, or a concatenation of such strings.

A pattern matching operation may be combined with a replacement operation, which is executed if the match succeeds. The general form of this type of statement is:

<string reference> ♭ <pattern string> ♭ = ♭ <string>

and interpreted as follows: "The string reference is scanned for the left-most occurrence of the pattern string; if the match succeeds, then the matched portion of the string reference is replaced by the replacement string. If the match fails, then the string reference is unchanged." For example, if X contains 'CAT', then the statement

X 'A' = 'ALPHA'

replaces X with 'CALPHAT', and the *success exit* is taken from the statement. Clearly, if the match had failed, then the *failure exit* would have been taken, and the replacement would not have been made. Similar to the pattern string, the replacement string may also be a concatenation of strings specified by string names or string literals.

Statement Labels and Branching

Any statement can have a name called a *statement label*. The general form of a statement with a label is:

<statement label> ♭ <rule> ♭ <goto>

e.g.,

NME1 STR = 'ABC'

To distinguish the above statement from a pattern matching statement followed by a replacement, the following rule is applied. Labels must start in the first column of the source document; the <rule> portion of the SNOBOL statement must start in the second column or later and must be separated from the label, if specified, by at least one blank character.

Normally, SNOBOL statements are executed sequentially. Sequential execution may be altered, however, by using the <goto> portion of the statement. For example, after the following statements have been executed:

```
X =      'A'
STR1 = 'MEN, WOMEN, AND CHILDREN'
STR2 = 'MEN'
STR1    STR2    /S(LBL2)
X = 'B'
```

LBL2 ....

X will contain the string 'A'. The slash character / is used to signify the beginning of the <goto> portion of the statement and must be preceded by a blank character. The success S, failure F, combined success and failure, and unconditional exits, respectively, from a statement are written as follows:

```
/S(<label1>)
/F(<label2>)
/S(<label3>)F(<label4>)
/(<label5>)
```

Example: Given a string X, replace all occurrences of the letter 'N' with the letter 'E' and vice versa.

```
        X = 'TENNESSEE'
2    X 'N' = '*'      /S(2)
EN    X 'E' = 'N'      /S(EN)F(3X)
3X    X '*' = 'E'      /S(3X)
```

After execution X would contain 'TNEENSSNN', which is the desired result.

System Symbols

After or during the execution of a program, it is quite natural for a user to want to inspect his results. Similarly, there are times when the user desires to read in data cards and operate upon them. Two reserved string names are reserved for this purpose: SYSPOT and SYSPIT.*

Any string can be printed on the system's printer by assigning its value to the special string name SYSPOT. For example, the statements

AB = '25'

SYSPOT = 'THE ANSWER IS '   AB

would cause the following line to be printed:

'THE ANSWER IS 25'

Input in SNOBOL is performed by referencing the special string name SYSPIT. A statement such as the following

CARD = SYSPIT

causes one card image to be read from the system input device and re-replace the contents of the string CARD.

It is often desirable to use the quote character in a character string, especially when printing results in a desired form. Since the character is also used as a delimiter for string literals, a special string name QUOTE is predefined to initially contain the quote character. Thus, the statement

SYSPOT = 'MISSION' QUOTE 'IMPOSSIBLE' QUOTE

would cause the line

MISSION 'IMPOSSIBLE'

to be printed.

SNOBOL Arithmetic

Although SNOBOL was not designed for numerical computations, there are many important applications which require a limited arithmetic capability. SNOBOL provides the facility to perform arithmetic operations on signed integers.

Any string name may be assigned a numeric value by making its contents a string of characters representing a signed or unsigned integer. For example,

A = '+125'

replaces A with the numeric value +125. As with string literals, numeric constants must be enclosed in quotation marks.

*In an original implementation of SNOBOL, SYSPOT stood for System Peripheral Output Tape and SYSPIT stood for System Peripheral Input Tape.

Numeric strings may be combined two at a time using the conventional arithmetic operators, i.e., + for addition, − for subtraction, * for multiplication, / for division, and ** for exponentiation. For example, the statement

$$\text{ALPHA} = \text{'}-17\text{'} + \text{'}3\text{'}$$

replaces ALPHA with the string '−14', whereas the statement

$$\text{ALPHA} = \text{'}-17\text{'}\text{'}+\text{'}\text{'}3\text{'}$$

replaces ALPHA with the string '−17+3'. Expressions requiring more than two operands must be simplified or completely parenthesized. *Example:* The following statements count the occurrence of the letter 'S' in the string STATE.

```
        STATE = 'MISSISSIPPI'
        NUM = '0'
SCAN    STATE 'S' = '*'   /F(REPL)
        NUM = NUM + '1'   /(SCAN)
REPL    STATE '*' = 'S'   /S(REPL)
        SYSPOT = 'S OCCURRED '   NUM   ' TIMES'
```

String Variables

As in the following example,

```
        STR1 = '/ *AB(.'
        STR2 = 'AB'
        STR1  '*'  STR2 = 'XY'
        SYSPOT = STR1
```

where '/ XY(.' would be printed, pattern matching clearly can be performed with a combination of strings as well as simply with a string name or a literal. The concept is extended to include a third type of string called a *string variable*. The contents of a string variable vary, as the name implies, and the concept can be used for determining an unknown part of a string, given a known part. A string variable is a string name enclosed in a pair of asterisks; it may only appear in the pattern portion of a rule. For example, the following statement:

```
        STRING    'ABC'    *VAR*    'XYZW'
```

searches the string STRING for any occurrence of the strings ABC and XYZW in order, possibly separated by other symbols. If the match is successful, any symbols which are found between ABC and XYZW replace the contents of VAR.

It should be emphasized that use of a string variable results in the formation of a new string, which is given the indicated name. However, the pattern match must be successful in order for a new string to be formed. Consider the following example:

LINE = '112358132134'
LINE   '123'   *S*   '132'
LINE   '123'   *S2*   '123'

The match in the second line would be successful, and S1 would contain the string '58'; however, the match in the third line is unsuccessful and S2 retains its old string or remains undefined.

Strings may be partitioned by using a combination of strings or string variables as the pattern in a SNOBOL rule. Given a string to be partitioned:

STR = 'ABC-DEF*GHI'

A *partition* statement such as:

STR   *PART1 * '—' *PART2* '*' *PART3*

would result in strings of the form

PART1 = 'ABC'
PART2 = 'DEF'
PART3 = 'GHI'

A length attribute may be given a string variable by following the string variable name with a slash and a numeric string, which denotes the desired length of the string to be formed. For example,

XY/'3'

and

XY/N

are equivalent if N = '3'. The statement

TEXT   *X/'1'*

replaces X with the first character of TEXT. Fixed length string variables may be used conveniently with the system symbol SYSPIT to read desired portions of a card. The next statement reads a card, assigns the first 34 characters to LEFT and the remainder to RGT:

SYSPIT   *LEFT/'34'*   *RGT*

Obviously, one can test for the occurrence of a character string, let's say one named X, followed by a character sequence of *unknown* composition, followed in turn by another known string Y. The statement might read as:

STR   X   **   Y   /S(SUCCESS)

Operationally, a nameless string variable is processed as a string variable with one exception: no name exists between the asterisks, and, therefore, no new string is formed. As an example, consider a string STR which contains extraneous characters, which are delimited on the left by '/*' and on the right by '*/'. The following program deletes the extraneous characters as well as the delimiters:

STR = 'XYZ/*NONSENSE*/ABC'
STR   *LFT*   '/*'   **   '*/'   *RGT* = LFT   RGT

Indirect Referencing

String names are sequences of characters, just as strings are. Moreover, in some cases they contain precisely the same characters; e.g.,

A = 'A'

Therefore, the contents of a variable may be a string name, without extending the character manipulation facilities of the language. All that is actually needed to use this capability is a means of indicating to the SNOBOL interpreter that a second order of referencing is desired. The dollar sign $ is used for this purpose, and the concept is known as *indirect referencing*. For example,

A = 'T'
LOC = 'A'
SYSPOT = $LOC

would cause the character T to be printed.

Indirect referencing is particularly useful for building symbol tables, since the user can utilize the table facilities built into the SNOBOL sysstem itself. Consider a symbol-value pair of the form (s,v), stored in the SNOBOL string named LBL and LOC, respectively; e.g.,

LBL = 'LOOPA'
LOC = '1738'

The following SNOBOL statement would entable this pair in the SNOBOL symbol table:

$LBL = LOC

Given the correct symbol name, e.g.,

OPND = 'LOOPA'

the value, e.g., '1738', is retrieved to replace the contents of string name ADDR in the following statement:

$$ADDR = \$OPND$$

Built-In Functions

The SNOBOL language contains several built-in functions designed to facilitate programming. A basic set is given in Table 3.1. The result of a function in SNOBOL has two parts: a value and an indication of success or failure. *Relational functions* such as EQUALS (X,Y) or .LE(X,Y) return a null result with an appropriate success or failure exit. *Data functions* such as, SIZE (X), return with a failure exit and a null result, only when the function could not be performed. Several examples will clarify these concepts:

1. The statements

$$X = `ABCD'$$
$$SYSPOT = SIZE (X)$$

   cause '4' to be printed.
2. The statement

$$EQUALS \quad (`0', `00') \qquad /S(ALPHA)F(BETA)$$

   causes control to be transferred to the string whose label is BETA.
3. The statement

$$.EQ(`2' \quad + \quad `2', `4') \qquad /S(ALPHA)F(BETA)$$

   causes control to be transferred to the string whose label is ALPHA. (Note the blank characters on either side of the + sign).

Operation of a SNOBOL Program

A SNOBOL program is an ordered sequence of statements which are executed in the given order, except for branching that may be specified in the <goto> part of a statement. Only one statement can have the label END, and this must be the last statement of the program. This END statement may optionally specify another statement label in the string reference position of the statement. If present, this reference indicates the initial program entry point. Otherwise, execution will begin with the first statement in the program. Any input string must follow the END statement.

3.4   WRITING AN ASSEMBLER PROGRAM IN SNOBOL

Pass one of the sample assembler program, which was considered in section 2.3, has been programmed in SNOBOL and is included here as an example. Several comments concerning the assembler language and the assembler language program are required: 1. Rather than writing the statements of the source program on an intermediate tape in preparation for pass two of the assembler, they are assigned to SYSPOT instead; 2. As a statement is assigned to SYSPOT, it is prefixed with a one character error field, indicating whether or not the statement was in error; 3. The assembler program uses the SNOBOL system's symbol-table capabilities, as suggested in the previous paragraph entitled *indirect referencing;* 4. All string names in the SNOBOL program are composed of five characters or more, eliminating a conflict with the assembler language program which limits the size of its symbols to four characters or less; 5. For the sake of simplicity, comments are not permitted in the assembler language statements.

In the SNOBOL program which follows, the statements are numbered on the left for easy reference. This facilitates the presentation of some descriptive notes which follow the program.

```
1    START     TYPEIII = ',TITLE,EJECT,SPACE,'
2              TYPEIV = ',EQUØØ,ORGØØ,ENDØØ,'
3              LOCCNT = '0'
4    RDCARD    SYSPIT *ALCARD*
5              ERRFLD = 'Ø'
6              ALCARD *COLUMN1/'1'*
7              EQUALS(COLUMN1, '*')     /S(WRITE)
8              ALCARD *LOCFLD/'4'* */'1'*  *OPRFLD/'5'* */'1'* *OPERAND*
9              OPERAND = TRIM(OPERAND)
10             TYPEIV ',' OPRFLD ','     /S(PGMCRL)
11             TYPEIII ',' OPRFLD ','    /S(WRITE)
12             EQUALS(LOCFLD, 'ØØØØ')     /S(INCLOC)
13             EQUALS(SIZE)$LOCFLD), '0')     /F(DUPERR1)
14             $LOCFLD = LOCCNT     /(INCLOC)
15   DUPERR1   ERRFLD = 'D'
16   INCLOC    LOCCNT = LOCCNT + '1'
17   WRITE     SYSPOT = ERRFLD   ALCARD     /(RDCARD)
18   PGMCRL    EQUALS(OPRFLD, 'ORGØØ')     /F(CHKEND)
19             .NUM(OPERAND)     /F(E..ERR)
20             LOCCNT = OPERAND
21             EQUALS(LOCFLD, 'ØØØØ')     /S(WRITE)
22             EQUALS(SIZE($LOCFLD), '0')     /F(DUPERR2)
23             $LOCFLD = LOCCNT     /(WRITE)
24   DUPERR2   ERRFLD = 'D'     /(WRITE)
25   CHKEND    EQUALS(OPRFLD, 'ENDØØ')     /S(LSTCRD)
26             EQUALS(LOCFLD,'ØØØØ')     /S(E..ERR)
27             EQUALS(SIZE($LOCFLD), '0')     /F(DUPERR2)
```

```
28                    .NUM(OPERAND)      /F(SYMOPND)
29                    $LOCFLD = OPERAND      /(WRITE)
30   SYMOPND   EQUALS(SIZE($OPERAND), '0')      /S(E..ERR)
31                    $LOCFLD = $OPERAND      /(WRITE)
32   E..ERR      ERRFLD = 'E'      /(WRITE)
33   LSTCRD      SYSPOT = ERRFLD      ALCARD
34   END          START
```

Notes:

1. Statements 1 and 2 set up lists of operations codes.
2. Statement 4 reads the assembler language statements.
3. Statements 6 and 7 check for an * in column one and process the statement as a comment.
4. Statements 8 and 9 break up the statement into location, operation, and operand and remove the trailing blanks from the operand.
5. Statements 10 and 11 classify assembler language statements.
6. Statement 13 tests if the symbol found in the location field has been previously defined.
7. Statement 14 enters the symbol found in the location field as well as the current value of the location counter into the SNOBOL symbol table.
8. Statement 16 updates the location counter by the length attribute of the generative instruction.
9. Statement 17 writes the error field and input card to SYSPOT and unconditionally branches to read the next assembler language statement.
10. Statement 19 checks if the operand of the ORG operation is a number, and statement 20 updates the location counter accordingly.
11. Statement 23 enters the symbol in the location field and the number in the operand field of the ORG instruction into the symbol table.
12. Statement 26 begins processing of the EQU instruction.
13. Statement 28 checks if the operand field of the EQU instruction is numeric.
14. Statement 29 enters the symbol in the location field of the EQU instruction and the numeric operand into the symbol table.
15. Statement 30 checks if the symbol in the operand field has been previously defined; if not, it is a programming error.
16. Statement 31 does two things. It retrieves a value from the symbol table, i.e., with the $OPERAND on the right-hand-side of the = sign, and also enters that value along with the symbol in the location field into the symbol table.
17. Statement 33 processes the last card.

PROBLEMS

3.1   Extend the basic string operations so that they include indications of *success* and *failure exits*. What general SNOBOL functions can be simulated using these extended operations?

3.2   Program pass two of the assembler program in SNOBOL.

REFERENCES

1. Desautels, E. J., and D. K. Smith, "An Introduction to the String Processing Language SNOBOL," (S. Rosen, Ed.) *Programming Systems and Languages*, New York, McGraw-Hill Book Co., 1967. Presents a complete overview of the SNOBOL language.
2. Forte, A., *SNOBOL3 Primer*, Cambridge, Massachusetts, The M.I.T. Press, 1967.   Introduces the SNOBOL language for the nonspecialist in computer programming.
3. Farber, D. J., *et al.*, "SNOBOL, A String Manipulation Language," *Journal of the ACM* (January, 1964). Surveys an early version of SNOBOL. The first published report on the language.
4. Ingerman, P. Z., *A Syntax-Oriented Translator*, New York, Academic Press, 1966. Contains an academic treatment of operations on symbolic objects and their theoretical implications.

4 | BASIC COMPILER METHODS

Programming languages have been a tremendous boon to the computing industry. In addition to giving more users access to the machine, they have decreased the lead time requirements for program development and the associated machine time as well. Moreover, the efficiency of the machine language programs generated by most modern compilers approaches that which could be attained by an experienced programmer using assembler language. When compared with inexperienced programmers, the compiler usually produces more efficient code.

Because of its impact on the industry, compiler writing has become practically a science in itself. To a large extent, the internal design of a compiler is dependent upon the programming language being compiled, although there is probably as much difference between compilers for the same language as there is between compilers for different languages. In spite of this, most compilers tend to have a similar overall structure, and some basic methods can be identified.

In this chapter, the original FORTRAN Automatic Coding System is covered in the first section. Next, Polish notation is introduced in preparation for stack compilation techniques which follow. Lastly, some identities and dualities useful for compiler writing are presented. Later in the book, compilers that operate in a batch processing environment are compared with those that operate conversationally and incrementally. A very general familiarity with the FORTRAN language, which can be obtained from Appendix C, is assumed.

4.1   THE FORTRAN AUTOMATIC CODING SYSTEM

The first higher level programming system which was commercially available was developed by the IBM Corporation in the years 1954–1956. It was named FORTRAN and is currently available in several versions. Although the effort was indeed a pioneering one, the methods used and the overall organization are still worthy of note and serve as a good basic model of the structure of a compiler. A major objective of the compiler was to generate efficient object code; accordingly, several passes of the compiler are devoted mainly to that end. The system is described in a paper by J. W. Backus, *et al.*[1]

The compiler transformed a program written in the FORTRAN language to machine language in six sections or passes over the source program. The six sections are described first. Later, the topic of arithmetic expressions is treated in detail.

The Structure of the FORTRAN Compiler

Some general observations on the structure of the FORTRAN compiler can be made: 1. The overall organization of the system is simple, with any complexities being caused by the attempt to make generated programs as efficient as handwritten ones. 2. Within the compiler, information is passed between sections in two forms: in tables and as compiled instructions. 3. Compiled instructions exist in an internal symbolic format until section 6, where they are converted to the internal coding conventions of the machine.

The six sections of the compiler are:

Section 1. Reads in and classifies statements. For arithmetic statements, compiles the machine language instructions. For nonarithmetic statements including input-output, does a partial compilation and records the remaining information in tables. All instructions compiled in this section are in the COMPAIL file (Compiled Arithmetic, Input-Output Logical file).

Section 2. Compiles the instructions associated with indexing, which result from DO statements and the occurrence of subscripted variables. These instructions are placed in the COMPDO file (Compiled DO file).

Section 3. Merges the COMPAIL and COMPDO files into a single file, while completing the compilation of nonarithmetic statements begun in Section 1. The machine language program is now complete but assumes a computer with a large number of index registers.

Section 4. Carries out an analysis of the flow of the machine language program, to be used by Section 5.

Section 5. Converts the machine language program to one which uses only the number of index registers available on the computer for which the program is being compiled.

Section 6. Produces the machine language program in a form ready for running, i.e., as a binary card deck. A listing of the machine language version of the program is also produced on demand.

In summary, the compiler generated as many machine instructions as it could in the initial (and only) pass over the program. Compiled instructions were kept in the COMPAIL and COMPDO files. Other information was kept in tables. As a result, only one pass over the program was required.

Arithmetic Expressions

In ordinary mathematics, an order of computation is implicit in every arithmetic expression. The usual order of precedence among arithmetic operators is (from highest to lowers): exponentiation, multiplication and division, followed by addition and subtraction. This convention has also been adopted in FORTRAN, where parentheses must be used only when it is desired to deviate from the established hierarchy of operations. This implicit ordering must be made explicit before the compilation of instructions can be performed. The original FORTRAN system used a very sophisticated but efficient algorithm for doing this. It is of historical significance and is described by example in the following paragraphs.

The method by which precedence relations are made explicit is as follows: an arithmetic operator of high precedence may be thought of as weakly separating the arguments on either side of it, while an operator of low precedence strongly separates the arguments on either side of it. Since there are three levels of operators to be considered, we can represent three levels of separation by placing one, two, or no pairs of parentheses to either side of the operator according to its order of hierarchy, i.e.,

$$A**B \qquad A ** B$$
$$A*B \qquad A) * (B$$
$$A+B \qquad A)) + ((B$$

This introduction of parentheses is balanced in that as many left as right parentheses are introduced. In addition, the entire expression is prefixed by two left parentheses and closed by two right parentheses. Each left parenthesis and operand is then prefixed with an arithmetic operator indicating its strength; e.g.,

$$A + B * C$$
$$((A)) + ((B)*(C))$$
$$+ (*(**A)) + (*(**B)*(**C))$$

The last expression is said to be in *normal form*, since the hierarchy of operators has been made explicit, and each left parenthesis is tagged with its strength.

The next step is to generate an unsorted list of *triples* described as follows:

$$(c_i, o_i, n_i)$$

where c_i = time when the operation should be performed

o_i = operation

n_i = operand

The triples are produced by an ill-defined process, best described by example. The scan begins with an arithmetic expression in normal form and proceeds from left to right with an indicator set initially at level zero. Each time a left parenthesis is encountered, the level indicator is increased by one. Similarly, the level is decreased by one when a right parenthesis is recognized. The levels are represented conceptually as follows;

$$\ell \overline{\begin{array}{c} \odot \ m \\ \end{array}}$$

where ℓ is the level indicator, $\odot$ is the operator, and m represents the next level or operand. The triples are generated from this latter form, as described in the following examples. Again consider the preceding example with the arithmetic expression in normal form. This is depicted as follows:

```
+( * ( ** A ))     +( * ( ** B ) * ( ** C ))

+1 * 2 ** A        +3 * 4 ** B    * 5 ** C
0 ⌐ 1 ⌐ 2 ⌐        0 ⌐ 3 ⌐ 4 ⌐    3 ⌐ 5 ⌐
```

The triples are formed and generated from left to right in (c_i, o_i, n_i) notation:

0+1	0+3.	3 * 5
1 * 2	3 * 4	5 * *C
2 * *A	4 * *B	

Next the triples are sorted, combined, and simplified:

Sorted	Combined	Simplified
0+1	$U_0 = +U_1 + U_3$	$U_0 = U_1 + U_3$
0+3	$U_1 = *U_2$	$U_1 = U_2$
1 * 2	$U_2 = **A$	$U_2 = A$
2 * *A	$U_3 = *U_4*U_5$	$U_3 = U_4*U_5$
3 * 4	$U_4 = **B$	$U_4 = B$
3 * 5	$U_5 = **C$	$U_5 = C$
4 * *B		
5 * *C		

This process is followed by a bottom-to-top replacement to represent the expression in an *intermediate notation*, from which machine language instructions can be generated (again, on a bottom-to-top basis):

Intermediate Notation

$$U_0 = A + U_3$$
$$U_3 = B * C$$

Although the explanation does not present the precise algorithm used, it is amenable to programming and was used successfully for many years. Another example will probably shed some light on the exact procedure followed. Consider the expression:

$$A + B**C*(E+F)$$

and its equivalent in normal form:

+(* (**A)) +(* (** B ** C) * (** (+(* (**E)) +(* (** F)))))

+1 * 2 **A   +3 * 4 ** B ** C   * 5 ** 6 +7 * 8 **E   +9 * 10 ** F

0 | 1 | 2   0 | 3 | 4 | 4   3 | 5 | 6 | 7 | 8   6 | 9 | 10

The associated triples and intermediate notation would appear, appropriately, as follows:

Triples	Sorted	Combined	Simplified	Intermediate Notation
0+1	0+1	$U_0 = +U_1 + U_3$	$U_0 = U_1 + U_3$	$U_0 = A + U_3$
1 * 2	0+3	$U_1 = *U_2$	$U_1 = U_2$	$U_3 = U_4 * U_5$
2 * * A	1 * 2	$U_2 = **A$	$U_2 = A$	$U_4 = B**C$
0+3	2 * * A	$U_3 = *U_4 *U_5$	$U_3 = U_4 * U_5$	$U_5 = E + F$
3 * 4	3 * 4	$U_4 = **B**C$	$U_4 = B**C$	
4 * * B	3 * 5	$U_5 = **U_6$	$U_5 = U_6$	
4 * * C	4 * * B	$U_6 = +U_7 + U_9$	$U_6 = U_7 + U_9$	
3 * 5	4 * * C	$U_7 = *U_8$	$U_7 = U_8$	
5 * * 6	5 * * 6	$U_8 = **E$	$U_8 = E$	
6+7	6+7	$U_9 = *U_{10}$	$U_9 = U_{10}$	
7 * 8	6+9	$U_{10} = **F$	$U_{10} = F$	
8 * * E	7 * 8			
6+9	8 * * E			
9 * 10	9 * 10			
10 * * F	10 * * F			

When read from bottom-to-top, the intermediate notation clearly represents an explicit ordering of the intended operations.

4.2 POLISH NOTATION

Polish notation is a form of mathematical notation, invented by the Polish logician Lukasiewicz. Its first use was in mathematical logic. It is of particular interest to those interested in compilers and translators, since it provides the facility to state complex expressions in a nonambiguous manner without relying on hierarchical delimiters such as parentheses. Subsequent scanning mechanisms are greatly simplified.

The basic difference between standard mathematical notation and Polish notation is the relative position of the operator ⊙ to its operands A:

1. Standard notation   A⊙A
2. Forward Polish notation ⊙AA
3. Reverse Polish notation AA⊙

The two Polish forms may also be varied by altering the order of the operands:

1. Forward Polish ⊙$A_1 A_2$
$$⊙A_2 A_1$$
2. Reverse Polish $A_1 A_2$⊙
$$A_2 A_1⊙$$

Moreover, each of the Polish forms can be applied to an arithmetic statement in two ways:

1. By forcing operators to occur in the Polish string as early as possible (Early Operator).
2. By forcing operators to occur in the Polish string as late as possible (Late Operator).

The following examples demonstrate the eight possible forms as applied to the arithmetic statement:

$$A \leftarrow B + C - D$$

Here, the replacement sign ← is interpreted as a dyadic operator, similar to the standard arithmetic operators.

1. Forward Polish
   a. ⊙$A_1 A_2$
      Early Operator ← A − +BCD
      Late Operator ← A+B−CD
   b. ⊙$A_2 A_1$
      Early Operator ← + −DCBA
      Late Operator ← −D+CBA

2. Reverse Polish

   a. $A_1 A_2 \odot$

     Early Operator ABC+D−←

     Late Operator   ABCD−+←

   b. $A_2 A_1 \odot$

     Early Operator DC−B+A ←

     Late Operator   DCB+−A ←

Clearly, some of the forms are more desirable than others. Some important factors to be used in selecting a form are as follows:

1. The relative complexity of the algorithm required to support language conversions from source language to Polish notation and from Polish notation to some target language.
2. The storage capacities required by each case.
3. The amount of data movement required by each case.
4. The sequence of object time execution typically assumed by the source programmer.

The most popular form has been the *Early Operator Reverse Polish* (EORP) with the operands in standard order (i.e., $A_1 A_2 \odot$). The next example which is slightly more complex provides additional insight into the notation (where ↑ denotes exponentiation):

$$\text{Standard notation: } X \leftarrow A + B \uparrow C * (D - E)$$
$$\text{EORP: } XABC \uparrow DE - * + \leftarrow$$

The reasons for the popularity of Polish notation are clear: 1. Operands can be moved directly from the source statement to the Polish string, requiring no intermediate storage; 2. The operands appear in a sequence expected by the user; and 3. The occurrence of an early operator during Polish to target language conversion allows immediate output (i.e., code generation), without requiring that the entire statement be available. EORP notation is used exclusively in the following section on stack compilation techniques.

4.3   STACK COMPILATION TECHNIQUES

The *stack* is an invaluable mechanism in source language translation. It may be used in processing (and executing) all constituents of a program. In this chapter, it is applied only to arithmetic statements. Later, it will be applied to other parts of a program.

Techniques for translating from source language to early operator reverse Polish notation (hereafter called reverse Polish or simply Polish)

are described. The succeeding step in the processing of airthmetic statements, which usually involves a translation from Polish to target language
or an interpretation of the Polish notation, will be left for the programmer.

Stacks

A stack or pushdown store is simply a list or chain of registers. It may be
implemented as a list structure* or an array. Regardless of implementation, it has the same property: data is removed on a *last-in-next-out* basis.
Common terminology would call this a LIFO stack for last-in-first-out.
It may be visualized as a stack of plates with a fixed bottom and a top,
whose level moves up and down with the number of plates in the stack.

Simple Arithmetic Statements

The notion of using a stack to translate an arithmetic statement from
standard mathematical notation to Polish notation is indeed an unusual
technique and is introduced by considering only simple arithmetic statements, i.e., those which do not contain parentheses or subscripted variables. The concept is extended for translating generalized arithmetic
statements in the next section.

The translation process is facilitated by the use of a T-junction, similar
in structure to a railway switching network:

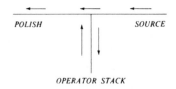

During translation, operands (identifiers and constants) pass directly
from *SOURCE* to *POLISH;* but, in general, operators reach the *POLISH*
list via the *OPERATOR STACK*. Before an operator is shunted to the
OPERATOR STACK, however, any operators at the top of the stack,
which have a hierarchy equal to or greater than that of the current operator (i.e., the one being processed), are allowed to pass to the POLISH
string. Table 4.1 gives a general operator and delimiter hierarchy table;
it is followed by Table 4.2, which gives the functions denoted by the operators and delimiters.

---

*For a discussion of list structures, see chapter 6.

TABLE 4.1   OPERATOR AND DELIMITER HIERARCHY TABLE

Hierarchy Number	0	1	2	3	4	5	6	7	8	9	10
Operators,	(⊢ ↓	) ⊣	∨	∧	¬	= ≠ ← < ≤ > ≥	,]	− +	* /	↑ ~	[

TABLE 4.2   FUNCTIONS DENOTED BY OPERATORS AND DELIMITERS

Operator(s) / Delimiter(s)	Function(s)
( )	Grouping
[ ]	Enclose subscripts
⊢ ⊣	Beginning of statement; end of statement
∧ ∨	Logical operators: and, or
+ − * / ↑	Arithmetic operators: plus, minus, multiply, divide, exponentiation
= ≠ > ≥ < ≤	Relational operators: equal to, not equal to, greater than, greater than or equal to, less than, less than or equal to
↓	Subscript operator
←	Replacement operator
,	Separates subscripts
~	Unary arithmetic operator: negation
¬	Unary logical operator: not

For example, consider the translation of the statement

$$Y \leftarrow A + B * C / 3$$

to Polish notation.

The identifier "Y" is passed to *POLISH* directly; the "←" cannot cause any operator unstacking, since the stack is empty and is stacked itself. Similarly, "A" is sent directly to *POLISH*, and the T-junction looks as follows:

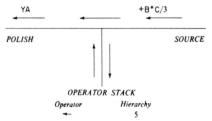

The "+" with a hierarchy of seven cannot cause the "←" to be unstacked before it and is stacked also. The identifier "B" is transferred to *POLISH*, and the T-junction looks as follows:

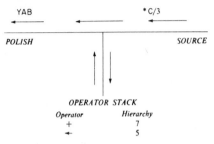

The "*" and "C" are handled similarly, since "*" has a hierarchy of eight:

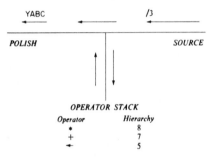

The current operator "/", having a hierarchy equal to that of "*" at the top of the *OPERATOR STACK*, causes "*" to be unstacked to the *POLISH* string. Then, the "/" is stacked. After the "3" has been processed, the T-junction looks as follows:

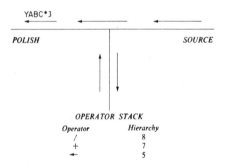

Since there is no *SOURCE* remaining, the *OPERATOR STACK* is emptied so that the *POLISH* string reads as follows:

$$YABC*3/+\leftarrow$$

The expression is read from left to right and is an early operator reverse Polish (EORP) representation of the original statement, which was written in standard mathematical form.

Generalized Arithmetic Statements

The preceding section simply introduced the topic of translating arithmetic statements from standard mathematical notation to EORP notation. Several extensions must be mentioned before the translation process can be treated in general:

1. The operation " ~ " replaces the operator " – ", when it is used as negation. This is recognized during initial scan, when the " – " is preceded by a "(", " = ", or " ↑ ". For example:

$$\text{Source:} \quad Y \leftarrow -A*B+(C*D)$$
$$\text{Polish:} \quad YA \sim B*CD*+\leftarrow$$

2. Relational and logical operators have also been included in the hierarchy table with appropriate priorities.
3. Subscripts on variables are denoted by opening and closing square brackets. The delimiter "," used between subscript expressions eventually gets routed to the *POLISH* string and serves to denote

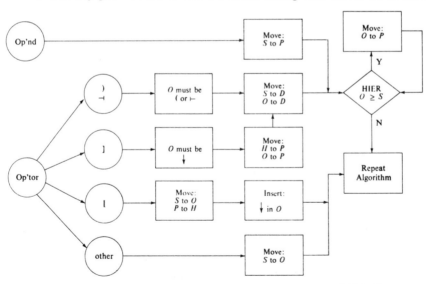

S–SOURCE STRING; O–OPERATOR STACK; P–POLISH STRING; H–HOLD STACK; D–DISCARD

Fig. 4.1   General flow diagram for an arithmetic statement translator.
S—SOURCE STRING; O—OPERATOR STACK; P—POLISH STRING; H—HOLD STACK; D—DISCARD

the number of subscripts to the Polish-to-target language translator or interpreter.

The generalized translation algorithm is straightforward and well-defined; it has been used in many compilers and interpreters as well. The flow diagram originated at the Burroughs Corporation and was used in conjunction with their B5000 system, the method has been published in several versions since. It is included as Fig. 4.1 and requires Table 4.1 as an operator table; both were used in the development of Table 4.3, which is an example of this more general technique.

TABLE 4.3   PICTORIAL REPRESENTATION OF STACK TRANSLATION TECHNIQUES
            FOR ARITHMETIC STATEMENTS

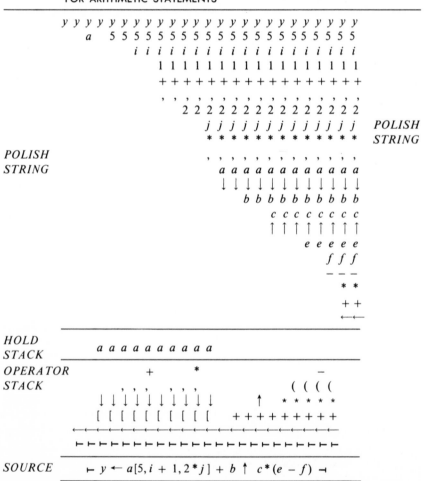

Figure 4.1 and Table 4.1, as well as Table 4.3, should serve as procedural references to the subject.

4.4   IDENTITIES AND DUALITY IN PROGRAMMING LANGUAGES

One of the main objectives of a good compiler is to decrease the size and minimize the execution time of the generated machine language program. This is usually discussed under the topic of optimization and is concerned mainly with common subexpressions and the removal of statements from iterative loops.* Optimization is also feasible at the operator level, which is the subject of this section. Two aspects are considered: formal identities and duality. *Formal identities* permit unnecessary operators to be removed from arithmetic expressions, resulting in a potential savings in program size and execution time. *Duality* of operators allows the inclusion of only one of a dual pair of operators. This is particularly useful when the operator turns out to be a programmed function which occupies a significant amount of storage space.

Formal Identities

The representation of an arithmetic statement in Polish notation makes it especially amenable to analysis for the removal of unnecessary operators. Heretofore, only the translation process from standard mathematical notation to Polish notation has been described. Although the reverse process, i.e., the translation from Polish notation to standard algebraic form, is indeed less complex, it is not as well known and is discussed here. The reverse process (termed retranslating or retranslation) is necessary for some examples that deal with formal identities.

Once an expression has been reduced to reverse Polish, retranslation is accomplished by scanning the string from left to right until the first operator is located. The operator is then placed between the two preceding operands with all three items becoming a parenthetical group in the string. The procedure is repeated, always initiating the scan from the left, until a fully parenthesized statement in standard mathematical notation is formed. For example, the Polish string

$$XABC*D/+\leftarrow$$

would be retranslated in the following steps:

1. In the left to right scan, the first operator * is placed between the two preceding operands, i.e., B*C, giving

$$XA(B*C)D/+\leftarrow$$

*See chapter 8 for a discussion of *common subexpressions* and *removable statements*.

with the parenthesized expression to be regarded henceforth as an operand.

2. The scan is repeated, and the / is recognized as the next operator; it is also placed between the two preceding operands, giving

$$XA((B*C)/D)+\leftarrow$$

3. The operator + is recognized next and processed accordingly

$$X(A+((B*C)/D))\leftarrow$$

4. Finally, the last operator is $\leftarrow$; the completely retranslated statement, therefore, is

$$(X\leftarrow(A+((B*C)/D))$$

or written in standard algebraic form as

$$X = A + \frac{BC}{D}$$

Historically, treatment of the unary minus has been a problem. It is recognized in an arithmetic statement as the first character following the replacement operator =, a left parenthesis, or the exponentiation operator ↑. It is of interest here because in many cases, its use is superfluous; for example, the arithmetic expression

$$(-A)*(-B)$$

may be replaced without question by A*B. Certain combinations of operators and the unary minus may be manipulated so that the number of unary minus operators in an expression are minimized. Table 4.4 contains a complete list of formal identities developed by Professor J. A. N. Lee, head of the Computer Science program at the University of Massachusetts.[4] In the table, π, ρ, and τ denote operands, and $\sim$ denotes the unary minus. Each identity is first given in standard mathematical form and then followed by its equivalent in Polish notation.

Using the identities is essentially a matter of moving the imbedded unary minus operators to the right in the Polish string; in the process, standard operand-operator sequences are replaced by reduced forms from the table of identities. As an example, consider the expression:

$$(-B)*(-A)$$

or in Polish notation

$$B \sim A \sim *$$

TABLE 4.4   FORMAL IDENTITIES†

Original Expression	Reduced Expression
1. $\pi+(-\rho)$	$\pi-\rho$
$\pi\rho\sim+$	$\pi\rho-$
2. $\pi-(-\rho)$	$\pi+\rho$
$\pi\rho\sim-$	$\pi\rho+$
3. $\pi*(-\rho)$	$-(\pi*\rho)$
$\pi\rho\sim*$	$\pi\rho*\sim$
4. $\pi/(-\rho)$	$-(\pi/\rho)$
$\pi\rho\sim/$	$\pi\rho/\sim$
5. $-\pi-\rho$	$-(\pi+\rho)$
$\pi\sim\rho-$	$\pi\rho+\sim$
6. $-\pi+\rho$ or $-(\pi-\rho)$	$\rho-\pi$
$\pi\sim\rho+$ $\pi\rho-\sim$	$\rho\pi-$
7. $-\pi*\rho$	$-(\pi*\rho)$
$\pi\sim\rho*$	$\pi\rho*\sim$
8. $-\pi/\rho$	$-(\pi/\rho)$
$\pi\sim\rho/$	$\pi\rho/\sim$
9. $(-(-\pi))$	π
$\pi\sim\sim$	π
10. $\pi*\rho\uparrow(-\tau)$	$\pi/(\rho\uparrow\tau)$
$\pi\rho\tau\sim\uparrow*$	$\pi\rho\tau\uparrow/$
11. $\pi/(\rho\uparrow(-\tau))$	$\pi*\rho\uparrow\tau$
$\pi\rho\tau\sim\uparrow/$	$\pi\rho\tau\uparrow*$

† Reproduced by permission of the publisher.

Using identity 3, this expression is transmuted to

$$B\sim A*\sim$$

or for clarity

$$[B\sim A*]\sim.$$

By identity 7

$$[BA*\sim]\sim$$

and by 9

$$BA*$$

which is retranslated to read

$$(B*A).$$

As another example, consider the expression,

$$-D-A+B*(-C)$$

i.e., in Polish notation,

$$D \sim A - BC \sim * +.$$

By identity 3,

$$D \sim A - BC* \sim +$$

and from identity 1,

$$D \sim A - BC* -$$

or more clearly,

$$[D \sim A-][BC*]-.$$

Using identity 5, this is transmuted to read,

$$[DA+] \sim [BC*]-$$

and again from 5,

$$[DA+BC*]+ \sim .$$

The latter expression can then be retranslated to the following algebraic form:

$$-((D+A)+(B*C))$$

thereby eliminating one operation from the expression.

Duality

With the exception of Iverson's paper on the subject,[3] very little is available in the literature, if anything at all, on the duality of operators in programming languages. The concept promises to be a fruitful one with the increased popularity of rich languages* currently being made available with interactive time-sharing systems. The large number of operators poses a potential problem, especially where internal storage may be of concern. The use of *dual operators*, therefore, is conceivably a means of reducing the total number of operators required.

---

*A "rich language" is generally regarded as one which allows a wide variety of data types extended to include structured operands, such as vectors and matrices. A wide variety of operators is also provided for effectively utilizing the extended operand types. The net result is that a significant amount of computation may be achieved with each interaction with the computing system.

A unary operator τ is defined to be *self-inverse* if $\tau(\tau X) \leftrightarrow X$. If ϕ, θ, and τ are unary operators and the following conditions hold:

1. τ is self-inverse,
2. $\phi X \longleftrightarrow \tau(\theta(\tau X))$

then $\theta X \longleftrightarrow \tau(\phi(\tau X))$ and ϕ and θ are said to be *dual with respect to τ.* * The floor and ceiling operators[†] are dual with respect to the minus operator e.g.,

$$\lfloor X \longleftrightarrow -\lceil(-X)$$

Moreover, some unary operators are *self dual* (i.e., $\phi = \theta$) and other operators are self dual but only with respect to themselves. The following expressions are examples of self duality (here $\div$ as a unary operator denotes reciprocation):

$$-X \longleftrightarrow -(-(-X))$$
$$\div X \longleftrightarrow -(\div(-X))$$
$$-X \longleftrightarrow \div(-(\div X))$$
$$\div X \longleftrightarrow \div(\div(\div X))$$

The duality of binary operators is developed in a similar fashion. If ϕ and θ are binary operators, if τ is a self-inverse unary operator, and if

$$X\phi Y \longleftrightarrow \tau((\tau X)\theta(\tau Y))$$

then $X\theta Y \longleftrightarrow \tau((\tau X)\phi(\tau Y))$ and ϕ and θ are said to be dual with respect to τ. As examples, the MAX and MIN operators[‡] are dual with respect to minus and the logical operators AND and OR ($\wedge$ and $\vee$) are dual with respect to logical negation, as are the relational operators $=$ and $\neq$.

The amount of duality among the basic operators of a programming language is obviously dependent upon the original design philosophy. When adding an operator (or function) to a language, however, there is certainly no harm in considering its dual operator, since the incremental cost of its implementation is minimal.

4.5   ADDITIONAL TOPICS

A large amount of information is available on compiler-writing methods; only the most elementary and straightforward of these have been pre-

---

* Abbreviated "dual wrt."

[†] The floor of X, written $\lfloor X$, is defined as the largest integer not exceeding X. Similarly, the ceiling of X, written $\lceil X$, is defined as the smallest integer not exceeded by X.

[‡] More precisely defined as functions.

sented. Several topics are of prime importance and should at least be mentioned.

Optimization is of major concern. The processing of *common subexpressions* and *removable statements** is desirable but requires that a program be analyzed into functional blocks with predecessor and successor relationships. The analysis of program flow is nontrivial, and much theoretical work has been performed in support of it.

Every programming language has a syntactic structure of some kind, and that fact is reflected, either explicitly or implicitly, in every compiler. The effective use of syntactical methods, as introduced in the next chapter, should be a challenge to every compiler writer.

Additional topics are too numerous to describe in detail. A basic list would necessarily include: the processing of data structures,† local and global variables, recursive techniques, file handling, and compilation in virtual machines. The list could go on for many paragraphs.

PROBLEMS

4.1   Show how the overall design of the original FORTRAN compiler would be modified to process a language such as COBOL (Appendix B).

4.2   Draw a flow diagram for evaluating an expression in reverse Polish notation and another for forward Polish notation. Compare the two.

4.3   Write a program in a popular programming language for adding items to and extracting items from a *stack*.

4.4   Program the "General Flow Diagram for an Arithmetic Statement Translator," Fig. 4.1.

REFERENCES

1. Backus, J. W., *et al.*, "The FORTRAN Automatic Coding System," *Proceedings of the Western Joint Computer Conference*, Vol. 11, p. 188, 1957. Describes the original FORTRAN language and compiler.

2. Baeker, H. C., and B. J. Gibbons, "A Commercial Use of Stacks," (R. Goodman, ed.), *Annual Review in Automatic Programming*, **4,** New York, Macmillan Company, 1964. Introduces the use of the push-down stack technique in the design of language processors.

3. Iverson, K. E., "Formalism in Programming Languages," *Communications of the ACM*, **7,** Number 2, p. 80 (February, 1964). Presents formal relationships between operators in a higher level programming language.

4. Lee, J. A. N., *The Anatomy of a Compiler*, New York, Reinhold Publishing Corp., 1967. Discusses basic compiler methods including Polish notation, identities, and compiler organization.

*See chapter 8.
†See chapter 6.

5. Randell, B., and L. J. Russell, *ALGOL 60 Implementation*, New York, Academic Press, 1964. Describes a complete compiler for the ALGOL language. The methods include Polish notation and use of the T-junction.
6. Wegner, P., (ed.), *Introduction to System Programming*, New York, Academic Press, 1964. Presents methods for translating arithmetic statements from infix to Polish notation.

5 | SYNTACTICAL METHODS

In spite of their obvious advantages, several problems were associated with programming languages and compilers right from the beginning and have continued to exist. The first problem is that of *denoting valid programs* in a given programming language; i.e., to what conventions should a programmer adhere so that his programs are acceptable to the compiler and will also give him the expected results. The next problem is the *multiplicity of compilers* required to support the various programming languages. Each language requires a compiler, which involves not only an initial investment but also a maintenance effort for an extended period of time. The last problem is *change*. Every time a change is made to a programming language, a corresponding modification to its compiler is required. Furthermore, a complete set of compilers has to be written each time a new generation of computers is produced.

What is desired, therefore, is a means of describing valid statements in a language that would aid a programmer in writing acceptable statements and that would ease the compiler problem, as well. In fact, it would be advantageous to have just one compiler that would accept a description of the language, in addition to the source language program. Changes to a programming language would then require only a modification to the language description instead of a modification to its compiler. A new language would not require a new compiler but simply an appropriate description of it. Finally, the development of a new generation of computers would require that only one compiler be rewritten. The total concept is known as *syntax-directed* compiling. This chapter is limited, how-ever, to some of the more significant aspects of syntactical methods.

The problem of satisfying both the human user and the computer is obviously nontrivial. As an example of this, consider the following description of an arithmetic expression. It is perhaps typical of the many ways in which such a description has been expressed.

Let E denote the set of permissible arithmetic expressions and let e denote any member of that set. Let c be any constant and v be any variable (subscripted or not) or value of a function. If $\oplus$ is an arithmetic operation, then

1. c is in E;
2. v is in E;
3. e is in E;
4. $+e$ or $-e$ is in E, provided that the leftmost character of e is not $+$ or $-$;
5. $e_1 \oplus e_2$ is in E, provided that two arithmetic operators do not appear in succession.
6. Only the expressions defined in 1 through 5 are in E.

The description gives us a fairly good idea of what an arithmetic expression is, providing we have prior knowledge of constants, variables, and functions. On the other hand, it would be totally unacceptable as input to a compiler or as a precise description of an arithmetic expression.

The generation and recognition of valid constructs in a language is a familiar problem—not only to programmers—but also to logicians and linguists. *Post production systems* were developed by the logician Emil Post, so that well-formed formulas (wff's) in symbolic logic could be determined. *Phrase-structure grammars* were developed by the linguist Chomsky in the study of natural languages for similar reasons. Lastly, *Backus normal form* was developed by the programmer John Backus for the study of programming languages.* All of these systems had the same basic objective, which was to specify rules of formation for acceptable sentences in their respective languages. This chapter is concerned primarily with rules and recognizers for programming languages.

5.1 GRAMMARS FOR PROGRAMMING LANGUAGES

A *syntax* or *grammar* for a programming language is a set of rules for denoting valid statements in that language. One of the most widely known

---

*See the references by Davis, Floyd, and Korfhage for background material on syntactical methods.

grammars is Backus normal form,[1] which was originally used for describing the ALGOL programming language. Many variations exist, of which Ingerman's *metasyntactic notation*[5] seems to be the most completely developed. Another form named *Inverted Notation*, which has been patterned after the metalanguage* used with COBOL, is introduced. The discussion returns to syntactical methods after some introductory material is presented.

Preliminary Information

Programs in a programming language are represented by strings of characters over a finite alphabet composed of letters, digits, and a number of punctuation characters, delimiters, and operation symbols. The set of all permissible characters is denoted by A and is termed the alphabet of the language L. The set of all finite strings over A of L will be denoted by $A*$. The purpose of a syntactical description is to distinguish strings of $A*$ which belong to L from those which do not belong to L.

A grammar G is required for a language L in order to specify it in a constructive manner. This is equivalent to saying: given a string α of $A*$, determine whether or not it is a valid string in $L(G)$.[†]

A *grammar* is a metalanguage for specifying sets of strings. Mathematically, elements of a set are simply listed; e.g.,

$$A = \{a_1, a_2, a_3\}$$

This notation has been varied somewhat as follows:

$$A = a_1 \mid a_2 \mid a_3$$

where " $\mid$ " denotes *exclusive or* and the statement is read, "an instance of A is $a_1, a_2,$ or a_3." The philosophy has been extended so that elements (we shall later call them constructions) may also be sets. The following sets are equivalent:

$$X = xy \mid yz \mid zw \mid wa$$

and

$$X = Y \mid Z$$
$$Y = xy \mid yz$$
$$Z = zw \mid wa$$

---

*A *metalanguage* is a language used to describe other languages. Essentially, inverted notation is the same as SRL notation used with IBM Systems Reference Library publications. It is included here because of its general use.

†Symbolically, $L(G)$ represents a language L specified by a grammar G.

Concatenation of sets is also permitted and defined as follows:

> If X and Y are sets, the notation XY is used to denote any element of the set X followed by any element of the set Y. For example, if $X = x \mid y$ and $Y = z \mid w$, then
>
> $$XY = xz \mid xw \mid yz \mid yw$$

Infinite sets can be defined recursively by including the left-hand side (later called defined type) on the right-hand side; e.g., the definition

$$X = a \mid Xa$$

would define the infinite set $\{a, aa, aaa, aaaa, \ldots\}$.

Grammars for Simple Arithmetic Statements

Consider a simple language for arithmetic statements which allows replacement, addition, and multiplication. It is specified syntactically in each of the metalanguages mentioned above.

1. *Backus Normal Form* (BNF).
   The symbol "$::=$" stands for "is defined to be"; "$\mid$" stands for "or" and is used to separate alternate forms of the definition. The angular brackets "$<>$" are used to enclose the name of a phrase type, distinguishing it as a name rather than as an object named. All other symbols are literals which represent themselves.

   ```
   <program> ::= <assignment> | <assignment>; <program>
   <assignment> ::= <variable> = <arith expr>
   <arith expr> ::= <term> | <arith expr> + <term>
   <term> ::= <factor> | <term> * <factor>
   <factor> ::= <variable> | <integer> | (<arith expr>)
   <variable> ::= <letter> | <variable> <letter> |
                  <variable> <digit>
   <integer> ::= <digit> | <integer> <digit>
   <letter> ::= A | B | ... | X | Y | Z
   <digit> ::= 0 | 1... | 7 | 8 | 9
   ```

   An obvious question might be, "Is the syntactic specification order dependent?" The answer is both yes and no and pertains to the other grammars as well as Backus normal form. If the user's objective is to determine the structure of a particular statement or to validate a statement by manual methods, then the order is certainly not important. If, on the other hand, the objective is to develop a computer algorithm for syntax checking, then the order may be important and contributes to the efficiency and effectiveness of the program.

2. *Ingerman's Metasyntactic Language.*

In this metasyntactic language, a *rule* has the general form of an accretion of *metacomponents* to the right of which is juxtaposed a *metaresult*. As an example, the rule

$$ABC <d>$$

should be read "the object A followed by the object B followed by the object C is given the name $<d>$". Again, the angular brackets "$<>$" denote the name of something, and literals stand for themselves.

A   <letter>
B   <letter>
C   <letter>
D   <letter>
E   <letter>
F   <letter>
G   <letter>
H   <letter>
I   <letter>
J   <letter>
K   <letter>
L   <letter>
M   <letter>
N   <letter>
O   <letter>
P   <letter>
Q   <letter>
R   <letter>
S   <letter>
T   <letter>
U   <letter>
V   <letter>
W   <letter>
X   <letter>
Y   <letter>
Z   <letter>
0   <digit>
1   <digit>
2   <digit>
3   <digit>
4   <digit>
5   <digit>

6   <digit>
7   <digit>
8   <digit>
9   <digit>
+   <add op>
*   <mult op>
<digit><integer>
<integer><digit><integer>
<letter><variable>
<variable><letter><variable>
<variable><digit><variable>
<variable><factor>
<integer><factor>
(<arith expr>) <factor>
<factor><term>
<term><mult op><factor><term>
<term><arith expr>
<arith expr><add op><term><arith expr>
<variable> = <arith expr><assignment>
<assignment><program>
<assignment>; <program><program>

3. *Inverted Notation.*
   Inverted notation is an attempt to combine the outstanding features
   of several notations. When many syntactic alternatives are available
   in the language which is being described, the Backus and Ingerman
   forms tend to become quite lengthy. Inverted notation attempts to
   reduce this tendency. Again, some definitions are required:

   [ ]   optional
   { }   take a choice of
   ...   repetition of the preceding component
   .n.   n repetitions of the preceding component
   =   is defined as
   | or
   ' '   encloses terminal characters

   The name inverted notation is derived from the fact that names of
   constructs are *not* enclosed in delimiters as are literals. Inverted
   notation is applicable to a wide variety of language types and is particularly useful for describing control languages.† It should be noted

†See chapter 7.

that in the example of a simple arithmetic statement, the power of inverted notation is not particularly exercised.

program = {assignment | assignment ';' program}
assignment = variable '=' arith-expr
arith-expr = {term | arith-expr '+' term}
term = {factor | term '*' factor}
factor = {variable | integer | '(' arith-expr ')'}
variable = letter [{letter | digit} ...]
integer = digit [digit ...]
letter = {A | B | ... | X | Y | Z}
digit = {0 | 1 | ... | 7 | 8 | 9}

5.2   ELEMENTS OF SYNTACTICAL SPECIFICATIONS

A *syntactic specification* of a language is a concise and compact represen-tation of the structure of that language, but is merely that, and does not by itself constitute a set of procedures either for generating valid strings in the language or for recognizing a valid string. In section 5.4, syntax-directed methods for syntax recognition are considered. By this it is meant that the syntactic structure of the language is not reflected in the internal coding of the *recognizer* itself. Instead, it is expressed in a *normal form*, such as inverted notation, and read into the recognizer as data along with the source program. Later, the recognizer will be referred to as a *syntax checker*.

In order to discuss the structure of a language, names are given to classes of strings in the metalanguage. These classes are called *syntactic types*.

One obvious syntactic type is the alphabet of the language. These char-acters are called *terminal types* or more specifically, *terminal characters*. Classes which are defined in terms of other classes are termed *defined types*. Consider the following specification in BNF:

$$<assignment> ::= <variable> = <arith expr>$$

The type which is defined on the left side of the "::=" is called the defined type of the definition; the *definition* is said to be a definition of its defined type. The right-hand side will be called the *definiens*. Any sequence of type designators within the definiens is termed a *construction*, and any type designator within a construction is a *component*. Consider the fol-lowing examples:

$$<assignment> ::= <variable> = <arith expr> \qquad (1)$$
$$<term> ::= <factor> | <term> * <factor> \qquad (2)$$

In (1), <assignment> is the defined type of the definition, and the definiens has one construction composed of three components. The first component, <variable>, is defined type; the next component, " = ", is a terminal character of the alphabet; and the last component, <arith expr>, is another defined type. In (2), the defined type of the definition, i.e., <term>, is composed of two constructions. The first construction, <factor>, has only one component. The second construction has three components which are <term>, "*", and <factor>, respectively.

In order that the syntax specification constitutes a useful set of rules, three conditions must be met:

c1: Any *defined type* which occurs as a *component* in a *definiens* must also occur as the *defined type* of some definition.

c2: Every *defined type* must ultimately be constructible entirely out of *terminal characters*.

c3: There must be exactly one *defined type* which does not appear as a *component* in any *definiens* except its own. This type is termed the *starting type* of the syntax specification.

When each definition in a syntax specification depends only on itself or on the defined types in the preceding lines, then the specification has the property of being *sequentially definable*. Moreover, recursion within definitions permits syntactical constructs to be composed of like constructs (phrases may be composed of phrases). *Phrase structure grammars* (PSG), therefore, are those which allow recursion and permit a deviation from sequential definition. This latitude allows what might be loosely called a *second order inclusion* of phrases. That is, phrases may be components of clauses, and clauses may be components of phrases.

It is evident that a complete definition of a programming language may be expressed far more concisely by a PSG than by the corresponding English sentence. Most of the rules defining the language can be neatly and compactly listed without explanation, conserving space and time, and insuring clarity. The rules of a PSG are analogous to axioms. One who has received a program and an understanding of its structure can use a PSG to show that the program is well-formed and demonstrate its structure to others.

5.3   PICTORIAL REPRESENTATION OF A GRAMMAR

Syntactical specifications of programming languages are admittedly difficult to decipher, at times. In fact, the utility of the time invested is often very low. Nevertheless, grammars are necessary, especially for the more sophisticated languages. Ingerman[5] has developed a pictorial representation of a grammar, which is based on a few simple concepts. His method is particularly useful for the occasional user who is employing manual methods.

Consider the grammar for simple arithmetic statements, discussed previously. Each definition may be considered a little piece of a directed graph. Recall the following rule:

<term> ::= <factor> | <term> * <factor>

Using + to represent juxtaposition and ∨ to indicate a selection among alternatives, this rule may be written in the form of a small directed graph:

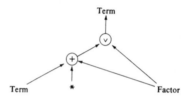

and may be further compressed to:

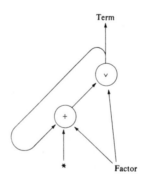

where the bifurcation in the above graph indicates the recursive nature of the grammar.

The entire set of rules of a language can be combined into a *graph of the language*. A graph of the grammar for simple arithmetic statements, introduced in section 5.1, is included as Fig. 5.1. The graph has loops in

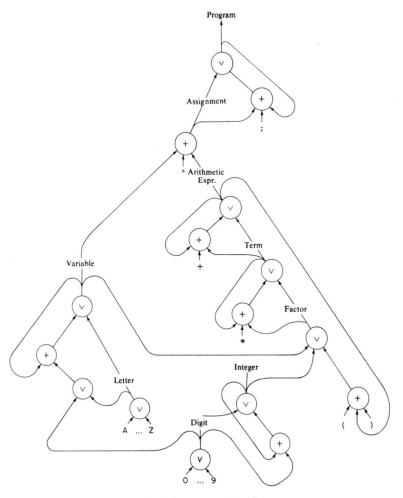

Fig. 5.1 Pictorial representation of a grammar.

it; however, this should be expected, since defined types can serve as components of other defined types. Even though a graph of a language can have loops in it, it should be noted that each rule appears only once.

5.4   SYNTAX ENCODING AND RECOGNITION

Earlier in this chapter, the concept of syntax recognition was introduced, implying some sort of recognizer which utilizes a syntactic description of the language and is capable of returning an indication of whether a particular statement is valid or invalid. Basically, the problem is as follows: Given a set of rules (syntax specification) for forming statements of a language, how is it determined whether any specific source string is a valid construct? The procedure begins by guessing or predicting how the statement is constructed, and either verifying this or backing up to try again, assuming some other method of construction. The process terminates when it is finally determined whether or not the statement is valid. As was mentioned earlier, the process is *syntax-directed* in that the syntax is encoded in a table rather than designed into the coding of the *syntax recognizer program*. Before proceeding with the recognizer program (hereafter called the *syntax checker*), some introductory material must be presented.

Basic Philosophy

At the beginning of the process, the syntax checker takes the starting specification as its first goal. The following procedure is then followed for subsequent defined types when they are selected as current goals:

> The syntax checker consults the definition of the defined type and considers the first alternative in the definition. It then successively takes each component of that alternative as a subgoal. If at any point it fails to find one of these subgoals, it abandons that alternative and considers the next alternative in that definition. If there is no next alternative, it has failed to realize its current goal and reports that to its *parent goal*. If it succeeds in finding the subgoals corresponding to each of the components of any alternative, it has found its goal and returns that indication.

Terminal Classes

An important consideration is the input and scanning of source statement. A SCAN routine is utilized which reads source records and keeps track of where in the input string the syntax checker is looking. When some component of an alternative has been verified and when the syntax checker desires to look at the next component, SCAN moves its input-string pointer to the following component. This is logical since a defined type which has been successfully recognized consists, ultimately, of a sequence of terminal characters, and the recognition of terminal characters is the job of the SCAN routine.

SCAN is the syntax checker's interface with the outside world. Therefore, the syntax checker is in a position to subordinate some of the detail ordinarily associated with syntax-directed methods to this routine. As a result, a concept of terminal classes is designated; some familiar examples are: *name*, *number*, and *literal*. Problems associated with these classes can be left entirely to the SCAN mechanism, which is sometimes required to operate in machine dependent fashion.

Encoding the Syntax Specification

To some extent, the manner in which the syntax is encoded is dependent upon the grammar. In spite of this, some general techniques can be developed. The techniques are oriented towards inverted notation. In fact, some modifications to our syntactical terminology are required to utilize this notation. In BNF, the major syntactical unit of the definiens is the construction which is composed of components. In inverted notation, the construction is not the major syntactical unit, but rather, the definiens is composed of *required elements, alternative elements,* and *optional elements.* Moreover, optional elements may be further composed of required or optional elements. The basic syntactical unit will still be called the component. The following examples demonstrate the new terminology ("eos" denotes end of statement):

$$\text{display} = \text{`DISPLAY'} \quad \{\text{name} \mid \text{literal}\} \quad \text{eos} \qquad (1)$$

$$\text{read} = \text{`READ'} \quad \text{name} \quad [\text{`RECORD'}] \quad [\text{`INTO'} \quad \text{name}] \quad \text{eos} \qquad (2)$$

In (1), 'DISPLAY' and *eos* are required elements; *name,* and *literal* are alternative elements. In (2), 'READ', *name,* and *eos* are required elements, while 'RECORD' and 'INTO' *name* are optional elements. If the element ['INTO' *name*] is selected, then both components are required.

A straightforward method of syntax encoding and recognition as well is presented. It is derived from a more general scheme developed by Cheatham and Sattley.[2] The encoding consists of two tables: the *syntax type table* and the *syntax structure table.* The syntax type table will contain an entry for each *syntactic type* which occurs anywhere in the syntax specification, whether it be a defined type or a *terminal type.* Each entry in the table consists of three items: a *type index,* a *yes-no item* indicating whether the type is terminal or not, and a *definition number* pointing to a line in the syntax structure table.

The syntax structure table will contain a line for each component of each element of each definiens in the syntax specification. Each line of the structure table will consist of these items:

1. *TYPECODE,* a pointer to a syntactic type in the syntax type table;
2. *SUCCESSOR,* a number representing lines in the syntax structure table—usually for the next component of a syntactical element, except for last components for which the field is set to OK; and
3. *ALTERNATE,* a number representing another line in the syntax structure table—usually for pointing to alternatives within the same syntactical element.

The syntax structure table is composed according to the following rules:

1. For each required element, set the *SUCCESSOR* to the line corresponding to the next syntactical element. Set the *ALTERNATIVE* to FAIL.
2. For each component, except the last, of an alternative element, set the *ALTERNATIVE* to the line number of the next component of *that* alternative element. Set the *ALTERNATIVE* of the last component to FAIL. Set the *SUCCESSOR* of all components to the line number of the next syntactical element. For all repeated alternative elements, set the *SUCCESSOR* of all components to the line number of the first component of that element.
3. For each component, except the last, of an optional element, set the *SUCCESSOR* to the next component in *that* element. Set the *SUCCESSOR* or the last component to the *next* syntactical element. Set all *ALTERNATIVES* to the next syntactical element.

As an introductory example, a restricted subset of COBOL has been selected for syntax checking and is presented as Table 5.1.

TABLE 5.1   MINI-COBOL

WRITE name [FROM name]
DISPLAY {name | literal}
READ   name   [RECORD][INTO   name]
ADD   {name | literal}[{name | literal} . . .]{TO | GIVING}   name
GOTO   name
MOVE   [name | literal}   TO   name

Accordingly, a syntax specification of this language in inverted notation has been developed as Table 5.2.

TABLE 5.2   SYNTAX SPECIFICATION OF MINI-COBOL

---

statement = {write | display | read | add | goto | move}
write = 'WRITE'   name   ['FROM' name]   eos
display = 'DISPLAY'   {name | literal}   eos
read = 'READ'   name   ['RECORD']['INTO'   name]   eos
add = 'ADD'{name | literal}[{name | literal} . . .]{'TO' | 'GIVING'}   name   eos
goto = 'GOTO'   name   eos
move = 'MOVE'   {name | literal}   'TO'   name   eos
eos = '⊥'
name = N
literal = L

The process of transforming the language description into a syntax specification is straightforward, which is partially the result of selecting an appropriate grammar. Using the rules given earlier in this section, the syntax type table and the syntax structure table are developed as Tables 5.3 and 5.4, respectively.

TABLE 5.3   SYNTAX TYPE TABLE

(*GOAL*) *Type*	*Index*	*Terminal*	*Definition*
statement	i	N	1
write	ii	N	7
display	iii	N	12
read	iv	N	16
add	v	N	22
goto	vi	N	31
move	vii	N	34
'WRITE'	viii	Y	
'FROM'	ix	Y	
'DISPLAY'	x	Y	
'READ'	xi	Y	
'RECORD'	xii	Y	
'INTO'	xiii	Y	
'ADD'	xiv	Y	
'TO'	xv	Y	
'GIVING'	xvi	Y	
'GOTO'	xvii	Y	
'MOVE'	xviii	Y	
eos	xix	Y	
name	xx	Y	
literal	xxi	Y	

The next section describes an algorithm for syntax checking, which uses a syntax type table and a syntax structure table as described. The procedures for building these tables are well-defined and amenable to machine processing. Clearly, a computer program could have been written to transform the grammar from inverted notation to the tabular form required by the syntax checker. Such a program is analogous to a metaprogram, except that it accepts syntactic specifications as input and produces syntactic specifications as output. It could appropriately be called a *metasyntactic translator.*

TABLE 5.4   SYNTAX STRUCTURE TABLE

SOURCE	Type	SUCCESSOR	ALTERNATE	Note
1	ii	OK	2	write
2	iii	OK	3	display
3	iv	OK	4	read
4	v	OK	5	add
5	vi	OK	6	goto
6	vii	OK	Fail	move
7	viii	8	Fail	WRITE
8	xx	9	Fail	name
9	ix	10	11	FROM
10	xx	11	Fail	name
11	xix	OK	Fail	eos
12	x	13	Fail	DISPLAY
13	xx	15	14	name
14	xxi	15	Fail	literal
15	xix	OK	Fail	eos
16	xi	17	Fail	READ
17	xx	18	Fail	name
18	xii	19	19	RECORD
19	xiii	20	21	INTO
20	xx	21	Fail	name
21	xix	OK	Fail	eos
22	xiv	23	Fail	ADD
23	xx	25	24	name
24	xxi	25	Fail	literal
25	xx	25	26	name
26	xxi	25	27	literal
27	xv	29	28	TO
28	xvi	29	Fail	GIVING
29	xx	30	Fail	name
30	xix	OK	Fail	eos
31	xvii	32	Fail	GOTO
32	xx	33	Fail	name
33	xix	OK	Fail	eos
34	xviii	35	Fail	MOVE
35	xx	37	36	name
36	xxi	37	Fail	literal
37	xv	38	Fail	TO
38	xx	39	Fail	name
39	xix	OK	Fail	eos

The Syntax-Checker Algorithm

A completely general purpose syntax checker is indeed beyond the scope of this treatment; in fact, there is some doubt (see Conclusions) whether its utility is worth the required investment in time, space, and complexity. However, the concept *is* worthy of note, and the intuitive notions involved should be a part of one's mental repertoire. For these reasons, an algorithm is presented for use with sequentially definable grammars without left recursion.

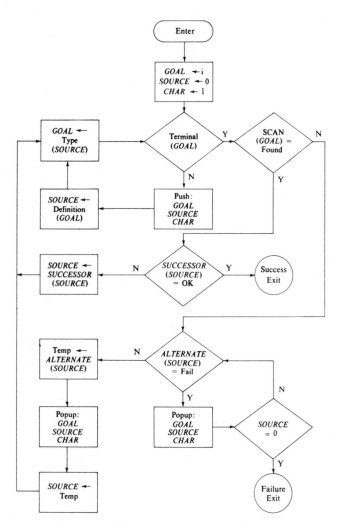

Fig. 5.2 The Syntax-checker algorithm.

The flow chart, Fig. 5.2, illustrates the algorithm working from syntax tables of the sort that have just been described. The following comments will help in following the diagram. The global variables *GOAL*, *SOURCE*, and *CHAR* denote push-down stacks and are used as follows:

1. *GOAL* is the line number in the syntax type table corresponding to the syntactic type currently being considered. It is obtained from the syntax structure table as a function of the *SOURCE* line number.
2. *SOURCE* is the line number in the syntax structure table of the component being considered. It is pointed to by the *DEFINITION* column of the syntax type table and by the *SUCCESSOR* and the *ALTERNATE* columns of the syntax structure table.
3. *CHAR* is a number pointing to the character or terminal type in the input string next to be considered. It is used primarily by the *SCAN* routine.

The SCAN routine looks for a specific terminal symbol or terminal class. It returns a *success* or *failure indicator*, which is tested in the *found box*. The *push* function pushes the *SOURCE*, *GOAL*, or *CHAR* stack entries down one position so that another value can be entered. The *popup* function eliminates the top entry of the specified stack.

At this point, it would be worthwhile for the reader to work through a few examples from Mini-COBOL using Tables 5.1, 5.3, and 5.4 and Fig. 5.2.

Conclusions

It is very evident that syntax-directed analyzers cannot be as efficient as keyword and operator-hierarchy techniques for the simple task of recognizing input structures. This follows from the fact that no matter how cleverly the language designer arranges the syntax specification, the analyzer will necessarily spend some of its time tracing blind alleys. Appropriate specifications can make the blind alleys less frequent and shorter, but there will always be some. One of the major advantages of syntax-directed techniques, however, is that it is very easy to change the specification or the language merely by changing the syntax tables, requiring no modifications to the algorithms. And this is indeed the case.

PROBLEMS

5.1   Given the following description of a simple assignment statement:

```
<statement> ::= <variable> = <expression>
<expression> ::= <term> | <term> + <expression>
<term> ::= <factor> | <factor> * <term>
```

<factor> ::= <variable> | (<expression>)
<variable> ::= *A* | *B* | *C*

Write a computer program to generate the 10 well-formed assignment statements which can be formed from the definition. [Hint: see Irwin, L., "Implementing Phrase-Structure Productions in PL/I," *Comm. ACM*, Vol. **10**, No. 7 (July, 1967), p. 424].

5.2 Consider the grammar of exercise (5.1). Convert the BNF to inverted notation and develop a syntax type table and a syntax structure table for it.

REFERENCES

1. Backus, J. W., "The Syntax and Semantics of the Proposed International Algebraic Language of the Zurich ACM-GAMM Conference," *Proceedings of the International Conference, Information Processing*, UNESCO, Paris, 1960. Describes the syntax used with the ALGOL programming language.
2. Cheatham, T. E., and K. Sattley, "Syntax Directed Compiling," *Proceedings of the Eastern Joint Computer Conference*, AFIPS, vol. **25,** 1964. Contains a complete description of the philosophy and techniques of syntax-directed compiling along with some practical applications.
3. Davis, M., *Computability and Unsolvability*, New York, McGraw-Hill Book Company, 1958. Provides background material on logical systems and well-formed formulas.
4. Floyd, R. W., "The Syntax of Programming Languages—A Survey," *Transactions on Electronic Computers*, IEEE, vol. **EC-13,** (Aug., 1964). Defines and explains such concepts as phrase-structure grammars and syntax-directed analysis.
5. Ingerman, P. Z., *A Syntax-Oriented Translator*, New York, Academic Press, 1966. Presents a single syntax-oriented translator along with definitions and an extensive bibliography.
6. Korfhage, R. R., *Logic and Algorithms: With Applications to the Computer and Information Sciences*, New York, John Wiley and Sons, Inc., 1966. Relates mathematical logic and formal language theory to the computer sciences.

6 | LIST PROCESSING

Many computer applications involve lists of objects. The different kinds of lists may vary between an inventory table composed of stock items and a multilinked structure used as a symbol table in a metaprogram. More formally, a *list* is a set of elements among which an explicit or implicit relationship exists. The relationship may be inherent in the nature of the data, in the manner in which it is organized, or in the structure of the list itself. An element may be a simple data type, such as a word or series of characters, or it may be a more complex structure composed of several fields, possibly possessing different type attributes.

6.1 TYPES OF LISTS

By definition, a list is a linear arrangement of elements, $E(0)$, $E(1)$, $E(2), \ldots, E(n)$, where $n \geq 0$. The only essential property of a list is the relative position of its elements, i.e., $E(i)$ precedes $E(i + 1)$ and is preceded by $E(i - 1)$ for $i > 1$ and $i < n$. Lists differ in the way they are represented in computer memory and in the properties of their elements.

A list whose elements represent simple data fields, regardless of whether they are of fixed length or of variable length, is termed a *simple list*. Accordingly, a list which contains at least one element which is not a data field but is another list is termed a *compound list*. Simple lists can reside in sequential locations in computer memory or in discontiguous blocks which are linked together. Compound lists may only exist in the latter form.

The method which is selected for storing a particular list in computer memory is dependent, clearly, upon the nature of the data and the operations that are to be performed on it. Considerations relating to the nature of the data will become clear as the types are described. A basic set of operations, however, can be listed beforehand and discussed in general. They are listed as follows:

1. Reference the ith element to examine it or modify it in some way;
2. Delete the ith element;
3. Insert a new element just before or after the ith element;
4. Combine two lists;
5. Divide a list into two other lists;
6. Copy a list;
7. Sort the elements of a list using a specific value (i.e., a key) within an element; and
8. Search for the occurrence of an element with a set of desired properties.

Given a particular method of representing a list, it is obvious that not all of the above operations can be performed efficiently. For example, it is more efficient to randomly access elements of a list which are fixed in length and are stored in sequential locations in computer memory than if the elements were stored in discontiguous blocks and linked together. On the other hand, inserting an element in the middle of a linked list would require the rearrangement of only a few pointers, whereas the same operation on a sequential list would require that elements of the list be physically moved to create a slot for the new element. Nevertheless, some generalizations* on the use of lists are given and should serve as a basic guideline on the subject:

1. Elements of linked lists require more memory space to include the link information; in many cases, however, more effective use is made of memory because of the absence of vacant table space.
2. Linked lists facilitate the insertion and deletion of elements compared with sequential lists in which large amounts of data may have to be moved.
3. Randomly accessing elements of sequential lists is more efficient than if the elements were structured as a linked list.
4. Linked lists can be divided and joined more conveniently than sequential lists.
5. Linked lists provide the capability for processing compound elements, such as other lists, while sequential lists, in general, do not.

*The generalizations, as well as the preceding list operations, are due to Knuth.[2]

Certain types of simple lists are commonly used and have obtained names of their own:

1. A *stack* is a list for which all insertions and deletions are made at one end.
2. A *queue* is a list for which all insertions are made at one end and all deletions are made at the other end.

The various types of lists are considered in more detail in the following paragraphs.

Simple Lists

A simple list contains elements which represent data. If the elements occupy consecutive locations in computer memory, then the list is termed a *sequential list*; furthermore, if the elements are a fixed size, then the memory address of any particular element can be computed, given its relative position in the list. If, for example, each element requires m memory units,* then

$$location\,[E(i + 1)] = location\,[E(i)] + m$$
$$location\,[E(i)] = L_0 + m * i$$

where L_0 is the base address (i.e., the address of the first element of the list or $E(0)$) and $E(i)$ is an element of the list.† Clearly, a character string, as discussed in chapter 3, is a sequential list where each element is comprised of one character. If, on the other hand, the elements are of a variable size, then the ith element cannot be addressed directly, even though the list occupies consecutive memory locations. For example, a sample sequential list composed of four fixed-size elements is pictured conceptually as follows:

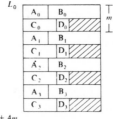

*The term *memory unit* refers to a byte, a word, or any other quantity which can be addressed directly by a machine language computer program.

†Zero-origin indexing is used. If one-origin indexing is required, the quantity m must be subtracted from each effective address.

A more general form of the simple list is the *linked list*, where the elements do not occupy consecutive memory locations but are linked together via pointer variables (i.e., words which contain addresses instead of data values), contained as fields in the element itself. The most primitive form of a linked list is the *unidirectional list*, where each element contains a forward pointer to the next element. Pictorially, the links are depicted by arrows, and the actual memory locations are not considered; realistically, it is recognized that each element possesses an actual memory location. A unidirectional list, containing the same elements as in the preceding example, is shown as follows:

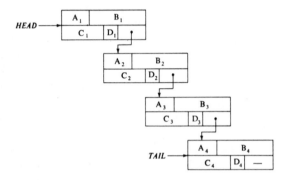

A linked list has to be rooted somewhere, and this is accomplished through a *HEAD* variable which points to the head of the list; similarly, a *TAIL* variable exists and points to the last element of the list. In some lists, called *circular lists*, the last element is linked to the first, forming a closed loop. The principal advantage of this structure is that all elements can be reached, regardless of where the list was entered. The *bidirectional list* is an extension to the unidirectional list, where every element is also linked to its predecessor. This facility permits the list to be searched in both directions, when appropriate, and is depicted in the following simple example:

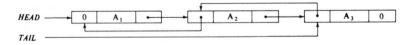

A bidirectional list also permits an element to be deleted, knowing only the address of the element itself. In a unidirectional list, additional information is required.

Clearly, a stack, a queue, or any other simple list can be represented by any one of the above structures; the specific choice of a structure is dependent, of course, on the particular application.

Compound Lists

In ordinary mathematics, it is often desired to replace a variable in a formula with a more complicated expression. In the following example, the second expression is derived from the first by the replacement of x by $(x + 1)$:

$$f(x) = x^2 + 2x + 1$$
$$f(x + 1) = (x + 1)^2 + 2(x + 1) + 1$$

In a general sense, this replacement operation characterizes a class of operations that is required in anomalous computer applications, such as symbolic mathematics, theorem proving, and mechanical linguistics. Although these operations can be performed with simple lists or even string manipulation systems, they can be performed more efficiently and more conveniently in systems designed for list manipulation, as compared to those designed to manipulate elements of lists. Compound lists facilitate this type of symbolic processing, and several programming languages have been developed to satisfy the need.

The remainder of the chapter, except for the last section on list processing in PL/I, is concerned with compound lists and their processing. The LISP language, developed at M.I.T. for list processing, is introduced as an appropriate programming language for computer applications requiring structures of this type.

6.2   COMPOUND LISTS AND WHY THEY ARE USEFUL

The objective of this section is to discuss the usefulness of compound lists and to engender an idea on how they can be represented in computer storage, such that they are amenable to use by a wide class of users. Compound lists are stored in a straightforward manner in the LISP system,[4] and that methodology is used to demonstrate the practicability of the concept. The original implementation of LISP was for a computer with a fixed word length, in which the locations in computer storage were called *memory registers*.* This terminology is used here, although it should be recognized that the techniques can be made to apply equally well to computers in which storage is organized differently.

A *compound list* is nothing more than a structure of elements strung together in a particular sequence. Clearly, the definition holds, regardless

---

*The term *memory register* should be interpreted to be synonomous with *memory location*, except that a fixed word length is assumed.

of the specific composition of the elements, as long as the facility exists for storing and processing sublists.   In LISP, an element is made to correspond to a memory register.   Each register is divided into two equal parts and, except for the terminal register of a list, the second part contains the address of the next register in the sequence; the second part of a terminal register contains a delimiter symbol, taken here to be zero. As with simple lists, the registers do not have to be consecutive in memory and a register can be inserted at any point in a list without disturbing the others.   When adding an element, an unused register is acquired, and its address is placed in the second part of the register after which it is to be inserted; the address of the following register is placed in its second half.

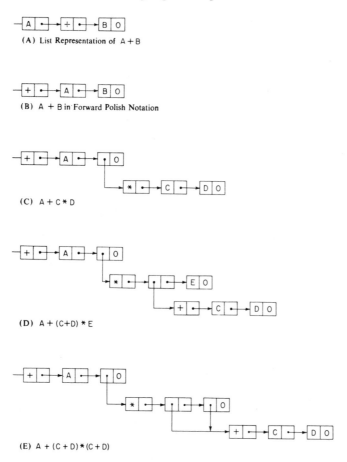

(A) List Representation of A + B

(B) A + B in Forward Polish Notation

(C) A + C * D

(D) A + (C+D) * E

(E) A + (C + D) * (C + D)

Fig. 6.1 Examples of compound lists.

Unused registers are linked together in a *free list*;* registers are taken from it and returned to it when appropriate.

The first part of a register is termed the **car**† of that register and the second half, the **cdr** (pronounced "cudder"). In what would correspond to a simple list, the **cdr** contains an address pointing to the next register on the list, while **car** is free and may contain a symbol or point to a symbol stored elsewhere. Fig. 6.1a shows a list representation of the expression A + B. It is shown in forward Polish notation in Fig. 6.1b.

The **car** of a register may alternately contain an address and point to a sublist. Thus, a *compound list structure* is formed. Fig. 6.1c is derived from Fig. 6.1b by replacing B with C * D. Complex expressions may be handled in this way, and changes may be easily made to their component parts. Other examples are shown in Figs. 6.1d and 6.1e. In the latter is contained a common sublist.

A list must start somewhere, and the address of its first register is stored in a register known as a *base register*.‡ These registers can be given names, so that a symbol table of the form:

$$(<name>, <base register>)$$

can be maintained. It follows that base registers can also point to sublists which are components of other list structures.

6.3   LIST MATHEMATICS

A number of mathematical concepts, involving expressions and functions, are required so that complex functions, involving list processing operations, can be defined. The concepts, due to McCarthy,[5] are generally well-known but should be reviewed. Conditional expressions, which may be new to some, permit the writing of recursive functions.

A *partial function* is a function that is defined only on part of its domain. Partial functions arise when functions are defined by computations; because for some values of the arguments, the calculations defining the value of the function may not terminate. Many of the functions we define will be partial functions.

A *propositional expression* is an expression whose possible values are T (true) or F (false). It is assumed that the student is familiar with the

---

*Unused memory registers are linked together in what is called a *free list*. The list is dynamic in the sense that insertions and deletions are constantly being made to it. The free list is usually formed, when the list processing program is initially loaded into the machine.

†**car** and **cdr** are acronyms for Computer Address Register and Computer Decrement Register, respectively. They refer to portions of a memory register in an early computer for which the LISP system was implemented.

‡Referred to earlier as the *head of the list*.

propositional connectives "∧" (and), "∨" (inclusive or), and "¬" (not); and also the relational operations >, <, =, ≥, ≤, ¬>, ¬<, and ¬=. Typical propositional expressions are:

$$x < y$$
$$(x \leq y) \wedge (c \neg= d)$$
$$m \wedge n \vee p$$

Conditional expressions are a device for expressing the dependence of quantities on propositional quantities. A conditional expression has the form:

$$[p_1 \rightarrow e_1; p_2 \rightarrow e_2; \ldots; p_n \rightarrow e_n]$$

where the p's are propositional quantities, and the e's are expressions. It may be read, "If p_1 then e_1, otherwise if p_2 then $e_2, \ldots$, otherwise if p_n then e_n.

The rules for determining whether $[p_1 \rightarrow e_1; p_2 \rightarrow e_2; \ldots; p_n \rightarrow e_n]$ is defined, and if so, what its value is are given as follows:

1. Examine the p's from left to right;
2. If a p whose value is T is encountered before any p whose value is undefined is encountered, then the value of the conditional expression is the value of the corresponding e (if this is defined);
3. If any undefined p is encountered before a true p, or if all p's are false, or if the e corresponding to the first true p is undefined, then the value of the conditional expression is undefined.

The concepts can be simplified, with some qualifications, as follows:
   "The value of $[p_1 \rightarrow e_1; p_2 \rightarrow e_2; \ldots; p_n \rightarrow e_n]$ is the value of the e corresponding to the first p that has the value T." For example:

$$[1 < 2 \rightarrow 4; 1 > 2 \rightarrow 3] = 4$$
$$[2 < 1 \rightarrow 4; 2 > 1 \rightarrow 3; 2 > 1 \rightarrow 2] = 3$$
$$[2 < 1 \rightarrow 4; T \rightarrow 3] = 3$$
$$[2 < 1 \rightarrow \tfrac{0}{0}; T \rightarrow 3] = 3$$
$$[2 < 1 \rightarrow 3; T \rightarrow \tfrac{0}{0}] = \text{undefined}$$
$$[2 < 1 \rightarrow 3; 4 < 1 \rightarrow 4] = \text{undefined}$$

Some common definitions usually expressed in natural language are given as follows:

$$|x| = [x < 0 \rightarrow -x; T \rightarrow x]$$
$$\textbf{sign}\,(x) = [x < 0 \rightarrow -1; x = 0 \rightarrow 0; T \rightarrow 1]$$

Using conditional expressions, we can, without circularity, define functions by expressions in which the subject function occurs. For example,

$$n! = [n = 0 \rightarrow 1; T \rightarrow n * (n - 1)!]$$

When 0! is evaluated, the answer 1 is calculated; the expression $0 *$ $(0 - 1)!$ never arises. The evaluation of 2! would proceed as follows:

$$2! = [2 = 0 \rightarrow 1; \mathsf{T} \rightarrow 2 * (2 - 1)!] = 2 * 1!$$
$$= 2 * [1 = 0 \rightarrow 1; \mathsf{T} \rightarrow 1 * (1 - 1)!] = 2 * 1 * 0!$$
$$= 2 * 1 * [0 = 0 \rightarrow 1; \mathsf{T} \rightarrow 0 * (0 - 1)!] = 2 * 1 * 1$$
$$= 2$$

A function, such as the factorial function, which includes itself in its definition, is termed a *recursive function*. Two other common examples are:

$$\textbf{gcd}(m, n) = [m > n \rightarrow \textbf{gcd}(n, m); \textbf{rem}(n, m) = 0 \rightarrow m;$$
$$\mathsf{T} \rightarrow \textbf{gcd}(\textbf{rem}(n, m), m)]$$

where $\textbf{rem}(n, m)$ denotes the remainder left when n is divided by m; and

$$\textbf{sqrt}(a, x, \epsilon) = \left[|x^2 - a| < \epsilon \rightarrow x; \quad \mathsf{T} \rightarrow \textbf{sqrt}\left(a, \frac{1}{2}\left(x + \frac{a}{x}\right), \epsilon\right)\right]$$

which computes the square root of a, given an initial approximation x. There is no guarantee that a function determined by a recursive function will ever terminate. If the computation does not terminate, the function must be regarded as undefined for the given arguments.

6.4   THE LISP LANGUAGE

LISP is a universal programming language designed for symbolic data processing and has proved useful for many applications in the field of artificial intelligence. It is also useful at the elementary level for simple list manipulation, and it is toward that end that this section is oriented. A complete description of the language can be obtained from the *LISP 1.5 Programmer's Manual*.[4] Of particular interest in LISP are symbolic expressions referred to as *S-expressions*, which is the concept by which data are represented in the system. The remainder of the language is designed around this concept, and that is what gives the language its power as a symbolic programming tool.

Symbolic Expressions

The most elementary type of S-expressions is an *atomic symbol*,* which is a string of numerals and capital letters, the first of which must be a letter.

---

*It follows that a literal, i.e., a quantity which represents itself, or a class of symbols similar to itself, is also composed of numerals and capital letters.

For example,

A
XPRIME
ABLEDOGBAKER
M14

are atomic and are considered as a whole rather than as a string of characters. All S-expressions can be built out of atomic symbols and the punctuation characters "(",")", and ".". An S-expression may be formed from two S-expressions as follows:

(X.Y)

More formally, an S-expression is either an atomic symbol, or it is composed of elements in the following order: a left parenthesis, an S-expression, a dot, an S-expression, and a right parenthesis. Thus, the following are S-expressions:

X
(X.Y)
((X.Y) . Z)
((X.Y) . (Z.W))

Functions

In LISP, function names are written as lowercase letters and are underlined. Arguments are enclosed in square brackets and separated by the semicolon.

The function *cons* has two arguments and is used to build an S-expression from two argument S-expressions; e.g.,

cons [X;Y] = (X.Y)
cons [(X.Y); Z] = ((X.Y) . Z)
cons [*cons* [X;Y]; Z] = ((X.Y) . Z)

The functions *car* and *cdr* have one argument and are used to subdivide a given expression. The value of the function *car* is the first part of its composite argument; the *car* of an atomic symbol is undefined. For example,

car [(X.Y)] = X
car [*cons* [X;Y]] = X
car [((X.Y) . Z)] = (X.Y)
car [X] is undefined

Similarly, *cdr* produces the second part of a composite argument and is undefined if the argument is atomic. For example,

$$cdr \text{ [X] is undefined}$$
$$cdr \text{ [(X.Y)] } = \text{ Y}$$
$$cdr \text{ [((X.Y) . Z)] } = \text{ Z}$$
$$car \text{ [}cdr \text{ [(X . (Y.Z))]] } = \text{ Y}$$

In LISP, variables are represented by lowercase letters and numerals, the first of which is a letter. For example, if x is composite, then

$$cons \text{ [}car[x]; \text{ }cdr \text{ }[x]] = x$$

Predicates

Functions which assume a *true* or *false* value are also defined. These functions are called *predicates*, and the values true and false are represented by the atomic symbols T and F, respectively.

The predicate *eq* tests for the equality of atomic symbols and is undefined if either of its arguments are nonatomic. For example,

$$eq \text{ [X;X] } = \text{ T}$$
$$eq \text{ [X;Y] } = \text{ F}$$
$$eq \text{ [}cons \text{ [X;Y]; Z] is undefined}$$

The predicate *atom* takes one argument and is true if its argument is atomic. Its value is false, otherwise; e.g.,

$$atom \text{ [X] } = \text{ T}$$
$$atom \text{ [}cons \text{ [X;Y]] } = \text{ F}$$
$$atom \text{ [}cdr \text{ [X;Y)]] } = \text{ T}$$

The predicate *null* takes one argument and is true if its argument is NIL (see next section). It is written in the form:

$$null \text{ }[x]$$

List Notation

S-expressions may also be written in *list notation*, which is a convenience when long lists are involved. In list notation, S-expressions are separated by blank characters or commas, and the entire list is enclosed in parentheses as follows:

$$(X \text{ } XY \text{ } AB2 \text{ } A)$$

which is equivalent to

$$(X, \text{ } XY, \text{ } AB2, \text{ } A)$$

Its equivalent in dot notation is

$$(X \ . \ (XY \ . \ (AB2 \ . \ (A.NIL))))$$

where NIL is a special atomic symbol which serves as a terminator. In general, elements of lists may be S-expressions in either dot or list notation. The list $(m_1 m_2 \ldots m_n)$ is equivalent to $(m_1 . (m_2 . (\ldots (m_n.NIL) \ldots)))$ in dot notation. For example,

$$(X \ Y \ Z) = (X. \ (Y. \ (Z.NIL)))$$
$$((X \ Y) \ Z) = ((X. \ (Y.NIL)) \ . \ (Z.NIL))$$
$$((X.Y) \ Z) = ((X.Y) \ . \ (Z.NIL))$$

Statements

LISP statements can be written in two ways: as composite functions and as conditional expressions. Composite functions utilize a combination of basic function and are written using nested sets of brackets, as follows:

$$caddr \ [x] \ = \ car \ [cdr \ [cdr \ [x]]]$$

For example,

$$caddr \ [(X \ Y \ Z \ W)] \ = \ Z$$

A much larger class of functions can be written by using conditional expressions of the form:

$$[p_1 \rightarrow e_1; \ p_2 \rightarrow e_2; \ \ldots ; \ p_n \rightarrow e_n]$$

which has been described in detail in section 6.3. In this context, each p_i or e_i can be either an S-expression, a function, a composition of functions, or another conditional expression. Several examples of the latter form are readily available:

1. The function *append* joins two S-expressions.
   $$append \ [x;y] \ = \ [null \ [x] \rightarrow y; \ T \rightarrow cons \ [car \ [x];$$
   $$append \ [cdr \ [x]; y]]]$$
   $$append \ [(X \ Y); \ (Z \ W)] \ = \ (X \ Y \ Z \ W)$$
2. The predicate *equal* returns the value T, if its arguments are identical S-expressions.
   $$equal \ [x;y] \ = \ [atom \ [x] \rightarrow [atom \ [y] \rightarrow eq \ [x;y]; \ T \rightarrow F];$$
   $$equal \ [car \ [x]; \ car \ [y]] \rightarrow equal \ [cdr \ [x]; \ cdr \ [y]];$$
   $$T \rightarrow F]$$
3. The predicate *member* is true, if the S-expression x occurs among the elements of the list y.
   $$member \ [x;y] \ = \ [null \ [y] \rightarrow F; \ equal \ [x; \ car \ [y]] \rightarrow T;$$
   $$T \rightarrow member \ [x; \ cdr \ [y]]]$$

Representation of List Structures

Because of the recursive nature of many LISP functions, it is frequently difficult to achieve a precise understanding of the operations that are performed. In cases like these, a picture is often very helpful.

Conceptually, lists are not stored in a computer as strings of characters but rather as structures built of memory registers. Earlier, memory registers were described as being composed of a *car* and a *cdr*, e.g.,

For the representation of atomic symbols, the *car* contains a pointer to the character string stored in memory somewhere; it is represented as follows:

For nonatomic symbols, the *car* or *cdr* contains a pointer to another S-expression which may be atomic or contains an S-expression itself. Finally, the S-expression (X.Y) is represented as

from which the structure of more complex S-expressions can be derived. For example,

(A B) = (A.(B.NIL))

and

((M.N) X (A.B))

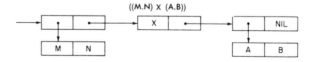

Other Features and a Final Example

As in almost all programming systems, input and output facilities are required, and LISP provides the functions *read* [x] and *print* [x] for reading cards and printing results, respectively. As one might expect, input lines must be written as S-expressions, and output is printed in the same general form.

Arithmetic functions on fixed and floating point values are provided in the language, and an input and output facility is designed to process these values as well. Arithmetic expressions are not permitted so that all computations must be written in a functional form, such as *plus* $[x_1; x_2; \ldots; x_n]$.

Most programming systems provide a means for defining functions, and LISP does not deviate from the established precedent. Through a facility similar to the Lambda calculus,[4,5] functions are defined and represented as S-expressions, like programs in the language itself. Both topics are beyond the scope of this treatment, however, and the reader is referred to the given references for additional information. Nevertheless, the basics of LISP have been presented for those interested in an overview or for those desiring to implement similar functions in more general programming languages.

LISP is frequently applied to symbolic mathematics on the computer. As a final example, a LISP function named *factoradd*, to be written as

$$\text{factoradd } [x; y]$$

is developed, which adds two factors symbolically. A factor is defined in BNF* as follows:

<factor> ::= <variable> | <variable> + <variable>
<variable> ::= $A \mid B \mid C \mid \ldots \mid Y \mid Z$

The factors are represented internally in forward Polish notation as lists, i.e.,

Standard Notation	LISP Notation
A + B	(+ A B)
A	(A)
2A + 2B	(+ (* 2 A) (* 2 B))

where the "+" and "*" are regarded as atomic symbols and would be replaced in a real life situation by appropriate character strings. The *factoradd* function is written as a conditional expression which uses other defined functions. Clearly, these functions could have been included, in detail, in *factoradd*; they were removed for clarity of presentation and are included after the main definition which follows:

---

*Backus normal form.

$$factoradd\,[x;y] \;=\; [atom\,[x] \rightarrow [atom\,[\,y] \rightarrow add\,[x;y],$$
$$\mathsf{T} \rightarrow tadd\,[x;y]],\; atom\,[\,y] \rightarrow tadd\,[\,y;x],$$
$$\mathsf{T} \rightarrow append\,['+';\; append\,[add\,[opnd1\,[x];$$
$$opnd1\,[\,y]];\; add\,[opnd2\,[x];\; opnd2\,[\,y]]]]]$$

where

$$add\,[x;y] \;=\; [eq\,[x;y] \rightarrow append\,['*';\; append\,['2';\; x]],$$
$$\mathsf{T} \rightarrow append\,['+';\; append\,[x;y]]]$$
$$opnd1\,[x] \;=\; car\,[cdr\,[x]]$$
$$opnd2\,[x] \;=\; car\,[cdr\,[cdr\,[x]]]$$
$$tadd\,[x;y] \;=\; [atom[x] \rightarrow [eq\,[x;\,opnd1\,[\,y]] \rightarrow append\,[car\,[\,y];$$
$$append\,[add\,[x;\,opnd1\,[\,y]];\; opnd2\,[\,y]]],$$
$$\mathsf{T} \rightarrow append\,[car\,[\,y];\; append\,[opnd1\,[\,y];$$
$$add\,[x;\,opnd2\,[\,y]]]]],\; \mathsf{T} \rightarrow tadd\,[\,y,x]]$$

6.5   LIST PROCESSING IN PL/I

Although list processing systems, such as LISP and IPL-V,[6] provide the user with a powerful tool for solving "pure" list processing problems, they impose constraints on the user that make the language inappropriate for more general use. Previously, the only recourse left to programmers with list processing applications was to learn basic list processing methods and to apply them with assembler language programming, when appropriate. The end result was that list processing techniques were not being applied, when they perhaps should have been, and that the techniques themselves were not being extended as a result of actual use. The first major programming language to include list processing facilities is PL/I, a description of which is included as Appendix D.

When programming in most higher level programming languages, the actual location of data in storage is not of major concern. In fact, most languages have no facility for using that information, even if it were available. In list processing applications, however, the location of data is of major concern, and a facility must be available for using the information. PL/I contains three facilities which make it amenable to list processing: a **CONTROLLED** storage class, the concept of a based variable, and a data class of type **POINTER**.

Pointer Variables

The data type **POINTER** implies an item that will be used to locate other data, as compared to one which might be used strictly as problem data.

As examples, consider the following declarations:

DECLARE PT POINTER, BETA FIXED
CONTROLLED (PT);
DECLARE (HEAD, TAIL) POINTER;

In the first statement, PT is a *pointer variable* which will be used to locate BETA. In the second statement, HEAD and TAIL are pointer variables which will be used explicitly to locate other data fields in computer storage.

Controlled Storage and Based Variables

When a data variable has the attribute CONTROLLED, storage allocation must be specified for that variable with the ALLOCATE statement. (Later, the same storage may be released with the FREE statement.) It is useful to combine this concept with that of the pointer variable, as shown in the following example:

DECLARE X (100) CONTROLLED (PTR);
ALLOCATE X SET (PTR);

Here, PTR is declared implicitly as a pointer variable; when storage is obtained for X, PTR is set to the corresponding address. Henceforth, when reference is made to array X, it is implicitly located via the storage address contained in pointer variable PTR. A controlled variable used in this manner is also termed a *based variable*. Use of the based variable concept has been extended to input-output processing, when records are read into and written out of buffers, instead of being assigned to fixed addresses in storage. Consider the following record structure:*

DECLARE 1 DRECRD BASED (DPTR),
2 ACCT CHARACTER (10),
2 NAME CHARACTER (30),
2 PAYRCD DECIMAL FIXED (7,2);

and an associated input statement:

READ FILE (DFILE) SET (DPTR);

*Data items of different sizes and/or of different data types, but which possess a logical relationship to one another, may be grouped into a hierarchy called a *structure*. This hierarchy is reflected in a level number which specifies the organization of elementary items within the structure.

Execution of the READ statement* would cause data to be read into an input buffer (or would have the next record located in a buffer) and have pointer variable DPTR set to point to the beginning of the record. In a sense, the location of the record and its corresponding substructure is *based* upon the specified pointer variable.

Pointer Qualifiers

A based variable may be qualified by a pointer variable other than the one that was implicitly declared with it. The supplementary pointer may be one that was implicitly declared for another based variable or one that was explicitly declared of type POINTER. The symbol -> , i.e., a hyphen followed by a "greater than" sign, is used for this purpose. For example,

```
DECLARE 1 X CONTROLLED (PTR),
          2 Y FLOAT,
          2 Z FIXED,
          2 W CHARACTER (15);
```

The statement Y = Z implies

```
PTR -> Y = PTR -> Z
```

and a reference to W implies PTR -> W.

List Structures

If components of the allocated structure are of type POINTER, list structures can be created where the elements are chained together. In the following example, three elements are chained together as described:

```
DECLARE (HEAD, TAIL) POINTER;
DECLARE 1 X CONTROLLED (PT),
            2 A POINTER,
            2 B FLOAT;
ALLOCATE X;
HEAD = PT;
TAIL = PT;
ALLOCATE X;
TAIL -> A = PT;
TAIL = PT;
ALLOCATE X;
TAIL -> A = PT;
A = NULL;
TAIL = PT;
```

*A similar facility exists for output transmission.

where HEAD points to the head of the list, TAIL points to the end of the list, and NULL is a special system symbol denoting a null entry.

List Processing Operations

As further examples of list processing in PL/I, two complete procedures are presented. The first procedure CHAIN adds an element to the end of a unidirectional list. The pointer variables HEAD and TAIL point to the beginning and end of the list, respectively.*

```
CHAIN: PROCEDURE (NEWELEM);
DECLARE 1 ELEMENT CONTROLLED (NEWELEM).
         2 PTR POINTER,
         2 NUMBER FIXED,
         (HEAD, TAIL) POINTER STATIC EXTERNAL
                  INITIAL (NULL);
PTR = NULL;
IF TAIL = NULL THEN HEAD, TAIL = NEWELEM;
ELSE TAIL -> PTR, TAIL = NEWELEM;
END CHAIN;
```

The second procedure, which is a function, counts the number of elements in a unidirectional list and returns the total. Again, HEAD points to the beginning of the list.

```
SUM: PROCEDURE FIXED;
DECLARE 1 NODE CONTROLLED (PT),
         2 QT POINTER,
         2 DATA FLOAT,
         HEAD POINTER STATIC EXTERNAL,
         N FIXED INITIAL (0);
IF HEAD = NULL THEN RETURN (0);
PT = HEAD;
ST: N = N + 1; PT = QT
IF PT ¬= NULL THEN GOTO ST;
RETURN (N);
END SUM;
```

List processing was never touted as a simple way of programming computers; yet, it was effective for a certain class of problems which probably would not have been programmed otherwise. The facilities in PL/I

*The attribute STATIC refers to storage that is allocated before execution of the program and is never released during execution. The attribute EXTERNAL permits the same data item to be referenced from several procedures. The INITIAL attribute specifies constants that are assigned to data names when computer storage is allocated.

have made list processing available to the programmer, in conjunction with his well-established techniques, and have uncovered several new applications as well. The practice of processing a data record in an I/O buffer, as mentioned earlier, instead of having to move it to a predetermined storage area can result in significant savings in execution time for some data processing applications. The implications for systems programming are many. Topics such as more general file design, symbol table methods, and compiler methodology, to mention only a few, are affected by this advancement.

PROBLEMS

6.1   Draw a flow diagram to delete an element from a bidirectional list.
6.2   Given the following input card in LISP:

$$(A \ (B \ C) \ (D \ B \ C) \ A)$$

apply the following statement to it

$$read \ [x]$$

and show how x is represented in memory.
6.3   Given the following function definitions:

push (list, symbol)—*symbol* is placed on the stack *list*, which is represented as a list structure. It is considered to be the element last-in. If *list* is null, the *symbol* is first-in and last-in.

pull (list, symbol)—The last-in of *list* is pruned from it and placed in *symbol*. If only one element is on *list* prior to *pull*, it becomes a null list after the operation.

Write two LISP functions named:

$$pull \ [list, symbol]$$

and

$$push \ [list, symbol]$$

Use conditional expressions, if necessary, and denote the free list by F.

REFERENCES

1. Flores, I., *Computer Programming*, Englewood Cliffs, N.J., Prentice-Hall, Inc., 1966. Introduces the various types of lists and presents basic list processing operations.
2. Knuth, D. E., *The Art of Programming*, Vol. I, *Fundamental Algorithms*,

Reading, Mass., Addison-Wesley Publishing Company, 1968. Contains a complete chapter on "Information Structures" and discusses methods, applications, and mathematical foundations.

3. Lawson, H. W., "PL/I List Processing," *Communications of the ACM* (June, 1967). Describes the PL/I list processing facility.

4. McCarthy, J., et al., *LISP 1.5 Programmer's Manual*, Cambridge, Mass., The M.I.T. Press, 1962. Presents a complete guide to the LISP system.

5. McCarthy, J., "Recursive Functions of Symbolic Expressions and Their Computation by Machine," *Communications of the ACM* (April, 1960). Describes conditional expressions and their relationship to the theory of computation.

6. Newell, A., et al., *IPL-V Manual*, Englewood Cliffs, N.J., Prentice-Hall, Inc., 1961. Presents the form and meaning of the IPL-V list processing system.

7. *PL/I Language Specifications*, New York, IBM Corporation, Form C28-6571, 1965. Contains a complete description of the PL/I language.

7 | COMPUTER LANGUAGES

One of the most popular topics in computer technology is the study of *computer languages*. Several different types of computer languages are recognized, although in many cases, the differences are obscured by conflicting terminology. The name which is probably most often misused is algorithmic language. The term algorithmic language, like the word algorithm,* is frequently used but rarely defined. Algorithmic language is often used synonymously with programming language. However, the distinction is an important one. A *programming language* implies a higher level procedure-oriented language for programming a computer; generally speaking, it is hoped that the associated syntax and semantics will transcend different computers and generations of computers. Nothing more is expected. An *algorithmic language*, on the other hand, implies a body of knowledge that can be passed from one generation to another. Clearly, the media, in the latter case, is the algorithmic language. Usually, algorithmic languages are programming languages, but this is not necessarily so. The distinction between the two is not always well-defined, with most languages of either type having properties of the other. Some familiar programming languages are FORTRAN, COBOL, and PL/I. A well-known algorithmic language is ALGOL. A slightly different type of computer language, namely *control language*, will also be introduced. Usually, control languages are degenerate forms of programming lan-

---

*For a definition of algorithm, see chapter 1.

guages. They are often used for communications with a computer operating system* but are used for specialized applications as well. The last type of language to be considered, which is a form of control language that would be placed somewhere between an assembler language and a programming language on a continuum of languages, is the *macro language*. Macro languages have interesting properties which are now being included in higher level languages.

7.1   CONTROL LANGUAGES

By definition, control languages are not intended to be used for the encoding of algorithms or for the programming of computer procedures. Instead, their function is to *direct*. The directed object may be a person, a computer operating system, or a computer program. Control languages are divided into two major categories: *command languages* and *macro languages*.

Command Languages

The syntax of a command language is usually trivial, with the syntax specification having only one or two defined types. The major syntactical element, in the terminology of inverted notation, is the *command*, which is a required element. *Statement prefixes* are used for identification purposes only; *operands* modify the command as required. *Skip logic* is permitted on occasion to prevent the execution of a given command if certain conditions exist. One command statement may refer to another with the statement prefix; on the other hand, from an execution point of view, once a command is executed, it should be considered as having been discarded. A generalized syntax specification with examples follow:

[*statement-prefix*] *command* [*operand* [, *operand*]...] [*conditional-expr*]

Examples:

```
SET   CNT = CNT + 1
RUN  FORTRAN
//STP  EXEC  M34I
TYPE  (ALPHA **2) − 34, (IF E< .003)
LIST  BLOCK 7
```

The most common use of command languages has been with operating systems for job control cards and for operator communications. The structure is convenient for problem-oriented languages, however, since

*A control language used for this purpose is often called a *command language* or a *job control language*.

the command itself may be a keyword in the vocabulary of a specialized application.

Macro Languages

A macro language is a language which enables the user to write, in abbreviated form, anything which involves a significant repetition of patterns. For example, the familiar sequence:

```
FETCH   A
ADD     B
STORE   C
```

could be more conveniently written as:

```
ADDX   A,B,C
```

where ADDX is defined as follows:

```
MACRO
ADDX    &A,&B,&C
FETCH   &A
ADD     &B
STORE   &C
MEND
```

and the character "&" indicates that the identifier which follows immediately is a parameter. The sequence MACRO...MEND is termed a macro definition. The use of ADDX is termed a macroinstruction.

The *macro language processor* generates a sequence of function language statements* for every occurrence of each macro instruction encountered. The generated statements are then processed as any other statement in the function language.

Before a macro instruction can be recognized and processed by the macro language processor, its characteristics must be made explicit with an appropriate declaration or definition. A *macro definition*, then, is a set of statements which provides the macro language processor with the following information:

1. The macro instruction code and format of the macro instruction; and
2. The sequence of function language statements to be generated when the macro instruction appears in the source program.

The amount of detailed information which must be supplied by the programmer to satisfy these requirements is listed minimally as follows:

---

*Although macro processors are usually a part of an assembler program, the concept is more general, and the processor may be a stand-alone metaprogram. In this context, it generates a program in a function language.

1. A macro definition header statement;
2. A macro instruction prototype statement;
3. One or more model statements; and
4. A macro definition trailer statement.

The macro definition header and trailer serve as statement parentheses and delimit the macro definition. The macro instruction prototype statement denotes the skeleton entry, which is completed by the programmer when the macro is used. The model statements form the set of function language elements from which the macro language processor generates function language statements corresponding to a specific macro instruction.

Inherently, macro languages are limited. The major limitation, however, is the function languages which they support. This reflects not only upon fixed formats, parameters, excessive detail, etc., but also upon the limited conditional and control facilities in the respective function language. In spite of these limitations, several innovations have found their way into macro languages and are worth mentioning:

1. Keyword parameters,
2. Conditional statements,
3. Global variables, and
4. Operand sublists.

Although these topics are beyond the scope of this treatment, further information is available from the references at the end of the chapter or from the reference manual for any general purpose macro assembly program.

7.2 PROGRAMMING LANGUAGES

As with machine and assembler languages, the function of programming languages is to direct the computer to execute a desired sequence of operations. Here, the implication is that a programming language is a higher level language, i.e., higher than assembler language. The major advantage, in using higher level languages, is that much of the detail that is ordinarily associated with assembler language is thereby subordinated to a metaprogram called a *compiler*.

Several similarities exist between programming languages (in the above sense) and assembler languages:

1. The sequence in which statements should be executed must be given explicitly or implied by the order in which they are presented to the metaprogram;

2. Data types and associated storage requirements must be stated (perhaps implicitly);
3. Methods for altering or directing the sequence of program control, conditionally, must be available to the programmer;
4. Input/output facilities must exist;
5. The capability for defining and using subprograms must exist in the language or system; with
[6. The computational aspects are being implied, in general.]

Conceptually, therefore, programming languages do not require a major change in thinking over more detailed languages.

The statements of programming languages are divided into five classes and introduced in the following paragraphs. The classes of statements are: data manipulation, program control, input and output, specification, and subprogram. Some concepts, characteristic of algorithmic languages, are considered later in the chapter.

Data Manipulation

Data manipulation statements perform the calculations, data movement, list processing, or string editing required by a particular application. As a result of a data manipulation statement, the value of a data variable is replaced.* In general, data manipulation is the major function of most computer processing. In scientific computing, data manipulation usually involves mathematical equations, as shown by the following FORTRAN example:

$$Y = A*B**2 + C$$

In commercial computing, data manipulation normally incorporates data movement and a limited amount of arithmetic computation. Two statements from COBOL are illustrative of commercial computing:

> MOVE RESULT TO ANSWER.
> ADD PAY, GROSS GIVING TOTAL.

Two examples from PL/I represent list processing and string manipulation, respectively:†

> TAIL − >PTR = EPTR;
> MSTR = 'MESSAGE NO' || SUBSTR(AMZT, I,7);

---

*However, some minor exceptions exist with respect to output and return statements in some new programming languages.

†The function SUBSTR forms a substring of a data field of type string, and the operator "||" denotes concatenation.

Program Control Statements

Program control statements are the mechanism by which sequential execution is altered in programs. Control statements are divided into four categories: 1. unconditional branches; 2. conditional branches and conditional statement execution; 3. looping; and 4. execution control.

Unconditional branches interrupt sequential execution and indicate the statement to be executed next, either singly or multiply as the result of some computation. In most languages, this statement takes the form of the GOTO, as shown in the following FORTRAN examples (where statements are labeled by statement numbers):

GOTO 25
GOTO (10, 20, 30), I

where in the second statement, control is transferred to statement 10, 20, or 30, depending upon whether I contains 1, 2, or 3.

In other languages such as COBOL and PL/I, paragraphs or statements may be labeled by names, as depicted in the following COBOL examples:

GOTO PAR-ONE.
GOTO P1, P2, P3 DEPENDING ON I.

Similar to FORTRAN, control is transferred to paragraphs P1, P2, or P3, depending upon I, in the latter statement. In PL/I, variables can have the attribute LABEL, so that they may contain label values instead of data values. For example (in PL/I),

GOTO SWITCH;

would transfer program control to the statement whose label is contained in the variable SWITCH. In general, this facility provides the programmer with a great amount of flexibility, since the contents of label variables can be modified with standard assignment statements.

Conditional statements allow the programmer to change the sequence of execution or to execute a given statement on a conditional basis. This feature can be used for iterative procedures, for providing a means of processing exceptional cases, or for making basic decisions during the course of program execution. The conditional element can be based on either a propositional or arithmetic expression; e.g. (in FORTRAN):

IF (A+1) 10, 20, 30
IF (A*B.GT.X) X = X+1

In the first statement, program control goes to statements 10, 20, or 30, if the expression A+1 is less than zero, equal to zero, or greater than zero, respectively. In the second case, the statement $X = X + 1$ is executed only if the logical expression has the value *true*. COBOL provides a slightly extended capability with a *condition name facility*, in addition to a logical if statement (first example):

> IF AGE IS GREATER THAN 400 MOVE 99 TO AGE.
> IF MALE NEXT SENTENCE OTHERWISE GOTO FEMALE-PAR.

In the second example, the condition name MALE is associated with a specific value of an appropriate variable. If the variable contains the specific value, then the condition name MALE has the value *true*. PL/I, perhaps, combines the best of both languages with an IF statement of the form:

> IF <expression> THEN <group> ELSE <group>

where *expression* can be a logical expression or a scalar expression. If the expression is a scalar expression, it is converted to a bit string and interpreted as being *true* if any bit is one. The element *group* may be a statement, a DO group (see below), or a begin block (see Appendix D). PL/I contains another conditional facility which is amenable to unusual or interrupt conditions. The ON statement, written as follows:

> ON<condition> <statement>

establishes supplementary processing, which should be initiated if the specified condition occurs; e.g.,

> ON ZERODIVIDE GOTO FIXIT;

The ability of a computer program to repeat the same operations with different data, called *looping*, is a powerful tool which greatly reduces programming effort and the size of programs, as well. In general, a loop has the following elements: 1. an indexing or induction variable; 2. a range of statements to be executed; and 3. indexing parameters or a conditional expression which controls the number of iterations. (In any given application, however, any one of the above elements may not be required.) In writing a loop, two components are required: 1. the *loop head* gives the *mode* of execution, the induction variable, and the indexing or control parameters; and 2. the *loop body* gives the range of statements to be executed iteratively. During the machine processing of a loop, one of three modes of iteration is implicitly selected from the information in the loop head. Either the loop body is executed a specified number of times; or it is executed until a specific condition is met; or it is executed as the induction variable assumes a given set of values. In the latter case, the loop may be terminated when the list of values is exhausted or when a predetermined condition is met. Clearly, the list of values may be listed explicitly or given as a range. The next examples demonstrate these concepts:

FORTRAN
DO 100 I = 1,10

.
.
.

100   ___

COBOL
PERFORM LOOP-ONE VARYING 1 FROM 1 BY 1
UNTIL 1 IS GREATER THAN 10.
PERFORM B-BLOCK THRU E-BLOCK 13 TIMES.

PL/I
LOOP: DO WHILE (A < B);

.
.
.

END LOOP;

The FORTRAN example contains a loop head, a loop body, and the mode of iteration permits the induction variable I to assume a set of values, given as a range. Two COBOL examples are given, and, in both cases, only a loop head is provided. The first example specifies a loop where the induction variable assumes a set of values which is terminated by a predetermined condition. In the second COBOL example, a loop is performed a given number of times. In the PL/I example, a loop head and a loop body are written, and the loop body is executed while a specified condition is satisfied.

Execution control statements halt or terminate program execution or supply the compiler with compile-time information. Execution control statements, in general, vary from language to language, with the STOP and END statements being the most common forms, and between different operating systems.

Input and Output Statements

Input and output statements are the facilities with which programs communicate with the outside world. The outside world may be a card deck supplied by the user on the system input stream, a printed page, or an intermediate storage device such as tape or disk. Two modes of input and output are usually available in higher level languages: formatted and unformatted. *Formatted output* goes through an editing procedure which converts the data from the internal representation of the machine to an external form required by a particular application. *Formatted input* reverses the process. With *unformatted input/output*, the data is stored externally in a manner which is closely akin to the form in which it is found internally. Consider the following FORTRAN examples:

READ(N,9000) (A(I),I = 1,20)
WRITE(10) A,B,(C(J),J = 1,5)

In the first statement, a formatted record is read from input unit N, utilizing a format denoted by the numeral 9000. In the second statement, an unformatted record is written on output unit 10. In COBOL, the programmer need not be concerned with the formatting problem, and any required conversions are made during the course of performing the desired computation; e.g.,

READ CHANGE-FILE INTO UPDATE-RECORD, AT END
    GOTO EOF.
WRITE SAVER.

Clearly, the mode of input and output in COBOL is determined either by the compiler or by the operating system under which the COBOL programs are to be run. PL/I provides the advantages of both FORTRAN and COBOL. Consider, for example, the following PL/I statements:

PUT EDIT (X,Y)(X(3), F(12,5), X(7), E(30, 15));
READ FILE (PERSONNEL_FILE) SET (PTR);

The first statement involves stream* input/output and puts the variables X and Y in formatted form in the system output stream. The second statement reads a record from the file named PERSONNEL_FILE and sets the pointer variable PTR to its location in computer storage.

Specification Statements

Specification statements declare problem and execution-control data, file types, establish storage requirements, inform the compiler of expected execution-time conditions (relating to machine configurations, etc.), and specify how exception-type conditions should be handled.

Data and storage declarations may be *static* or *dynamic*, as required. Static declarations are effective at load time. Dynamic declarations are effective at execution time and are explicitly invoked or implicitly specified. Problem data declaration may specify the base, scale, mode, or pre-

---

*With *stream-oriented input/output*, the respective unit is considered to be a continuous stream of data items, in character form, to be assigned from the stream to variables or from variables to the stream. It is contrasted to *record input/output*, where the input or output exists in the form of physically separate records.

cision of *arithmetic data* and the mode and length of string data, as well as initial values for both. Execution-control data declarations may specify *label data*, *event data*, and the manner in which storage should be allocated. In general, *file types* are denoted implicitly, although most programming languages, which are used for commercial applications, have facilities for declaring them [and associated records] explicitly. *Environment* declarations extend the compatibility of programming languages among different machine types and may be used to specify run-time system configurations, as well. *Exceptional-condition* specifications may be handled on either a specific or general basis. That is, all occurrences of a given exception (e.g., a floating-point overflow) may be processed in the same way, or facilities may be available to handle each occurrence on an individual statement basis. A complete set of examples, in this category, would be quite lengthy and beyond the intent of this introduction. Some problem data declarations are included, however, to give the reader an intuitive notion of how declarations are made in the various languages:

FORTRAN

```
INTEGER A/10/, MTX(100,10)
REAL MAT1(10,10,10)
COMMON MAT1
```

COBOL

```
01   EMPLOYEE-RECORD, CLASS IS ALPHANUMERIC, USAGE IS DISPLAY.
        02   NAME, SIZE IS 30 CHARACTERS.
        02   BADGE, SIZE IS 4, CLASS IS NUMERIC.
           03   LOCATION, SIZE 2.
           03   DEPT, SIZE 2.
        02   SALARY, SIZE IS 12, PICTURE IS $,$$$,$$$.99.
```

PL/I

```
DECLARE ALPHA CHAR(20), SWITCH BIT(1), (X REAL, Y COMPLEX)
           FLOAT BINARY, TOT BINARY FIXED (17,2),
           CNT DECIMAL FIXED(8);
DECLARE   1 FORMAT_1 BASED (PTR),
           2 FORMAT CHARACTER (1),
           2 PAY_NUMBER CHARACTER (7),
           2 WAGES FIXED DECIMAL (5,2);
```

Subprogram Statements

It is often desirable to execute identical kinds of computation with different data. The process is simplified by using the subprogram concept, where sequences of computation are specified by the programmer as sub-programs or where prewritten routines are available from a central library. Two types of subprograms exist: subroutine subprograms and function subprograms. *Subroutines* are invoked by a separate statement in the programming language and are classed as closed subprograms, as noted below. Functions assume a functional value by their appearance in an arithmetic expression and may be classed as open subprograms or closed subprograms.* For *each* reference to an open subprogram, a copy of the generated machine language instructions are included with the program being compiled. Conversely, only one copy of a closed subprogram is included per program and a standard linkage is made to it for each time that it is referenced. The two classes of subprograms can be depicted as follows:

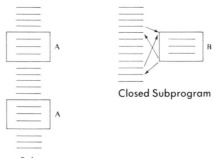

Closed Subprogram

Open Subprogram

In discussing subprograms, two topics are of particular interest: 1. The constituent parts of a subprogram definition; and 2. The process of invoking subprograms.

A *subprogram definition* is composed of two parts, a subprogram head and a subprogram body. A *subprogram head* names the subprogram, denotes its attributes, and specifies its parameters. The parameters indicate which variables are to be replaced when the subprogram is invoked. The *subprogram body* gives the statements to be executed when the subprogram is used, and usually all statements which are ordinarily available in the programming language are permitted to be used when a subprogram is being developed.

When invoking a subprogram, the programmer specifies what arguments are to replace the dummy parameters given in the subprogram definition. During actual processing of an open subprogram, the machine language instructions are executed directly, since no parameters need be

---

*Other common names for open and closed subprograms are *in-line* and *out-of-line*, respectively.

set up.*   During the execution of a closed subprogram, the parameters are replaced by the given arguments, and the statements are executed as if they were one of a kind.

Facilities for defining and using subprograms differ between programming languages, although most languages provide the CALL statement to invoke a subroutine subprogram. As with the previous class of statements, several examples are provided to clarify the concepts. A FUNCTION definition in FORTRAN would look somewhat as follows:

FUNCTION   ABCD(X,Y,Z)

———
———
... X
———
———
... Y
———
———
... Z
———
———
ABCD =
———
———
END

It could be invoked by the term ABCD (a_1, a_2, a_3) in an arithmetic expression. Similarly, the *subprogram head* of a COBOL subroutine definition might look somewhat as follows:†

U1.   ENTER LINKAGE-MODE.
         CALL 'GETREC' USING NUMBER, ADDRESS, COUNT.
U2.   ENTER COBOL.

and the *subprogram body* would follow accordingly.

Subprogram facilities provided in PL/I are similar in concept to those provided in FORTRAN, although the syntactic appearance seems to be quite different. Both types of subprograms are available and are declared by the same subprogram definition statement PROCEDURE. They differ,

*Arguments are processed by the compiler, and appropriate storage addresses are inserted into the open subprogram skeleton at compile-time.

†Implementors of the COBOL language are given considerable freedom in implementing the ENTER verb. The sample given is perhaps typical of the many versions which exist.

however, in the manner in which control is returned to the calling program. A function type subprogram returns an explicit result with the RETURN (*expression*), while the subroutine subprogram returns an implied result with the RETURN statement without an operand. As an example of both types combined, consider the following random number generator which is entered as a subroutine to set the starting numbers and entered as a function for obtaining a random number:

```
SETRAND:   PROCEDURE(M,N);
           DECLARE(GENNUM, RANDNUM) FIXED STATIC;
           GENNUM = M;   RANDNUM = N;
           RETURN;
RAND:      ENTRY;
           RANDNUM = GENNUM*RANDNUM;
           RETURN(RANDNUM);
           END;
```

The subprogram would be invoked for initialization and for obtaining a random number by statements such as:

```
CALL SETRAND(I, J);
       .
       .
       .
ALPHA = RAND;
```

In the first case, it is used as a subroutine; in the second, as a function.

Summary

It is obvious from the above discussion, and the FORTRAN, COBOL, and PL/I examples, that the objectives behind higher level (or programming) languages were met well. The language facilities have been classed into a small number of categories, and the kinds of different statements have been kept to a minimum. For the task of computer programming, this is desirable. Moreover, the truth of the preceding sentence is supported by the widespread use of the languages mentioned.

On the other hand, these languages are not totally satisfactory for expressing algorithms in a rigorous and consistent manner and tend to support eventual computer processing.* What if the objective is to express algorithms? This was the problem faced by the ALGOL designers; as a result, the computer processing aspects were de-emphasized, and features

---

*This is not precisely true. Pl/I, which was developed after FORTRAN, COBOL, and ALGOL, has virtually all of the facilities of ALGOL. Nevertheless, it has been emphasized by the PL/I designers that PL/I is intended to be a programming language and not an algorithmic language.

were added to give the language conciseness and consistency. These features are covered in the next section.

7.3   ALGORITHMIC LANGUAGES*

As was mentioned earlier, the distinction between programming languages and algorithmic languages is not a rigorous one. However, a definite difference does exist in their basic objectives. The objective in programming languages is to subordinate programming detail. The basic objective in algorithmic languages is to represent an algorithm in the most natural way with the fewest language primitives. Following this line of thinking, the following topics are presented in order: (1) compound statements; (2) blocks; (3) local and global variables; and (4) procedures.

Compound Statements

It is often desirable to be able to treat a number of consecutive statements as a unit. A *compound statement* is such a unit and consists of a set of statements (S_i) enclosed in the system symbols **begin** and **end**.

$$\textbf{begin } S_1; S_2; \ldots; S_n \textbf{ end}$$

The statements composing a compound statement as well as the compound statement itself may be labeled. Compound statements may be nested as required. For example:

```
begin
    if X = 0 then begin
                  X: = 1;
                  COUNT: = COUNT + 1;
              end
         FACTOR: = (Y ÷ X) ↑ 2
end
```

A compound statement may be used wherever a single statement can be used.

Blocks

A *block* is a compound statement in which one or more declarations (i.e., specification statements) precede the first statement, S_1. The symbol **begin** followed by the declaration is termed the *blockhead*. The statements of

---

*The algorithmic language ALGOL is used to present features basic to algorithmic languages. ALGOL, as described in Appendix A, contains many other features which enable it to be useful as a programming language, as well.

the block followed by the symbol **end** is termed the *block body*. Blocks may also be nested, as required.

In addition to specifying a group of statements, the *block* also indicates the range of statements over which variables retain their meaning. This will be covered in the next section.

Blocks which overlap are called *disjoint* and are not permitted in most algorithmic languages. Blocks containing imbedded blocks are termed *nested*. Statement labels are local to the block in which they are enclosed, disallowing transfers into the middle of a block. This is tantamount to saying that blocks can only be entered through their blockheads.

Generalizing, a block is a statement that can be used anywhere that a simple statement can be used. Conceptually, a block is a compound statement in which local variables can be declared; conversely, a compound statement is a block with no declarations.

Local and Global Variables

Variables must be declared in blocks in which they are used. This is done *explicitly* by including declarations in the blockhead; these variables are *local* to the block in which they are declared, and the block is said to be the *scope* of the variable. Variables can also be defined *implicitly* by not being declared in the blockhead of a particular block while being referenced in that block. These variables are *global* to the block and must be declared in an outer (or enclosing) block. In the following example:

```
begin real X, Y, Z; ...
···begin real X, W;
   Y: = X + W;
   end
   ...
end
```

X is local to both blocks (representing different storage locations, as well); Y and Z are local to the outer block and global to the inner block, and W is local to (i.e., retains its definition in) the inner block.

This can be stated in a slightly different manner with another orientation. Variables declared in blocks containing nested blocks retain their definition throughout the block, except in subblocks in which the same variable is declared. Making two declarations of the same variable in the same blockhead is illegal. On the other hand, two declarations of the same variable in different blockheads are allowed and result in two names representing different data values in different blocks.

Variables declared in a blockhead are created upon entry to that block and deleted upon exit from the block; i.e., every time a block is entered, a new copy of the variables, local to the block, is defined. It is often desirable to have declared variables retain their definitions between activations of a given block. This declarative facility is available with most algorithmic languages with the concept extending to arrays as well.*

Procedures

Another type of block is the *procedure* which permits the programmer to define subroutines and functions by means of a procedure definition. A procedure definition is composed of a *procedure head* and a *procedure body*. The procedure head names a procedure, provides a list of variables known as *formal parameters*, and declares local variables. The statements composing the procedure, in which the parameters appear, followed by a procedure terminator, are termed the procedure body.

A *procedure call* or *procedure statement* consists of the procedure name followed by a list of actual parameters. The procedure call is a representation of the procedure body in which the formal parameters have been replaced by actual arguments. The following statements define a procedure which forms the product of the first N elements of an array and assigns them to a given variable:

```
procedure  PROD(C,N,RESULT);
      real array C; integer N; real RESULT;
      begin integer I;
          RESULT: = 1;
          for I:=1 step 1 until N do
          RESULT:=RESULT×C[I];
      end
```

It would be used in a procedure call as follows:

```
begin real array  VECTOR [1:15]; real P;
      .
      .
      .
  PROD(VECTOR, 15, P);
      .
      .
      .

      end
```

If the procedure definition declares a function, then the procedure call is not a separate statement but rather a *function designator* which may be used as a primary† in an expression. The above procedure is rewritten as

*In ALGOL, these variables are declared as **own** variables.

† A *primary* is a constituent of an arithmetic or logical expression and generically denotes a constant, variable, function designator, or an expression enclosed in parentheses.

a *function-type procedure* which serves the same purpose:

```
real procedure  PROD(C,N);
real array C; integer N;
begin integer I; real  TEMP;
TEMP: = 1;
for I: = 1 step 1 until N do
TEMP: = TEMP × C(I);
PROD: = TEMP;
end
```

The function PROD is used in the following example which adds the product of the first 10 elements of array X and the product of the first 20 elements of array Y and places the scalar result in Z:

$$Z: = PROD(X,10)+PROD(Y,20);$$

Actual parameters in procedure calls and function references can be expressions as well as constants and variables. Because of this, two general ways of initializing parameters have been developed:

1. *Call by value.* This results in evaluation of the expression at the instant of call and assignment of this value to a local variable within the procedure.
2. *Call by name.* This results in evaluation of the expression every time the parameter is used during the execution of the procedure.

The following example, due to Wegner[11], illustrates the difference:

```
real procedure  P(A);
    real  A;
    begin
        K: = 5;
        P: = A;
    end
```

Let P(K) be a reference of the function P. If A is called by name, then a one-to-one correspondence is established between the address of parameter A and the address of argument K such that the value of P(K) is always 5. If A is called by value, then the value of A is established upon entry to the procedure such that P(K) is given by the value of K at that time.

7.4   MACRO FACILITIES IN HIGHER-LEVEL LANGUAGES

Macro facilities have been available in assembler languages for some time, but few higher level programming languages have included such features.

One noteworthy language which includes these facilities is PL/I, where they are referred to as *compile-time facilities*.* The name chosen is indeed accurate in that macro processing does take place at compile time. Historically, several attempts have been made in this direction, as shown in the references. Generally, the efforts can be classified by where they make themselves evident in the compiler process. Therefore, to simply state that macro facilities are needed is misleading; where they are needed and how they are to be provided must also be noted. Briefly, three kinds are identified as follows:

1. *Text macros* are employed for text editing and for incorporating prepared text into a program during lexical analysis.
2. *Syntactic macros* are employed during syntactic analysis and allow the introduction of new structures into the language.
3. *Functional macros* are employed during the code generation phase of compilation and are used primarily for incorporating open coding, for various procedures and functions, into the generated machine language program.

Relationship to the Compiler Model

In order that macro facilities be discussed adequately, a generalized model of a compiler is required. By *compiler model* is meant a division of the compiling task into a collection of conceptually distinct phases, each performing identifiable subtasks, such as lexical analysis, syntactic analysis, optimization, or code generation. Using the compiler model given in chapter 8 as a reference, it is readily seen that lexical and syntactic analysis occur in phase 1, and code generation is performed in phase 4. Clearly then, *text* and *syntactic macros* would be processed during phase 1, and *functional macros* would be processed during phase 4.

More detailed information on the compiler processes of interest is necessary for a clear understanding of macros. The three subtasks are further described in the following paragraphs:

1. *Lexical analysis* is the process of interfacing with the source of program text and identifying, isolating, and disposing of the terminal symbols and token symbols occurring in the program text, and outputting a sequence of descriptors of these terminal and token symbols.
2. *Syntactic analysis* is the process of identifying the syntactic units (with respect to some particular syntax) occurring in the stream of descriptors produced by the lexical analysis process, resulting in a parse of the program text.

*See section 7.5.

3. *Code generation* is the process of inspecting the pseudo-code representation of the computation and, using the information developed during the optimization phase, generating the sequence of machine language coding for carrying out the computation.

Text Macros

By *text macros* is meant a macro facility that is available to the programmer during the lexical analysis phase of compiling. This is the most primitive form of macro capability and allows simple text replacement on a many-one basis. For example, in B5000 ALGOL one could define a macro with the statement:

define LOOP1 for I step 1 until N #

and later write statements like:

LOOP1 N do A[I]←0

which would be expanded into:

for I = 1 step 1 until N do A[I]←0

by the compiler.

The concepts used in text macros are certainly not sophisticated by any stretch of the imagination; however, providing the user with a definitional tool for representing his program in a language natural to him has a lot to do with the solution of complex problems. The compile-time facilities provided with the PL/I language fall into the category of text macros. They differ only in that they are processed during a preprocessing pass over the source program, instead of during the lexical analysis phase of compilation.

Syntactical Macros*

The objective of syntactic macros is to provide a facility which allows one to define new syntactic structures in terms of the given syntax of a programming language. Three additions to the compiler are required: 1. a syntactic augment to the programming language to allow the definition and the invocation of macro; 2. a facility within the syntax analyzer for storing and recording the macro definitions; and 3. a mechanism within the syntactic analyzer to handle the call of the macros.

A language extension to provide syntactic macro capability would look like the following (in BNF notation):

<macro-param>::= **LET** <name> **BE** <syntactic type>
<macro-def>:: = **MACRO** <macro-form> **MEANS** '<defining string>'

*Cheatham[2] has done extensive work on syntactical macros, and this section is primarily the result of his efforts.

A call of the defined macro would be of the form:

$$\% <\text{macro-call}>$$

where $\%$ is a special character not in the programming language, and which takes special precedence over every symbol to the left of it. For example, the syntactic macro definition:

LET N BE INTEGER
MACRO MATRIX(N) MEANS 'ARRAY(1:N, 1:N)'

(which is essentially equivalent to a syntactic definition of the form: MACRO:: = '%"MATRIX"('INTEGER')'), followed by a macro statement of the form:

$$\% \text{MATRIX}(25)$$

would result in the compilation of:

ARRAY (1:25, 1:25)

Similarly, the definition:

MACRO A MEANS '+B*C+'

followed by the statement:

$$X = Y \quad \% A Z$$

would result in the compilation of:

$$X = Y + B*C + Z$$

Functional Macros

The name *functional macro* is derived from the fact that a compiler meta-program translates a program written in an argument language to its equivalent in a function language. Accordingly, the objective of a functional macro is to provide the programmer with the option of placing function language statements in his argument program and to have the compiler include them in the resultant function language program. Again, augments are needed in the language and language processor to incorporate the facilities.

Functional macros can be *implicitly* defined in the language or be *explicitly* defined by the programmer.

Implicit functional macros are open subroutines, as found in most programming languages. In many cases, the execution-time is less if in-line coding is inserted in the object program rather than a branch and link to a closed subroutine. In many cases, the amount of in-line coding is less than the number of required linkage instructions. Some typical examples from FORTRAN (or another algebraic language, as well) are:

$$ABS(X)$$
$$MAX(x_1, x_2, \ldots, x_n)$$

Explicit functional macros are written by the programmer and may be parameterized, as required. They use the code generation phase of the compiler but may affect earlier phases as well. Two forms of explicit functional macros are recognized:

Type I. This type is used simply to insert function language statements, directly in-line. Two keywords—GENERATE and ENDGEN are used:

GENERATE

$$\begin{bmatrix} \text{function} \\ \text{language} \\ \text{statements} \end{bmatrix}$$

ENDGEN

Type II. This type utilized defined macros or a macro library. Type II macros are *defined* with or without parameters as follows:

DEFINE *name*

$$\begin{bmatrix} \text{function} \\ \text{language} \\ \text{statements} \end{bmatrix}$$

ENDDEF

or with parameters:

DEFINE *name* (& A, & B, ...)

... & A ...

& B ...

ENDDEF

They may be later called by the GENERATE statement, using the "name" option:

GENERATE *name*

or with parameters:

GENERATE *name* (X,Y,...)

Of the three types of macro facilities, functional macros are the most elementary and the type that occurs most frequently. An obvious example is the facility for including assembler language statements in a FORTRAN program. As higher level programming languages have become more powerful, the need for functional macros has diminished. Nevertheless, functional macros tend to be used heavily with systems programming languages in which efficiency and the utilization of special machine language instructions are of prime importance.

7.5   COMPILE-TIME FACILITIES IN PL/I

The programming language PL/I (see Appendix D) contains a compile-time macro facility that would probably fall into the category of text macros. Instead of being processed during the lexical analysis phase of compilation, the PL/I macros are identified during a preprocessor stage, and the source program is modified accordingly. In other words, the programmer has some control over his source program while it is being compiled. The source program may optionally contain special statements (identified by a leading % and named preprocessor statements) that cause portions of the program to be altered as follows:

1. Any variable appearing in the program can be changed;
2. The programmer may indicate conditional compilation by specifying which parts of his program are to be compiled; and
3. Statements residing in a user library or system library can be included in the program.

Preprocessor statements take the form of standard PL/I statements, with the addition of the leading %, and permit the programmer to perform computations on his program as data. A subset of the PL/I language is permitted in preprocessor statements.

Preprocessor Scan

The source program is scanned sequentially on a character-by-character and statement-by-statement basis. Preprocessor statements encountered during the scan can cause the source program to be altered in either of two ways:

1. The preprocessor statement can cause the preprocessor to continue scanning from a different point in the program (including a point that has already been scanned); and
2. The preprocessor statement can cause variables in the source program to be replaced by preprocessor variables.

Before a variable in a source program can be replaced during preprocessor scan, that variable must have been activated for replacement with the % DECLARE statement and be given a replacement value with a preprocessor assignment statement. Once this is done, any further occurrence of that variable in the source program, excluding preprocessor statements, is replaced by the given value. For example, if a PL/I source program contained the following statements:

```
%DECLARE X CHARACTER, Z FIXED;
%X='Y+Z';
%Z=5;
A=X;
```

then the following statement would be placed into the preprocessed program (i.e., the output of the preprocessor):

$$A=Y+5$$

Preprocessor variables can be deactivated for replacement with the %DEACTIVATE statement and activated again, while retaining their former value, with the %ACTIVATE statement. Looping, conditional expressions, and arithmetic operations are also permitted in preprocessor statements, as evidenced in the next example. Consider a program which might contain the following statements:

```
DO I=1 TO 10;
Z(I)=X(I)+Y(I);
END;
```

The following preprocessor statements would accomplish the same thing without requiring that looping and testing instructions be placed in the object program:

```
%DECLARE I FIXED;
%I=1;
%L1:;
Z(I)=Z(I)+Y(I);
%I=I+1;
%IF I<=10    %THEN %GOTO L1;
%DEACTIVATE I;
```

A program of the form:

```
Z(1)=X(1) + Y(1);
Z(2)=X(2)+Y(2);
        .
        .
        .
Z(10)=X(10)+Y(10);
```

would be generated by the preprocessor.

A preprocessor DO loop is provided to facilitate macro programming.

For example, the previous example written in DO form would look as follows:

```
% DECLARE I FIXED;
% DO I = 1 TO 10;
Z(I) = X(I) + Y(I);
% END;
% DEACTIVATE I;
```

External text may also be included from a user library or a system library with the % INCLUDE statement. Furthermore, the included text may consist of both preprocessor and nonpreprocessor statements. The text retrieved by a % INCLUDE statement is incorporated into the source program at the point where the % INCLUDE statement was executed. Therefore, the scan continues with the first statement which has been included.

Preprocessor Statements

This section gives a summary of the preprocessor statements available in PL/I. Several statements support a facility which allows the writing of function-type procedures for execution during preprocessor scan. The functions may operate on character strings and are written using the given preprocessor statements. Of these statements, the % PROCEDURE statement, the ENTRY attribute in the % DECLARE statement, and the RETURN as a preprocessor statement are included specifically for writing compile-time procedures. In the following statements, the square brackets [] indicate optional items, and the braces {} indicate that a choice must be made from among enclosed items.

1. *The Activate Statement.* The % ACTIVATE statement is used to make a preprocessor variable eligible for replacement. If it had been previously deactivated, it is activated with its former value. Format:

   % [*label*:] . . . ACTIVATE *identifier*[,*identifier*] . . . ;

2. *The Assignment Statement.* The compile-time assignment statement is used to evaluate compile-time expression and to replace a preprocessor-variable with the result. Format:

   % [*label*:] . . . *preprocessor-variable* = *preprocessor-expression;*

3. *The Deactivate Statement.* The % DEACTIVATE statement is used to make a preprocessor variable ineligible for replacement. Subsequent use of that variable in the source program causes no replacement. Format:

   % [*label*:] . . . DEACTIVATE   *identifier* [, *identifier*] . . . ;

4. *The Declare Statement.* The %DECLARE statement is used to establish an identifier as a compile-time variable or as an entry to a compile-time procedure and *activates* that identifier as well. Format:

%[*label*:] ... DECLARE *identifier* {FIXED | CHARACTER | *entry-declaration*} [, *identifier* {FIXED | CHARACTER | *entry-declaration*}] ... ;

where the format of "entry-declaration" is:

ENTRY[([CHARACTER | FIXED][,[CHARACTER | FIXED]] ...)]
RETURNS({CHARACTER | FIXED})

5. *The Do Statement.* The %DO statement provides a controlled looping facility; the range of the DO may include preprocessor and nonprocessor statements. Format:

$$\%[\textit{label};] \ldots \text{DO} \left[i = m1 \left[\left\{ \begin{array}{ll} \text{TO } m2 & [\text{BY } m3] \\ \text{BY } m3 & \text{TO } m2 \end{array} \right\} \right] \right];$$

where "*i*" represents a preprocessor variable, and "*m*1," "*m*2," and "*m*3" are preprocessor expressions.

6. *The End Statement.* The %END statement is used to denote the end of a compile-time DO group or a compile-time procedure. Format:

%[*label*:] ... END [*preprocessor-statement-label*];

7. *The Goto Statement.* The %GOTO statement causes the preprocessor to resume its scan at the specified statement label. Format:

%[*label*] ... {GO TO | GOTO} *preprocessor-statement-label;*

8. *The If Statement.* The %IF is used to control the scan of a program by the preprocessor on a conditional basis. Format:

%[*label*:] ... IF *preprocessor-expression*
%THEN *preprocessor-clause*-1
[%ELSE *preprocessor-clause*-2]

9. *The Include Statement.* The %INCLUDE statement is used to incorporate strings of external text into the program text being formed. Format:

%[*label*:] ... INCLUDE *identifier* [, *identifier*] ... ;

10. *The Null Statement.* The null statement is used to insert preprocessor statement labels into program text. Format:

%[*label*:] ... ;

11. *The Procedure Statement.* The %PROCEDURE statement declares a compile-time procedure, establishes its parameters, and gives the attribute of the value to be returned. Format:

$$\% \ label: [label:] \ldots \text{PROCEDURE} \ [(identifier$$
$$[, identifier] \ldots)] \ \{\text{CHARACTER} \mid \text{FIXED}\};$$

12. *The Return Statement.** The RETURN statement provides an exit from a compile-time procedure. Format:

$$[label:] \ldots \text{RETURN} \ (expression);$$

Summary

Although PL/I provides a comprehensive macro facility previously unavailable in a higher level programming language, its most significant aspect is perhaps the fact that preprocessor statements and nonpreprocessor statements are written in the same base language. The implications of this fact are far-reaching in that preprocessing can theoretically be extended to as many levels as are desired without requiring that the language primitives grow without bound. Only time can indicate if this will influence the direction of future programming languages.

PROBLEMS

7.1 Some common properties which can be applied to computer languages are: generality, simplicity, succinctness, naturalness, consistency, and efficiency. Apply these properties to the language of this chapter. Is it possible to assign a quantitative value to the properties so that the language can be compared?

7.2 In what way could FORTRAN be modified to make it more useful for commercial programming? Similarly, how would COBOL be modified to make it more amenable to scientific programming? To what extent does PL/I satisfy these needs?

7.3 *Call by name* is a useful concept in scientific computing. How might the notion be utilized in FORTRAN within the constraints of the language as described in Appendix C? Consider the technique of passing subprogram names as arguments in function references and subroutine calls and of using COMMON storage.

REFERENCES

1. Brown, P. J., "The ML/I Macro Processor," *Comm. ACM,* Vol. **10,** No. 10 (Oct., 1967). Describes a syntactic macro processor capable of generating code in any *base language.*

*PL/I statements within preprocessor procedures do not require the prefix character %. As a result, none is required with RETURN.

2. Cheatham, T. E., *The Introduction of Definitional Facilities into Higher Level Programming Languages,* CA-6605-0611, Computer Associates, Inc., 1966. Presents basic concepts for extending programming languages by providing definitional facilities which will enable the programmer to define higher level macros.
3. Feldman, J., and D. Gries, "Translator Writing Systems," *Comm. ACM,* Vol. **11,** No. 2 (February, 1968). Contains a complete survey of translator writing techniques and macro extensions of programming languages.
4. "FORTRAN vs. Basic FORTRAN," *Comm. ACM,* Vol. **7,** No. 10 (Oct., 1964). Contains a concise and comprehensive description of the FORTRAN language.
5. Lawson, H. W., "PL/I List Processing," *Comm. ACM,* Vol. **10,** No. 6 (June, 1967). Introduces the basics of the list processing facility in PL/I.
6. Leavenworth, B. M., "Syntax Macros and Extended Translation," *Comm. ACM,* Vol. **9,** No. 11 (Nov., 1966). Reports a syntactic macro facility which attempts to solve the semantic problems usually associated with macro processors.
7. Naur, P. (ed), "Revised Report on the Algorithmic Language Algol 60," *Comm. ACM,* Vol. **6,** No. 1 (Jan., 1963). Describes the algorithmic language, ALGOL 60.
8. Radin, G., and H. P. Rogoway, "Highlights of a New Programming Language," *Comm. ACM,* Vol. **8,** No. 1 (Jan., 1965). Presents an early review of PL/I then called NPL.
9. Sammet, J. E., "Basic Elements of COBOL 61," *Comm. ACM,* Vol. **5,** No. 5 (May, 1962). Presents an early but complete description of COBOL.
10. Waite, W. M., "A Language Independent Macro Processor," *Comm. ACM,* Vol. **10,** No. 7 (July, 1967). Discusses a macro processor which utilizes template matching techniques and the notion of nested functional expressions.
11. Wegner, P., *Programming Languages, Information Structures, and Machine Organization,* New York, McGraw-Hill Book Company, 1968. Contains a chapter on procedure-oriented languages and another on symbolic macros.
12. *An Introduction to the Compile-Time Facilities of PL/I,* IBM Corporation, White Plains, N.Y., Form C20-1689, 1968. Introduces the text macro facilities available with the PL/I language.
13. *PL/I Language Specifications,* IBM Corporation, New York, Form C28-6571, 1965. Contains a technical description of the complete PL/I language.

8 | ADVANCED COMPILER SYSTEMS

Compiler-writing techniques have received a great deal of pragmatic and academic attention and are now well-defined.* It was and still is generally felt that the compiler is independent of the operating system in which it resides, if it resides in one at all. The invention of time-sharing systems with conversational capability, however, has required that compiler experts reevaluate existing concepts to make better use of external facilities. This was done, and conversational and incremental compilers have evolved. A generalized and consolidated discussion of these relatively new concepts is the subject of this chapter.† First, a model of a batch compiler is introduced.‡ The concepts are then modified and extended for a conversational programming environment. Finally, a recent development termed *incremental compilation*, which satisfies the needs of both batch and conversational compiling, as well as interactive computing, is presented. First, some introductory material is required.

8.1 BASIC CONCEPTS

In the classical data processing environment§ (Fig. 8.1), the *compile phase* or *source language processing phase* (Fig. 8.2) is of prime impor-

---

*Two books devoted entirely to the subject are worth mentioning: Lee[5], *The Anatomy of a Compiler;* and Randell and Russel[10], *Algol 60 Implementation.*

†This chapter is reproduced in part, with permission, from the Proceedings of the AFIPS Conference, Vol. 34, p. 47–56; see Katzan.[4]

‡This model is basically the same as the one presented in chapter 4, which describes the original FORTRAN system. More detail is given here, when necessary, so that additional topics can be introduced.

§See Lee[6], p. 9.

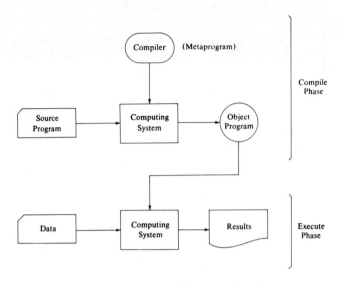

Fig. 8.1   Generalized data processing environment.

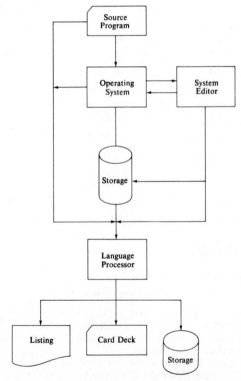

Fig. 8.2   Source language processing.

tance, as are definitions of *source program* and *object program*. The latter are redefined in terms of the time-sharing or interactive environment. Extraneous items, such as where the object program is stored or whether or not the compiler should produce assembler language coding, are practically ignored.

The *source program* is the program as written by the programmer. It is coded in symbolic form and punched on cards or typed in at the terminal. The *object program* is the program that has been transformed by the compiler into a machine-oriented form, which can be read into the computer and executed with very few (if any) modifications. Also of interest is the *information vector*, which gives initial conditions for compilation and denotes the types of output desired. A sample of specifications which might be found in an information vector follow:

1. Location of the source program;
2. Name of the program;
3. The extent of compiler processing, i.e., syntax check only, optimize, etc.;
4. Computer system parameters;
5. Compiler output desired; and
6. Disposition of the object module.

The form of the source program is sometimes required, although in most cases this information is known implicitly. This pertains to different BCD codes and file types, which may range from sequential or indexed files on conventional systems to list-structured files in virtual machines.

Similarly for output, the user can request a specialized form of object module or none at all, source or object program listing, and cross-reference listings. The object module is known as a *program module*, which contains the machine language text and relocation information. Additionally, it may contain an *internal symbol dictionary* for use during execution-time debugging. The internal symbol dictionary is especially useful in conversational time-sharing systems, where execution can be stopped on a conditional basis and the values of internal variables can be displayed or modified.

8.2 BATCH COMPILATION

Batch compilation methods are required, quite naturally, in a batch processing environment. The term *batch processing* stems from the days when the programmer submitted his job to the computer center and received his results later in time. A collection of different jobs was accumulated by operations personnel, and the batch was then presented to the computer system on an input tape. The important point is that the programmer has no contact with his job between the time it is submitted to operations and when he receives his output. The concept has been extended to cover *multiprogramming systems, remote job entry*, and the trivial case where no operating system exists and the programmer runs the compiler to completion.

The Generalized Batch Environment

The most significant aspect of the batch processing environment is that the entire source program is available to the compiler initially and that all compiler output can be postponed until a later phase. The compiler writer, therefore, is provided with a liberal amount of flexibility in designing his language processor. For example, specification (i.e., declarative) statements can be recognized and processed in an initial phase and storage allocated immediately. In the same pass, statement labels are recognized and entabled; then in a later phase, validity decisions for statements that use statement labels can be made immediately rather than making a later analysis on the basis of table entries. If desired, source program error diagnostics can be postponed. Moreover, the designer may specify his compiler, so that the source program is passed by the compiler, or so that the compiler is passed over the source program, which resides semipermanently in memory.

This inherent flexibility is not exploited in the compiler model which follows. Instead, an attempt has been made to present the material in a conceptually straightforward manner.

A Generalized Batch Compiler

By itself, a model of a generalized batch compiler is of limited interest. The concept is useful, however, for comparison with those designed to operate in time-shared computer systems. Therefore, the presentation is pedagogical in nature, in comparison with one which might present a step–by–step procedure for building one.

Processing by the compiler is naturally divided into several phases that tend to be more logical than physical. Each phase has one or more specific tasks to perform. In so doing, it operates on tables and lists, possibly modifying them and producing new ones. One phase, of course, works on the source program from the system input device or external storage, and another produces the required output. The entire compiler is described, therefore, by listing the tasks each phase is to perform; ordinarily, the description would also denote which tables and lists each phase uses and which tables and lists it creates or modifies. The specific tables and lists required, however, tend to be language dependent and are beyond the scope of this treatment.

The compiler model is composed of five phases and an executive routine, as follows:

The Compiler Executive (EXEC).   The various phases run under the control of a compiler executive routine (EXEC), which is the only communication with the outside world.   It establishes initial conditions and calls the different phases as required.   It can be assumed that EXEC performs all system input/output services upon demand from the phase modules. More specifically, the EXEC has five major and distinct functions:

1. To interface with the compiler's environment;
2. To prepare the source statements for processing by phase one;
3. To control and order the operation of the phases;
4. To prepare edited lines for output; and
5. To provide compiler diagnostic information.

Phase 1.   Phase 1 performs the source program syntactic analysis, error analysis, and translation of the program into tabular representation.   Each variable or constant is given an entry in the symbol table, with formal arguments being flagged as such.   Initial values and array dimensions are stored in a table of preset data.   Lastly, information from specification statements is stored in the specification table.   The most significant processing, however, occurs with respect to the *program reference file* and the *expression reference file.*

Each executable statement and statement label is placed in the program reference file in skeletal form.   In addition to standard program reference file entries, the program reference file contains pointers to the expression reference file for statements involving arithmetic or logical expressions.

The expression reference file stores expressions in an internal notation, using pointers to the symbol table when necessary.   As with the expression reference file, the program reference file also contains pointers to the symbol table.

Phase 2.   In general, phase 2 performs analyses that cannot be performed in phase 1.   It makes storage assignments in the program module for all variables that are not formal parameters.   It detects illegal flow in loops and recognizes early exits therefrom.   It also determines blocks of a program with no path of control to them; and lastly, it detects statement labels which are referenced but not defined.

Phase 3.   The object of phase 3 is to perform the global optimizations used during object code generation, which is accomplished in phase 4.

The first major function of phase 3 is the recognition and processing of *common subexpressions.*   Phase 3 determines which arithmetic expressions need to be computed only once and then saved for later use.   In addition, it determines the range of statements over which expressions are not re-defined by the definition of one or more of their constituents. If the occur-rence of an expression in that range is contained in one or more DO* loops, which are also entirely contained in that range, Phase 3 determines the outermost such loop outside from which such an expression may be computed, and physically moves the expression to the front of that DO loop. Only the evaluation process is removed from the loop; any state-ment label or replacement operation is retained in its original position. The moved expression is linked to a place reserved for that purpose in the program reference file entries corresponding to the beginning of the re-spective DO loops.

The second major function of phase 3 is the recognition and processing of *removable statements*. A *removable statement* is one whose individual operands do not have *definition points* inside the loop; obviously, the exe-cution of this statement for each iteration would be unnecessary. A defi-nition point is a statement in which the variable has, or may have, a new variable stored in it (e.g., appears on the left-hand side of an equal sign). In removing statements, they are usually placed before the DO statement.

Phase 3 also processes formal parameters and develops the prologue to the program; it optimizes the use of registers; and it merges the program reference file and the expression reference file to form a *complete program file* in preparation for phase 4.

Phase 4.   Phase 4 performs the code generation function. Its input con-sists of the symbol table and the complete program file and its output is the *code file*, which represents completed machine instructions and con-trol information.

Phase 5.   Phase 5 is the output phase and generates the *program module*, the source and object listings, and the cross reference listing. Upon re-quest, an *internal symbol dictionary* is also included in the program module.

Any compiler model of this type is clearly an abstraction; moreover, there is almost as much variation between different compilers for the same programming language as there is between compilers for different lan-guages. The model does serve a useful purpose, which is to present a con-ceptual foundation from which conversational and incremental compilers can be introduced.

---

*Although the DO keyboard is a constituent part of several programming languages, it should be interpreted as representing the class of statements from different languages which effectively enable the programmer to write program loops in a straightforward manner.

8.3   CONVERSATIONAL COMPILATION

Compared with the *batch* environment in which the user had no contact with his job once it was submitted, the conversational environment provides the exact opposite. A general purpose time-sharing system of one kind or another is assumed,* with users having access to the computing system via terminal devices.

In the batch environment, the user was required to make successive runs on the system to eliminate syntax and setup errors with the intervening time ranging from minutes to days. Excluding execution-time *bugs*, it often took weeks to get a program running. In the conversational mode, syntactical and setup errors can be eliminated in one terminal session. Similarly, execution-time debugging is also possible in a time-sharing system on a dynamic basis.

Conversational programming places a heavy load on a compiler and an operating system; the magnitude of the load is reflected in the basic additions necessary to support the conversational environment.

The Time-Sharing Environment

The time-sharing environment is characterized by versatility. Tasks can exist in the *batch* or *conversational* mode. Furthermore, source program input can reside on the system input device or be prestored. The time-sharing operating system is able to distinguish between batch and conversational tasks; therefore, batch tasks are recognized as such and processed as in any operating system. The ensuing discussion will concern conversational tasks. It is assumed, also, that the user resides at a terminal and is able to respond to requests by the system.

During the compile phase, the source program may be entered on a statement-by-statement basis or be prestored. In either case, the compiler responds immediately to the terminal with local syntactic errors. The user, therefore, is able to make changes to the source program immediately. Changes to the source program other than in response to immediate diagnostics cause a restart of the compilation process. Obviously, the system must keep a fresh copy of the source program for the restart case. To satisfy this need, a copy of the current up-to-date source program is maintained on external storage; if the source was prestored, the original version is updated with change requests; if the source program is not prestored, the compiler saves all source (and changes) as they are entered line-by-line. With the user at a terminal, the compiler is also able to stop midway during compilation (usually after the global statement analysis

*Two typical general purpose time-sharing systems are TSS/360[1,3] and MULTICS[2].

and before optimization) to inquire whether or not the user wants to continue. Under error conditions, the user may abort the compilation or make changes and restart the compilation process. Moreover, the user can utilize this pause to have his program syntax checked only.

During the execution phase, dynamic debugging is often desirable. This facility is usually a part of the command structure of the operating system. In preparation for execution-time debugging, the user would probably request an internal symbol dictionary during compilation so that internal variables can be addressed symbolically. Since execution-time debugging is a relatively new concept, it is discussed briefly.

Debugging commands usually fall into three categories: 1. program control; 2. program modification; and 3. debugging output. Debugging commands may be imbedded in the program itself, or the program can be stopped (either asynchronously or with an AT command) and the actions performed immediately. Examples of typical *program control* commands are:

> AT   *symbolic-location* ... STOP
> RUN
> RUN   *symbolic-location*

Examples of *program modification* commands are:

> SET A = 1.0
> IF A < 0; SET A = 0

Examples of *debugging output* commands are:

> DISPLAY MAIN.I: MAIN.A
> DUMP ARRAY

Furthermore, they can be used in combination as follows:

> AT   PTWO.100;   IF   A = 0;   STOP
> AT   T34.360;   DUMP   T34.A;   SET   CNT = CNT + 1

As mentioned earlier, a considerable amount of the compiler's effort is devoted to producing an efficient object program. As a result, the instructions to perform certain computations are sometimes not located where one would expect to find them. In fact, this is a direct consequence of *common subexpressions* and *removable statements*, which were discussed previously. Although these processes contribute to efficiency, they have a side effect which hinders the debugging effort. Therefore, when expecting to use dynamic debugging, the user would request an internal symbol dictionary and select the option which does not produce optimized code.

The conversational compiler and the time-sharing operating system must support several aspects of the conversational environment. These are summarized as follows: 1. the ability to change or forget the effects of the preceding statement; 2. restart logic; 3. maintenance of the entire source program in up-to-date form on external storage; 4. the ability to scan statements and produce diagnostics on an individual statement basis; and 5. the option to produce optimized or unoptimized code.

The Conversational Compiler

Basically, the conversational compiler[12] is a conventional batch-processor, containing special features making it suitable for conversational, terminal-oriented operation.

Structually, the major addition over a batch compiler is a *compiler control program* (CCP), which in effect controls compilation. CCP is cognizant of whether the mode of operation is batch or conversational and is able to fetch source records and dispose of output print lines, accordingly. CCP is the facility which maintains the source program on external storage and is able to tell if a new source record is indeed new, a change to the last one entered, or a change to a previous one. When processing a request to fetch a source record for the compiler, CCP can use this information to simply return the record, return it with the *forget flag* on, or call the compiler at its initial entry for the restart case. The function to fetch a source record is termed GETLINE and is summarized in Table 8.1. Accordingly, an overview of the CCP is given in Fig. 8.3.

The overall logic of the conversational compiler is shown in Fig. 8.4.

TABLE 8.1 GETLINE FUNCTION OF THE COMPILER CONTROL PROGRAM (CCP)

GETLINE	Conversational		Batch	
	Prestored	Not Prest.	Prestored	Not Prest.
	A	B	A	C

A. Fetches the next source record from external storage and returns it to compiler EXEC.
B. Fetches another source record from the terminal input device and updates the source file on external storage. If it is the next source record, the line is returned to the compiler with the *forget flag* off. If the given source record is to replace the previous one, the forget flag is turned on and the line is again returned. Otherwise, a previous line has been modified and the compiler is entered at the *initial entry point* for the restart case.
C. Fetches the next source record from the system input device and updates the source file on external storage; the line is returned to EXEC with the forget flag off.

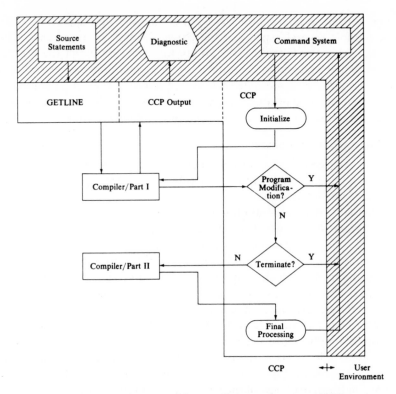

Fig. 8.3   An overview of the compiler control program (CCP).

Clearly, it differs very little from the batch version. The differences in the compiler itself are found in phase one and at the end of phase two. In phase one, as shown in Fig. 8.5, the compiler uses CCP as its external interface. Moreover, the compiler always compiles a statement conditionally; later it uses the forget flag to freeze or delete the compiled information.

After phase two, as shown in Figs. 8.3 and 8.4, the conversational compiler again exits to CCP. In the batch mode of course, CCP simply returns to the compiler. In the conversational mode, as shown in Fig. 8.3, the user is asked for changes and whether he wants to continue. At the user's request, CCP can change the source program, still residing on external storage, and restart the compiler at the *initial entry*. If the user desires to continue, the compiler is entered at the *continue entry*. Otherwise, CCP exits to the command system, and the remainder of the compilation is aborted.

Conversational compilation offers significant advantages over standard

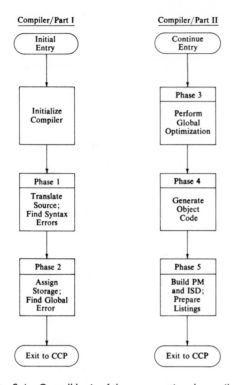

Compiler/Part I

Initial
Entry

Initialize
Compiler

Phase 1

Translate
Source;
Find Syntax
Errors

Phase 2

Assign
Storage;
Find Global
Error

Exit to CCP

Compiler/Part II

Continue
Entry

Phase 3

Perform
Global
Optimization

Phase 4

Generate
Object
Code

Phase 5

Build PM
and ISD;
Prepare
Listings

Exit to CCP

Fig. 8.4   Overall logic of the conversational compiler.

batch processing, most of which deal with the interactive mode of operation. The major disadvantage is that the entire source program must be available before execution can be attempted. In other words, one would like the versatility and flexibility of a language interpreter with the performance of a conversational or batch processor. Moreover, the performance must be reflected in the execution time as well as the compile time.

8.4   INCREMENTAL COMPILATION

One of the most promising ideas in this era of on-line computing is a concept termed *incremental compilation*. In an interactive programming environment, one would like to achieve both the speed factors inherent in compiled programs and the flexibility available with interpretive systems. Incremental compilers are an attempt to achieve these goals. In order that these goals can be realized, the following capabilities are required:

1. The ability to execute a statement immediately;

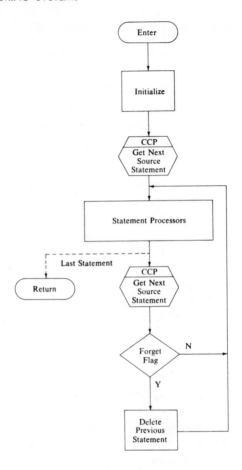

Fig. 8.5   Compiler/Part I interface with CCP.

2. The ability to modify a prior statement without forcing a recompilation;
3. The ability to execute a source program as it is being input;
4. The ability to execute selected portions of programs; and
5. A language processor that can also operate in the batch mode.

Clearly, all of the above requirements, except speed, are met with an appropriate interpretive program. In a large time-sharing environment, however, this resource is of prime importance, especially when a large number of terminals are being serviced.

The Environment for Incremental Compilation

Basically, the environment for incremental compilation is the same as for its conversational counterpart. By assuming a sophisticated operating system, such as TSS/360[1,3] or MULTICS[2], many of the problems described in early papers by Lock[7] and by Ryan[11], such as memory protection among users, an effective command system, and memory organization and management, are obviated. Dynamic loading facilities for utilizing hand coded subroutines, and a memory relocation feature[9] for mapping virtual addresses to real addresses, simplify problems involving the execution of code compiled incrementally and are also assumed. The programming language is naturally of importance and of great interest to most systems programmers. A language more powerful than standard FORTRAN or assembler language is expected, although the techniques would work satisfactorily therewith. A rich language which would enable a significant amount of computation per interaction is most desirable. Languages such as PL/I[8] and Iverson's language[5] are well suited to incremental compiling and executing.

The Incremental Compiler

This method of compilation permits two modes of operation: batch and incremental. In the *batch mode*, the user may compile a prestored source program but may not modify or execute the program during compilation. In the *incremental mode*, normally used only conversationally, special facilities are available to permit the modification, execution, and checkout of the program during compilation. These operations are performed through a combination of control and source language statements.

Incremental compilation consists of accepting a source program on a statement-by-statement basis. Each statement is compiled as it is received, and the code generated for it is immediately made available for execution. Associative links between the source program and object code are maintained, thus permitting the user, during compilation, to modify his source program and have the modification immediately reflected in the object code. The ability to compile, execute, and modify a program on a statement-by-statement basis gives the user a degree of flexibility over his program usually available only with an interpreter, yet reduces the principal objection to interpreters—that of requiring an excessive amount of execution time. While each statement in an interpreter must be processed each time it is executed, in an incremental compiler the statement has to be processed only when entered initially or when the user makes a source program modification. The incremental compiler has the added advantage of ensuring that the object code the user tests incrementally is virtually the same as the code produced for an object module, since the same code generators are used in both modes.

When an incremental compiler is used in the batch mode, all of the usual facilities are available to the user. When used in the incremental mode, all of the batch facilities are available, in addition to those provided to control the execution and debugging of the generated code. During both modes of compilation, the following options are permitted:

1. Analyze the program only for syntactic errors; do not perform a global analysis or generate code.
2. Analyze the program for syntactic and global errors; do not generate code.
3. Analyze the program for syntactic and global errors and generate object code as well.

The object program may be executed, in either the batch or incremental mode, only if the third option is selected. In most compilers of this type, the user may select one of several modes of executing the incremental code concurrently with compilation. As errors are uncovered, he may make modifications to the source language, without, in most cases, requiring a recompilation of the existing code or affecting previous execution.

In order to provide the user with the degree of control desired, two categories of *control statements* are necessary: transient statements and commands. A *transient statement* is a statement in the source language being compiled which is executed and discarded immediately. It allows the user to intervene during the execution of his program and print results or change values. *Commands* are control statements which allow the user to make modifications outside the scope of the source language. A good example would be to change the control point of the program.

Source program compilation and execution in the incremental mode is under direct control of a *language controller* (LC). Each interaction, by LC, with the user is divided into a processing cycle and/or an execution cycle, depending upon the input parameters. The compiler is called by LC to process source language and transient statements and if execution is requested, it is initiated and monitored accordingly. After execution, transient statements are discarded, whereas source language statements are retained. The command system of the operating system is called by the language controller to process commands. Clearly, there is a need to tie the various elements of a program together for operational reasons, and this requirement is satisfied by the *program structure table*, described below. Since the language controller controls a major portion of the processing when in the incremental mode, it is structured accordingly. As pictured in Fig. 8.6, it contains program elements for maintaining the

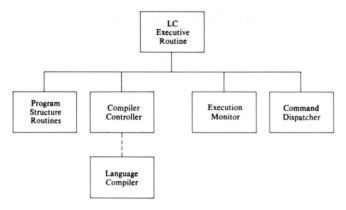

Fig. 8.6   Language controller.

source program and the program structure table, for controlling the compiler, for monitoring the execution of incremental code, and for interpreting and then dispatching or processing control statements. These functions are summarized in the following descriptions of the modules which comprise the language controller:

1. *Program Structure Routines.*   The program structure routines maintain the source program on external storage and manage the program structure table, which contains an entry for each source language statement in the program being compiled. The relationship of statements is also established for subsequent use by the execution monitor.

2. *Compiler Controller.*   The compiler controller provides the interface between the user and the compiler. It passes the identity and location of source statements to the compiler EXEC and receives the location of the compiled code in return. In so doing, it handles diagnostics and updates the program structure table.

3. *Execution Monitor.*   The execution monitor controls program execution as determined by the established mode of operation. It passes control between statements or halts execution after specific statements, as required. It utilizes the dynamic loader of the operating system and evokes other program modules when requested to do so.

4. *Command Interpreter and Dispatcher.*   The command interpreter analyzes control statements and calls either the compiler controller or the command system of the operating system, depending upon whether a transient statement or a command is being processed.

The program structure table is obviously of great importance, since it indicates the relationship of statements and the static properties of the program. Elements in the table are generated dynamically as source language statements are entered and are composed from the following quantities:*

1. A *type indicator* specifying the type of statement;
2. A list of *structure pointers* linking this statement to preceding and succeeding statements and to any function module† in which it might be contained;
3. A pointer to the *compiled machine code* for the statement;
4. A locator, such as data set name or physical location, of the *source program* on external storage; and
5. A statement identification, such as a *line number*, used for referencing the statement and for making insertions, deletions, and changes to the program.

Due to the nature of the incremental compilation process and the program structure table, it is not necessary that the incremental code for a given program reside in contiguous memory locations. In fact, only rarely will this be the case. Although this is conceptually different from the established practice of generating object code, it poses no serious problem in the incremental mode of operation.

In general, the incremental compiler is composed of the same basic components as the batch and conversational versions. Some differences, which tend to be related to the interrelationship of statements, do exist but are relatively minor. The *global analysis* of statements, for example, is severely crippled by the fact that all statements in a source module may not be available for analysis. The *global optimization* of statements is in the same category but must be eliminated entirely. It is very feasible, however, to include it as a special phase in the batch mode or provide a mechanism to convert from incremental to object code, including global optimization, in the conversational mode.

The basic compiler processing cycle begins when it is called at its source input entry. (Another entry could conceivably exist that might convert incremental code to object code.) The compiler EXEC obtains the source text to be processed from the language controller and builds a *program table* consisting of the text to be processed during the cycle; information on additions, insertions, and deletions; location of the existing symbol table; and parameter data relating to mode of compilation, listing options,

---

*The article by Lock[7] contains a comprehensive description of internal program structure in a programming environment such as this.

†The term function module is used to represent either a *block* or internal *procedure* as found in ALGOL or PL/I.

BCD codes, etc. The EXEC then invokes Phase 1 of the compiler, which performs a statement classification and syntax analysis and builds the program reference file and expression reference file from all of the statements specified in the program table.   Pointers to the encoded statements are then returned to the EXEC, where the encoded statements are linked back to the program table. Phase 2 is then invoked to perform a global analysis, when possible, and to assign storage for the statements indicated in the program table. This phase updates the symbol table and merges the program reference file and expression reference file to form the complete program file, maintaining the links to the program table as required. Phase 4* is now called to translate the encoded statements into object code, forming the code file.   Phase 5, which must generate either object code or incremental code, is considered below.

Operation of the compiler for each of the two basic modes, batch and incremental, can now be described. In a *batch compilation*, the source text available at entry consists of the complete program.   The program table passed to each component points to every statement in the source program, so that in a single cycle, the complete compilation is produced. Other than the executive, the only phase which must be aware of the batch parameter is Phase 5, which must build an object module instead of generating incremental code. Again, the object module consists of a program module (i.e., text and relocation data) and optionally, an internal symbol dictionary. The text portion consists of the object code produced and is entirely self-contained, with the code generated for a statement linking directly to the code for the next statement. The source text available at entry to an *incremental compilation* may represent anything from a single statement to a complete program.   Normally, however, the source text available represents only a portion of a program.   The program table, therefore, contains a group of statements to be added or deleted in the current program. The program table is in the same form as for a batch compilation and does not require different handling by Phases 1, 2, and 4. In this mode, Phase 5 generates incremental code.   Incremental code differs from an object module in that the program module (i.e., the relocation information) must be dynamically generated, requiring some special processing by the language controller and the system's dynamic loader. The text is organized on a statement-by-statement basis with interstatement linkage provided to allow the intervention by the language controller† at statement boundaries.

---

* Recognizing that no Phase 3 exists.
† That is, the execution monitor.

As a result of the incremental process, four modes of execution are possible: automatic, controlled, block, and step. In the *automatic mode*, statements are executed by the language controller immediately after they are processed by the compiler. In the *controlled mode*, statements are executed only when explicitly requested by a RUN command, which may designate a range of statements. In the block and step modes, an entire program (i.e., an external procedure) is available for execution. For the *block case*, the language controller pauses for user intervention after each block (or possible subroutine) in the program. When the *step* mode is specified, language controller suspends object program execution after each statement.

8.5   CONCLUSIONS

The world of time-sharing and its potential for interactive computing at a general level have raised some interesting topics.

First, it should be recognized that although batch techniques are currently very efficient and well-defined, they were developed of necessity. When these techniques gained their acceptance, the batch mode was the only operational procedure available for using the computer. The programming community should also recognize that program development in a batch environment may not be the most natural or the optimum method.

Second, it should be recognized further that conversational techniques do not offer a complete solution in that execution of parts of a program is usually not permitted. Clearly, language syntax errors can be detected during input, and this is certainly a step in the right direction. But if a programmer has to develop his algorithm completely before any of it can be executed, he might as well compile in the batch mode and rely on execution-time debugging.

Some form of incremental compiling, therefore, seems to be the only answer in sight to questions regarding the development of algorithms in an interactive computing environment. The ability to execute a program as it is being compiled is certainly natural and very well may be optimum from a developmental point of view. It remains to be seen if the gains can justify the complexity of an incremental compiler.

PROBLEMS

8.1   Using *batch compilation* techniques, take the following program through the various phases of compilation:

```
        REAL    T1, T2, T3
        INTEGER G
  10    READ    9000, T1, T2, T3
        IF   (T1)   100, 200, 100
  100   G = (T1 + T2 + T3)/3.0 + 0.5
        PRINT   9001, T1, T2, T3, G
        GO TO   10
  200   STOP
  9000  FORMAT (3F10.3)
  9001  FORMAT (1H, 3F10.3, I8)
        END
```

Show the tables and lists at the end of each phase. Use your own creativity in designing the lists and tables; however, they should be structured for the general and *not* the specific case.

8.2 Using an appropriate form of the *program structure table* for incremental compilation, prepare a detailed design of the *language controller*. In what ways can the design be simplified by eliminating the batch processing requirement? In light of this design, try to determine the major inefficiencies in the concept. How do these inefficiencies compare with interpretive execution?

REFERENCES

1. Comfort, W. T., "A Computing System Design for User Service," *Proceedings of the Fall Joint Computer Conference*, 1965. Presents an overview of the TSS/360 time sharing system from a user's point of view.
2. Corbato, F. J. and V. A. Vyssotsky, "Introduction and Overview of the MULTICS System," *Proceedings of the Fall Joint Computer Conference*, 1965. Presents a designer's overview of the MULTICS system.
3. Gibson, C. T., "Time-Sharing in the IBM System/360: Model 67," *Proceedings of the Spring Joint Computer Conference*, 1966. Describes the relocation hardware and system configuration of the TSS/360 system.
4. Katzan, H., "Batch, Conversational, and Incremental Compilers," *Proceedings of the Spring Joint Computer Conference*, 1969. Covers essentially the same material that was presented in this chapter.
5. Iverson, K. E., *A Programming Language*, New York, John Wiley and Sons, Inc., 1962. Presents a general programming language, utilizing structured operands and a multiplicity of operators.
6. Lee, J.A.N., *The Anatomy of a Compiler*, New York, Reinhold Book Co., 1967. Describes and discusses a complete FORTRAN compiler.
7. Lock, K., "Structuring Programs for Multiprogram Time-Sharing On-Line Applications," *Proceedings of the Fall Joint Computer Conference*, 1965. Discusses the structuring of programs for incremental compilation in an experimental time-sharing system for the IBM 7040 computer.
8. Radin, G., and H. P. Rogoway, "Highlights of a New Programming Language," *Communications of the ACM*, Vol. **8**, No. 1 (Jan. 1965). Presents an early description of the PL/I programming language.

9. Randell, B., and C. J. Kuchner, "Dynamic Storage Allocation Systems," *Communications of the ACM*, Vol. **11,** No. 5 (May, 1968). Surveys and evaluates techniques for dynamic storage allocation, automatic program relocation, and dynamic address translation.

10. Randell, B., and L. J. Russel, *Algol 60 Implementation*, New York, Academic Press, 1964. Contains a survey of ALGOL implementation techniques and a description of a compiler for the KDF9 computer.

11. Ryan, J. L., R. L. Crandall, and M. C. Medwedeff, "A Conversational System for Incremental Compilation and Execution in a Time-Sharing Environment," *Proceedings of the Fall Joint Computer Conference*, 1966. Describes an incremental compiler facility which is the major component of a conversational time-sharing system for the SDS 940 computer.

12. IBM System/360 Time Sharing System, *FORTRAN IV Program Logic Manual*, Y28-2019, IBM Corporation, Yorktown Heights, N.Y., 1967. Describes the internal logic of the conversational FORTRAN compiler for the TSS/360 time-sharing system.

9 | DECISION LOGIC TABLES

Although flowcharts are a widely accepted means of describing the logic of computer programs for both development and documentation purposes, they have several significant disadvantages which should encourage the analyst to seek alternate methods for stating the pertinent aspects of a problem. *Decision logic tables* provide an alternative. First, some of the disadvantages of the flowcharting techniques should be listed:

1. Although flowcharts are often very appropriate for describing scientific programs where each box can represent a certain amount of computation, they are very often *not* appropriate for programs in systems programming, business data processing, or information retrieval where a long sequence of logical decisions must be made;

2. Flow charts for complex programs tend to become lengthy, involved, and difficult to follow; and

3. Flowcharting requires that the analyst describe his problem and develop his computer program in the same operation.

Decision logic tables tend to overcome these disadvantages while providing some advantages, as well. With the use of decision logic tables, the following advantages can be listed:

1. Logic is stated precisely and compactly;
2. Complex logic is easier to understand and the relationship between variables is readily understood;
3. Decision logic tables lend themselves to update and change; and
4. The tables are appropriate for independent review and documentation.

The use of decision logic tables is not restricted to computer programming. In general, they can be used anywhere that complex logic must be described. McDaniel[3] describes several examples which relate to business, science and government.

9.1 BASIC CONCEPTS

A decision logic table is a tabular display of all pertinent aspects of a problem situation. The table contains all relevant conditions, relationships, and actions to be taken under each set of circumstances. For example, consider the following decision process: "If credit is OK, approve order; if credit is not OK, but payment record is favorable, approve order; if credit is not OK, payment record is not favorable, but special approval has been obtained, approve order; otherwise, return order to sales. The process would normally be flowcharted as shown in Fig. 9.1.

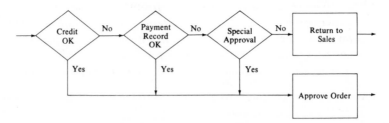

Fig. 9.1   Credit approval flow chart.

A decision logic table to represent the same procedure would appear as Table 9.1.

In the decision logic table, the sets of conditions and their related sets of actions are presented as vertical *rules* represented side-by-side. Whereas flow charts depict decision processes serially, decision logic tables represent the same processes in parallel.

TABLE 9.1. DECISION LOGIC TABLE FOR CREDIT APPROVAL

	Rule 1	Rule 2	Rule 3	Rule 4
Credit OK?	Y	N	N	N
Payment record favorable?	—	Y	N	N
Special approval obtained?	—	—	Y	N
Approve Order	X	X	X	—
Return to Sales	—	—	—	X

A decision logic table has four major sections, described in Table 9.2, and listed as follows: condition stub, action stub, condition entry, action entry.

TABLE 9.2 SKELETON
OF A LIMITED ENTRY
DECISION LOGIC TABLE

Condition Stub	Condition Entry
Action Stub	Action Entry

The *condition stub* is the upper left quadrant and contains descriptions of conditions on which decisions are to be based. Conditions are usually represented as questions. The *action stub* occupies the lower left quadrant and supplies all possible actions for the conditions listed above. The *condition entry* section is found in the upper right quadrant and answers the questions found in the condition stub. All feasible combinations of answers to the questions are formed here where the responses are restricted to "Y" to indicate yes and "N" to indicate no. If no response is indicated, then the response need not be checked for that particular question. The *action entry* is the remaining quadrant of the table and indicates the appropriate actions resulting from the conditions above. The only permissible entry here is the "X" to indicate, "Take this action." One or more actions may be designed for each combination of responses. The various combinations of responses and the indicated actions for each (combination) is called a *rule*. The various rules are normally numbered or lettered for identification purposes.

9.2 TYPES OF DECISION LOGIC TABLES

The vehicle used in the preceding section for introducing decision logic tables has been the limited-entry table. Two other types are in general use: extended-entry tables and mixed-entry tables.

Limited-Entry Tables

Limited-entry decision logic tables (see Table 9.1) are the most widely used type. They are readily identified by the fact that the condition entries are restricted to "Y", "N", or are not considered at all (represented perhaps by " – ") and that the action entries may contain only the character "X" which indicates that a particular action should be taken. In this type of table, entries in one quadrant (the condition-entry section, for example) do not extend to another quadrant (the condition stub). Table 9.3 contains a limited-entry decision logic table* for a personnel classification problem. It will be used later for comparison purposes.

TABLE 9.3.   LEDT FOR PERSONNEL CLASSIFICATION PROBLEM

	1	2	3	4	5	6	7	8
Bachelor's degree	—	—	—	—	Y	Y	N	N
Master's degree	—	—	Y	Y	N	N	N	N
Ph.D.	Y	Y	N	N	N	N	N	N
Less than 5 yrs. exper.	Y	N	Y	N	Y	N	Y	N
Greater than or equal to 5 yrs. exper.	N	Y	N	Y	N	Y	N	Y
Assign-grade 4							X	
Assign-grade 8					X			X
Assign-grade 12			X			X		
Assign-grade 16	X			X				
Assign-grade 20		X						

Extended-Entry Tables

In extended-entry decision logic tables, the condition stub and action stub serve only to identify the variables to be tested and the actions to be taken respectively. The condition entries must then contain a value or condition to be tested. Similarly, the action entries must contain specific procedures or data for the actions to be taken. Table 9.4 depicts an extended-entry version of Table 9.3. The number of entries in the condition and action stubs tends to be less in this form compared to limited-entry tables; how-

TABLE 9.4   EXTENDED-ENTRY TABLE FOR THE PERSONNEL CLASSIFICATION PROBLEM

	1	2	3	4	5	6	7	8
Degree	B	B	M	M	Ph.D.	Ph.D.	N	N
Experience (years)	LT 5	GE 5	LT 5	GE 5	LT 5	GE 5	LT 5	GE 5
Grade	8	12	12	16	16	20	4	8

*Often called a LEDT in the literature.

ever, in many cases extended-entry tables must be converted to their LEDT counterparts before computer processing can be attempted.

Mixed-Entry Tables

Features characteristic of both limited-entry and extended-entry tables may be combined into a single table called a mixed-entry table. In any one horizontal row, however, entries are limited to one of the two types, exclusively. Table 9.5 describes the personnel classification problem with a mixed-entry table. Mixed-entry tables have one major advantage. Conditions that can be appropriately expressed by binary values (i.e., Y or N) may be represented in that fashion and conditions that must be expressed by relational expressions may be written in that manner. In the personnel classification problem, a data item such as "degree" remains relatively stable while "years of experience" must be updated every year. Action entries may be considered similarly. Data items such as personnel "grades" are updated periodically by wage-and-salary studies and are amenable to extended-entry logic.

TABLE 9.5   MIXED-ENTRY TABLE FOR THE PERSONNEL CLASSIFICATION
PROBLEM

	1	2	3	4	5	6	7	8
Bachelor's degree	—	—	—	—	Y	Y	N	N
Master's degree	—	—	Y	Y	N	N	N	N
Ph.D.	Y	Y	N	N	N	N	N	N
Experience (years)	LT 5	GE 5	LT 5	GE 5	LT 5	GE 5	LT 5	GE 5
Grade	16	20	12	16	8	12	4	8

The use of decision logic tables for systems analysis and computer programming has some distinct advantages* which can be appropriately listed at this point:

1. It forces a clear problem statement and shows where information is missing.
2. It forces a complete logical description of the problem.
3. It completely defines, at system level, decisions to be implemented.
4. It leads to low-cost translation of a defined system into a working computer program.
5. It permits development and orderly presentation of systems too complex for effective charting.
6. It provides extreme subroutinization by forcing the segmentation of the overall system into logically manageable tables.

*See reference [5].

7. It is suitable for documentation, and for communication of system and program design between people.
8. It assists in implementing system changes, and quickly points out consequences of any one change, even in a complex system.
9. It permits system definition and description that are distinct from procedural content.
10. It is a technique that is easily learned.
11. Decision table language and presentation are suitable for direct translation into machine language; i.e., it lends itself to direct compiling.
12. It is useful for presenting management policies and rules, and for communicating system design to management for evaluation.

9.3 CONVERSION OF DECISION LOGIC TABLES TO COMPUTER PROGRAMS

When describing a computer processing problem with decision logic tables, it is assumed that, eventually, the decision logic will be transformed into equivalent computer programs. The transformation process contains three topics of general interest: (1) transforming decision logic tables to computer programs by manual methods; (2) transforming decision logic tables to computer programs by automatic methods; and (3) generating computer programs with minimum average processing time. Topics (1) and (3) are covered in this chapter. Topic (2) has been given substantial attention by the CODASYL* Systems Development Committee with the objective of developing a decision table language and associated processors. Although this topic is not covered here, the reader is referred to publications of the various computer manufacturers for further information.

Topic (1) is covered in this section and in 9.4. Topic (3) is considered briefly in section 9.5. Regardless of its particular format (or type) any decision logic table can be converted to a LEDT, as discussed previously. Only this type is considered in this and succeeding sections. Moreover, particular *conditions* and specific *actions* are of limited interest and are denoted by the variables C_i and A_j, respectively. The analysis also requires that the *rules* satisfy two constraints: 1. they are mutually exclusive; and 2. the order in which the conditions are tested must be irrelevant.

Equivalent LEDTs

When two rules result in the same action, they are said to possess one or more *irrelevant conditions*. In this case, the LEDT can be reduced, possi-

*Committee on Data Systems Languages.

bly, to an *equivalent LEDT* with fewer rules. Thus, the ignore indication (i.e., "—") is used to indicate that a specific condition is irrelevant. An example of LEDT simplification is given in Table 9.6. In rules 1 and 2, action A_1 is the desired result whether or not condition C_3 is tested; therefore, this test may be eliminated. Rules 5 and 6 can be analyzed similarly; action A_1 is selected independently of conditions C_2 and C_3. The simplified LEDT in Table 9.6 is mutually exhaustive while the expanded LEDT is not.

TABLE 9.6   SIMPLIFICATION OF LEDTS

(Expanded Table)

Condition	Rule					
	1	2	3	4	5	6
C_1	Y	Y	Y	Y	N	N
C_2	Y	Y	N	N	N	N
C_3	Y	N	Y	N	Y	N
Action	A_1	A_1	A_2	A_3	A_1	A_1

(Simplified Form)

Condition	Rule			
	1	2	3	4
C_1	Y	Y	Y	N
C_2	Y	N	N	—
C_3	—	Y	N	—
Action	A_1	A_2	A_3	A_1

In general, the objective of simplification is to reduce the number of eventual branch point in the computer program, saving both execution time and computer storage.

Sequential Testing Procedures

Sequential testing procedures (STPs) are decision trees generated when an LEDT is converted to a flowchart for computer programming. Figure 9.2 shows an STP corresponding to the simplified table in Table 9.6. The STP is entered at the top and branches are taken as input data and matched against the conditions in the LEDT. STPs are particularly useful for verifying the constraints mentioned earlier and for eliminating unnecessary nodes.*

*Elements of an STP may be referred to generically as nodes, regardless if they are *decision* boxes or *action* boxes.

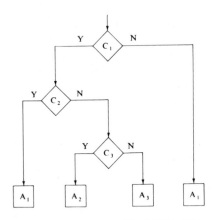

Fig. 9.2   An STP for the simplified LEDT of Table 9.6.

Press[4] has outlined three general steps for converting LEDTs to STPs in an orderly fashion:

Step 1. Choose the key condition from the set of rows with the minimum number of indifferent (irrelevant) entries.

Step 2. If one of the rows contain all "Y" or all "N" entries, discriminate on that condition.

Step 3. Discriminate on the condition row which maximizes CS_i where

$$CS_i = \sum_{i=1}^{n} C_{ij} - C_{ii},$$ and where n equals number of conditions in the table.

(Step three needs further explanation: a condition row C_i is made up of two sets of elements, those with "Y" or "—" entries (the positive elements) and those with "N" or "—" entries (the negative elements). C_j is said to be the *complement* of C_i if the negative rules in C_i have only "Y" or only "N" elements in C_j or the positive rules in C_i have only "Y" or only "N" elements in C_j. The number of complementary rules is known as C_{ij}, the count of the C_i with complements in C_j.) For example, in

	1	2	3
1	N	N	Y
2	N	Y	N
3	Y	Y	N

$$CS_1 = C_{11} + C_{12} + C_{13} - C_{11} = 3 + 1 + 3 - 3 = 4$$
$$CS_2 = C_{21} + C_{22} + C_{23} - C_{22} = 1 + 3 + 1 - 3 = 2$$
$$CS_3 = C_{31} + C_{32} + C_{33} - C_{33} = 3 + 1 + 3 - 3 = 4$$

As an application of the three steps, consider the following LEDT:

	1	2	3	4
C_1	N	N	N	N
C_2	N	N	N	Y
C_3	Y	—	N	N
C_4	N	Y	N	Y
	A_1	A_2	A_3	A_4

Use of step two would indicate that C_1 is the key condition thereby reducing the STP to an "error condition" and the following reduced table:

	1	2	3	4
C_2	N	N	N	Y
C_3	Y	—	N	N
C_4	N	Y	N	Y
	A_1	A_2	A_3	A_4

Step one then indicates that conditions (i.e., row) C_2 and C_4 are candidates for the key condition in the reduced table. Applying step three, i.e.,

$$CS_2 = C_{24} = 1$$
$$CS_4 = C_{42} = 2$$

indicates that C_4 should be used for the next decision. Repeated application of the steps would yield the following STP:

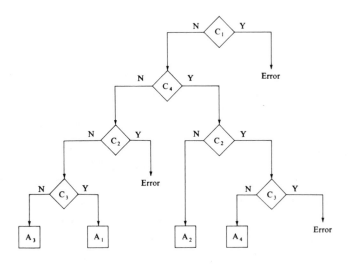

LEDTs of this sort might well be called *binary decision logic tables* in that any irrelevant condition could be converted to a superfluous binary decision. Veinott[7] has considered the programming of binary decision logic tables in FORTRAN, COBOL, or ALGOL. It is the subject of the next section.

9.4   PROGRAMMING DECISION LOGIC TABLES IN HIGHER-LEVEL LANGUAGES

Binary decision logic tables may be viewed as a convenient form for expressing a decision process that is dependent upon a combination of a number of conditions. For this purpose, flowcharts become quite lengthy and the generated computer programs often include duplicate sets of instructions for testing the same condition.

The process involves assigning a number to each *possible* combination of conditions and using these numbers in a multiple branch statement, such as the computed GOTO in FORTRAN. Clearly, then, 2^n combinations of n conditions exist. It should be noted, however, that more than one rule may exit to the same procedure.

Consider two vectors B and W, each of dimension n, where n is the number of conditions in the binary decision logic table. Let the components of B be denoted by b_i where $b_i = 1$ if condition C_i is true (i.e., "Y") and $b_i = 0$ otherwise. W is a weighting vector where each component is denoted by w_i and $w_i = 2^{i-1}$. Similarly, S_i is a statement label corresponding to the statements that will do the processing when the ith rule is satisfied. FORTRAN statements, appropriate for the branching process, would then be:

$$I = 1 + \sum_{i=1}^{n} (b_i * w_i)$$

$$GOTO \quad (S_1, S_2, \ldots, S_n), \ I$$

Similarly in COBOL:

$$COMPUTE \ I = 1 + \sum_{i=1}^{n} (b_i * w_i).$$

$$GOTO \quad S_1 \quad S_2 \ldots S_n \quad DEPENDING \ ON \ I.$$

As an example, consider the example of Table 9.1, rewritten as Table 9.7. If arrays W and B were declared appropriately and if S_1 and S_2 were valid statement numbers, then the following FORTRAN statements would perform the required processing:

$$I = 1 + B(1) * W(1) + B(2) * W(2) + B(3) * W(3)$$

$$GO \ TO \ (S_2, S_1, S_1, S_1, S_1, S_1, S_1, S_1), \ I$$

TABLE 9.7

Rule/B

		W	1	2	3	4	5	6	7	8
C_1	Credit OK?	1	1	1	1	1	0	0	0	0
C_2	Payment Record Favorable	2	1	1	0	0	1	1	0	0
C_3	Special Approval	4	1	0	0	1	1	0	1	0
	Approve Order	S_1	X	X	X	X	X	X	X	
	Return to Sales	S_2								X

Although the methods, presented above, involve testing every condition in the binary decision logic table, the size of the equivalent computer program is minimal since instructions to test each condition are included at most once. On the other hand, resultant execution time is not as low as with an optimal STP (sequential testing procedure).

Obviously, some conditions are simple to test and others are more difficult. Similarly, some rules are more probable than others. Both of these considerations have been ignored thus far but are important when minimum processing time is an objective. Reinwald and Soland[6], in a classic paper on decision logic tables, have used both topics for generating optimal computer programs. Their paper forms the basis for the next section.

9.5   OPTIMAL COMPUTER PROGRAMS

For production programs, minimizing execution time is of great significance. The problem is related to "equivalent LEDTs," which were discussed previously. A good question then is, "Given an STP, what is its expected cost?"

Expected Cost

Consider the LEDT* given in Table 9.8 and equivalent STPs pictured in Figure 9.3. Clearly, the C_i's are the costs involved with testing conditions x_i. For case (a), the expected cost is $(1.0) \times (50) + (.45) \times (68) + (.55) \times (.68) + (.40) \times (25) = \underline{128.00}$. For case (b), the expected cost is $(1.0) \times (25) + (.25) \times (50) + (.05) \times (68) + (.75) \times (68) + (.40) \times (50) = \underline{111.90}$ Similarly for case (c), the expected cost is $(1.0) \times (68) + (.55) \times (25) + (.20) \times (50) + (.45) \times (50) = \underline{114.25}$. Obviously, the magnitude of the expected cost cannot be estimated directly by considering the simplicity or complexity of the STP. The process of computing an

*For a thorough analysis of equivalent LEDTs, see Reinwald and Soland[6].

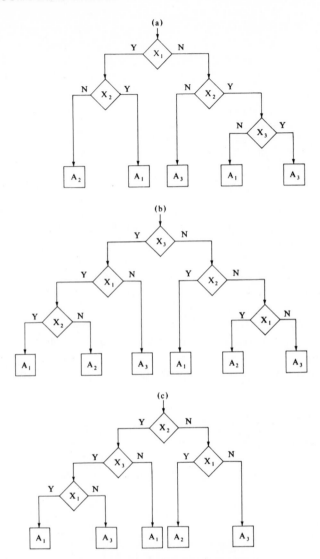

Fig. 9.3   STPs for the example of Table 9.8.

expected cost is one of multiplying the probability of reaching a node by the cost of testing for that condition and summing these values for all nodes in the STP. Given several equivalent STPs, the minimum average processing time can be computed in this fashion.

TABLE 9.8   EXAMPLE OF EXPECTED COST

Rule

Conditions	1	2	3	4	5	6	7	8	C_i
				Probabilities					
	.00	.15	.20	.05	.25	.20	.00	.15	
x_1	Y	Y	N	Y	Y	N	N	N	50
x_2	Y	Y	Y	N	N	Y	N	N	68
x_3	Y	N	N	Y	N	Y	Y	N	25
	A_1			A_2			A_3		143

Optimal STPs

Reinwald and Soland[6] have developed a direct method of generating optimal STPs, i.e., those with minimal average processing time. Although the technique is too lengthy for presentation here, the basic idea is given as follows:

The process begins with the set of all feasible STPs (i.e., all STPs equivalent to a given LEDT) and selectively divides this set into mutually exclusive subsets of STPs computing a lower bound to the expected cost of STPs in any particular subset. At each stage, the subset with the lowest cost is further subdivided until finally a subset is developed which contains only one complete STP with a cost equal to or less than the lower bound for every other subset. This is the optimal STP.

The reader is directed to the indicated reference for further details.

PROBLEMS

9.1   Given the following LEDT:

Probability

Cond.	.10	.10	.15	.05	.20	.25	.15	Cost
x_1	Y	Y	N	Y	Y	N	N	10
x_2	Y	Y	Y	N	N	Y	N	50
x_3	Y	N	N	Y	N	Y	—	70
	A_1		A_2			A_3		

Using the steps given for converting LEDTs to STPs, convert it to an STP indicating which rules were used. Then compute its expected cost.

9.2   Given the following definitions from Mathematical logic [see Korfhage, R. R., *Logic and Algorithms*. Wiley, 1966]:

p	q	$p \lor q$	$p \subset q$	$p \supset q$	$p \equiv q$	$p \land q$	$p \mid q$	$p \not\equiv q$	$\sim q$	$p \not\supset q$	$\sim p$	$p \not\subset q$	$p \downarrow q$
T	T	T	T	T	T	T	F	F	F	F	F	F	F
T	F	T	T	F	F	F	T	T	T	T	F	F	F
F	T	T	F	T	F	F	T	T	F	F	T	T	F
F	F	F	T	T	T	F	T	F	T	F	T	F	T

Develop a mixed-entry decision logic table showing either a true or false result if the condition stub contains p, q, and the operation.

REFERENCES

1. Chapin, N., "Parsing of Decision Tables," *Comm. ACM*, Vol. 10, No. 8, August, 1967. Presents practical techniques for reducing the size of large limited-entry decision tables.
2. Kirk, H. W., "Use of Decision Tables in Computer Programming," *Comm. ACM*, Vol. 8, No. 1, January, 1965. Describes a method of representing decision tables and data in computer storage and presents techniques for efficient processing with minimum storage requirements.
3. McDaniel, H., *An Introduction to Decision Logic Tables*, New York, John Wiley and Sons, Inc., 1968. Provides an introduction to limited-entry, extended-entry, and mixed-entry decision logic tables, for the non-programmer, along with a varied assortment of examples and exercises.
4. Press, L. I., "Conversion of Decision Tables to Computer Programs," *Comm. ACM*, Vol. 8, No. 6, June, 1965. Presents and evaluates procedures for the conversion of decision tables to computer programs considering storage requirements, execution time, and compile time.
5. *Proceedings of the Decision Table Symposium*, CODASYL Systems Group and Joint Users Group of the ACM, September, 1962. Introduces the concept of decision tables, gives several user's experience with them, and surveys conclusions drawn by users on their practicability.
6. Reinwald, L. T., and R. M. Soland, "Conversion of Limited-Entry Decision Tables to Optimal Computer Programs I: Minimum Average Processing Time," *Journal ACM*, Vol. 13, No. 3, July, 1966. Contains a theoretical treatment of procedures for converting limited-entry decision tables to computer programs with an emphasis on minimum processing time.
7. Veinott, C. G., "Programming Decision Tables in FORTRAN, COBOL, or ALGOL," *Comm. ACM*, Vol. 9, No. 1, January, 1966. Develops a simple broad-base approach for programming decision tables in FORTRAN, COBOL, or ALGOL.

PART TWO:

OPERATING SYSTEMS

10 | THE STRUCTURE OF OPERATING SYSTEMS

In general, the effectiveness of a computer installation is measured by its ability to satisfy needs for computation. To a large extent, effectiveness is influenced by the speed and configuration of the available computer. To an equally large extent, however, it is affected by the manner in which the hardware system is used and by how the installation meets its demands for service and for programming. The hardware system, along with the programmed facilities available for using it, is termed the *computer system*, which affects the work situation in the following ways:

1. By its ability to keep the system's hardware facilities as busy as possible;
2. By the extent to which the computer system is available for program development, program debugging, and for priority processing, i.e., in addition to the normal production workload;
3. By the versatility that the system provides for interchanging input/output device types and for accepting varied file organizations; and
4. By the reliability of the system so that it is available upon demand.

Effectiveness is also affected by less tangible aspects of the programming and user environment; they are termed *user considerations* and influence overall system effectiveness in a related manner:

1. By the programmer time (or the required lead time) necessary to develop computer programs;

2. By the time necessary to modify programs to satisfy unusual conditions existing at run time;
3. By the setup time required to run jobs;
4. By the versatility that must necessarily be built into programs; and
5. By the amount of priority processing that is required.

Clearly, then, three needs exist: 1. to maximize the use of the system's resources, 2. to reduce the complexity involved in preparing a program for execution on a computer, and 3. to give the user increased control over the way his program is processed by the computer system. An *operating system*, introduced in chapter 1* as an integrated set of control programs and processing programs designed to maximize the use of the system's resources and to reduce the complexity involved in preparing a program for execution on a computer, satisfies these needs.†

It is the objective of this chapter to consider the structure of operating systems from a user's point of view and from a system's point of view. In preparation for the material which follows, it is first necessary to discuss the functions, in general, that are performed by each on an *individual job basis*.

10.1   BASIC FUNCTIONS

Two basic functions are of interest: user functions and system functions. In preparing a program for execution, it is important that the user is aware of the facilities provided by the operating system and that the most efficient use possible is made of them. When designing an operating system, system designers must respond similarly. A thorough analysis should be made of the facilities which users need, and they should be provided within design limits.

User Functions

The first step in preparing a program for execution on a computer is the design phase, where the problem is formally stated, the constraints are listed, and the overall logic is determined. The next step is a specification of the input and output requirements, which include the organization of files, the types of access methods, and the external devices to be used. This latter category is generally called *Data Management*. This step is followed by a choice of the programming language(s) to be used. Pro-

---

*Section 1.3 should be reviewed at this time.
†It follows that the degree to which these needs are satisfied is dependent upon the comprehensiveness of the operating system. Given a comprehensive operating system, however, it must be understood and used before its objectives can be said to have been met.

gramming languages are usually selected so as to minimize development and debugging time and to facilitate future program modifications as well. Language processors are included in an operating system as processing programs and are treated as any other unit of work by the system. Programs may be structured into a main program and several subprograms as required; overall program structure is developed both in this step and in the succeeding one in which the actual programming is performed.

The programs are then ready for computer processing, which requires use of the operating system. The following information must be available before computer processing can begin:

1. Job control information,
2. Input/output requirements,
3. Source program(s), and
4. Data.

Job control information is presented in a command language,* which is interpreted by the operating system and provides the following information: job identification, priorities, and passwords;† a specification of input/output requirements; and requests to have specific processing programs executed. Two types of data exist: problem data and source programs. *Source programs* are data to the language processors; e.g., a FORTRAN or COBOL compiler. *Problem data* usually follows a request to have a problem program executed and exists in a form determined by the particular application. Depending upon the stage of program development, the job control information provided to the operating system may also contain debugging commands and request the services of *service programs* provided by the operating system.

Normally, many users will be contending for the use of the computer system; it is the function of the operating system to recognize priorities and maintain job schedules in accordance with installation guidelines.

System Functions

The objective of the operating system is to maximize the use of the system's resources and to provide services needed by the programmer. A specification of desired services is usually given with the job control information and is supplied on an as-needed basis. The remainder of this section introduces the functions performed by the system in response to a job.

---

*See chapter 7.

†The use of *passwords* in the command language is the method by which programs and data are protected from other users. This feature is especially significant in a comprehensive operating system which uses the concept of *public storage* for the storage of information.

The system first reads the entire job (i.e., job control information, programs, and data) into main storage and places it on external storage as an input job stream; it then initiates the job as a unit of work to the operating system.* This involves creating an initial program structure and forming a *job control block*, which will contain execution-control data and identify the job to the operating system. This function is accomplished by the *System Management* control program, which also performs the following job-oriented functions for each job on a system-wide basis:

1. Schedules the job for execution on either a priority or sequential basis;
2. Performs actual input/output for all jobs;
3. Processes normal and abnormal job terminations;
4. Allocates main storage; and
5. Controls the printing and punching of output files by peripheral devices.

System-oriented functions are described in a succeeding section.

Many control functions are subordinated to routines which run as ordinary jobs to the system. In the preceding paragraphs, for example, it was noted that the system first reads an entire job into memory and creates an input job stream. This function is normally performed by a utility routine which is treated as any other unit of work by the operating system. Other control program functions are made a part of the job itself. *Job Management* and *Data Management* fall into this category. Job Management routines which interpret job control information, execute service requests, and monitor the execution of processing programs are included in the memory space of every job. The same holds true for Data Management routines which initiate input and output for the processing program, maintain catalogs and libraries, and manage storage buffers; i.e., they reside in the memory space of each job which requests the functions they perform.† Systems structured in this manner facilitate multiprogramming in that several jobs performing different kinds of work can coexist in the system at the same time.

10.2   THE USER ENVIRONMENT

The most significant aspect of the user environment is the *command language* used to pass job control information to the operating system.

*In primitive operating systems, all constituents read the input device (e.g., card reader or tape) individually; this pertains to both control programs and processing programs.

†In sophisticated operating systems, *sharing* of system routines is often permitted and contributes to overall system efficiency.

Commands are available for initiating a job, for running programs, for informing the operating system of input/output requirements, and for using the various services provided. System and Data Management services are also available through macros, which are processed by the assembler system and which establish linkage between a processing program and the various control programs.

Another facet of the user environment is *Data Management*. Data Management facilities permit *data sets** to be named and then have these names along with the location of the data set and its various attributes[†] reflected in a central *catalog* in which each user has appropriate entries. Afterwards, data sets can be retrieved by name alone. Data Management facilities also allow files to be organized in a variety of ways and allow different access methods to be employed when reading and writing them. Lastly, a general purpose Data Management facility usually controls the allocation of space on direct-access devices[‡] and provides a comprehensive set of data-oriented utility programs.

The remaining major facet of the user environment is a rather general category called *user services*. Included here are facilities for loading and unloading programs, for requesting information from the system, for communicating with the system operator, and for using the *dynamic storage allocation*§ and *interrupt*□ features of the operating system.

Familiarity with Data Management concepts is necessary for a comprehensive understanding of command language facilities. For that reason, the subject of Data Management is discussed first.

Data Management

Input/output operations are of great importance in many data processing applications. The objectives of the Data Management functions are to achieve maximum efficiency in performing these operations while providing for versatility and convenience of use. Seven basic input/output operations are listed:

1. Read data;
2. Write data;
3. Block and deblock records;

---

*In this context, *data set* should be taken to be synonymous with *file*; it is defined in subsequent sections.

† Sample attributes might be device type and type of data set organization.

‡ A direct-access storage device is one in which the access time is effectively independent of the location of the data.

§*Dynamic storage allocation* is a method of assigning main storage such that the location of programs and data is determined at the moment of need.

□To *interrupt* a program means to stop it in such a way that execution can be resumed.

4. Overlap reading, writing, and processing operations;
5. Read, write, and verify data set labels*;
6. Automatically position data set volumes†; and
7. Detect and correct error conditions.

In order to perform these operations and to satisfy the stated objectives, Data Management facilities are usually designed to provide an effective means of organizing, naming, cataloging, storing, and retrieving a wide variety of types of data. These concepts are introduced in the following paragraphs.

The concept of a data set is basic to an understanding of data management. A *data set* is a collection of data records with a logical relation to one another. A *data record* is defined similarly as a collection of related data items treated as a unit. A record which is considered independently of its physical representation is termed a *logical record*, while a record that is defined in terms of its physical qualities is a *physical record*.‡ Physical records are separated by an area on the data medium that is used to indicate the end of block or record; the separator is called a *record gap*, which is used synonymously with the words *inter-record gap*. It is often convenient to group logical records to form a single physical record. The process of grouping records prior to output is termed *blocking* and decreases the number of required input/output operations and the amount of physical storage needed.§   Records may be combined, using one of three formats: fixed-length records F, variable-length records V, and undefined-length records U. The size of *fixed-length* records is constant for all physical records in a data set;□ similarly, the number of logical records in a physical record is also fixed. Fig. 10.1 depicts blocked and unblocked fixed-length records.

Fig. 10.1   Fixed-length records.

---

*A *data set label* is a collection of information that describes the attributes of a data set, and that is normally stored with the data set.

†A *volume* is a single unit of storage media, such as a single tape reel or a disc pack.

‡Confusion sometimes arises over logical and physical records. For that reason, a physical record is frequently called a *block*.

§This is so because inter-record gaps are eliminated.

□This is true except perhaps for the last physical record of a data set which is usually permitted to be short; the need for "padding" is thus eliminated.

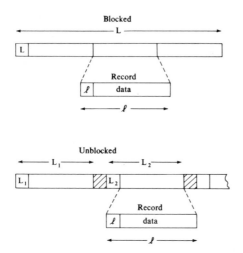

Fig. 10.2   Variable-length records.

The *variable-length* record type allows variable-length blocks of records, as well as variable-length logical records. The length (denoted by L) of the physical record is included as part of the record and precedes the data. A logical record is formed analogously with a length field (denoted by $\mathcal{L}$) preceding the data. Fig. 10.2 demonstrates this type of data format. The *undefined-length* record type is provided to allow processing of records that do not meet the requirements of the preceding types. As shown in Fig. 10.3, each block is treated as a record, and any deblocking must be performed by the user.

Irrespective of its particular representation on a storage medium, the structure of information* within a data set is usually determined by a particular application or by installation guidelines. *Data set organization* refers to established conventions for the arrangement of information in a data set. Three basic types exist and are supplied with most operating systems:

1. *Sequential.* This type of data organization is characterized by the fact that records are written and retrieved in physical rather than logical sequence. This type of organization is normally used for

Block	Block	Blk.	Block
Record	Record	Rec.	Record

Fig. 10.3   Undefined-length records.

*Here, the arrangement of records within a data set are of interest.

magnetic tapes, punched cards and tape, and printed output. Moreover, it may be provided for direct-access devices, as well.

2. *Indexed Sequential.* In this type of organization, records are arranged in collating sequence, according to a key that is part of every
record. This organization is normally used with direct-access devices
and permits direct as well as sequential access to any record.

3. *Direct.* Records within data sets on direct-access devices may be retrieved directly if their physical locations are known. Direct organization provides for this type of processing.

Different techniques are normally available to the user for transferring
data between main storage and an input/output device. These are termed
access methods, which are available through macro instructions recognized by the assembler system. The techniques are classified by their
treatment of buffering* and input/output synchronization with processing. The two techniques are named basic access and queued access and
are defined as follows:

1. *Basic access.* An access method in which each input/output macro
instruction causes a corresponding machine operation to be executed.

2. *Queued access.* An access method in which the transfer of data between the program and input/output devices is automatically syn-
chronized, eliminating delays for input/output operations.

The concepts of a named data set and of a system catalog permit data
set names, locations, and attributes to be entered into the catalog once
and thereafter be referred to by name alone. The facility is particularly
useful when data sets are used frequently or when they are shared by a
number of users. A *data set name* is a sequence of one or more simple
names, called components, arranged such that levels of qualification are
implied. For example, the data set name PAYROLL.SALARIED.PROF has two
levels of qualification. A *fully qualified name* is one where all levels are
specifically given. Data set names are used in Data Management commands to identify input and output data sets for processing programs and
to utilize the other data management services. In most operating systems,
the first level of qualification is the user's ID, which immediately partitions the catalog by users. *Partially qualified names* are also permitted in
commands where it is convenient to specify data sets as a group. Fig.
10.4 gives examples of the above concepts. The *system catalog* is a special

Buffering is generally regarded as a technique used to compensate for a difference in
the rate of flow of information or the time occurrence of events when transferring information from one device to another.

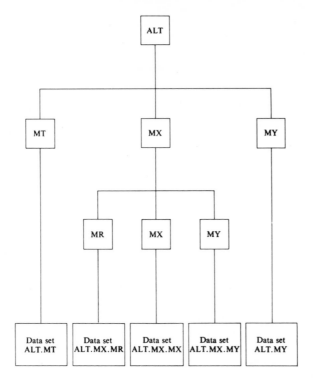

Fig. 10.4   Data set name structure.

data set that resides on direct–access devices or in bulk storage and is maintained by the operating system.   The catalog is organized into a hierarchy of indexes as follows:

1. The highest index, called the *master index*, is usually a set of user identification codes. The master index is maintained by the system itself and partitions the catalog so that all qualified users have access to it.

2. Subordinate entries are determined by the user and by how he adopts the data set name structure to his individual needs. Data set names are established by the **DEFINE DATA** and **CATALOG** commands discussed in the next section on command language.

Fig. 10.5 depicts a sample catalog structure.

Command Language

The objective of the command language is to direct the operating system to perform desired functions. The general format of operating system

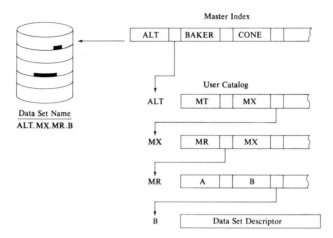

Fig. 10.5   Catalog structure.

command language statements* is patterned after the command language introduced in chapter 7.   A statement contains two fields—a command field and an operand field, pictured as follows:

Command	*Operand*
Command Name	One or more operands delimited by commas

The *command field* contains a command name, such as RUN or DATA, and identifies the requested operation. The *operand field* is separated from the command by one or more blanks and provides information required by the particular command.

Commands are divided into three general categories: program management, data management, and user services. Five typical *program management commands* are described; they allow the user to initiate or terminate a job and to control how his job is processed by the operating system. The typical program management commands and the functions they request of the system are given in Table 10.1. Ten typical *data management* commands are identified; they permit the user to operate on his data sets and to inform the system of his input/output requirements.   The typical data management commands are given in Table 10.2. Four typical *user service* commands enable the user to load and unload programs, to obtain information on data sets, and to communicate with the operator. These commands and their functions are given in Table 10.3.

*That is, the statements which pass *job control information* to the operating system.

TABLE 10.1   PROGRAM MANAGEMENT COMMANDS

Command	Function
JOB	Identify user to system for initiation of his job.
ENDJOB	Signifies the last card of a job.
RUN	Requests that the system execute a given program.
RESERVE	Identify types of I/O devices needed for private data sets.
TIME	Establish time limit for job.

TABLE 10.2   DATA MANAGEMENT COMMANDS

Command	Function
CATALOG	Enter data set name and control information into the catalog.
DELETE	Delete data set name from catalog.
DATA	Build a data set.
DEFINE DATA	Define data set and describe its characteristics to the system.
COPY DATA SET	Make a duplicate copy of a specified data set.
ERASE	Release the space on a direct-access storage device occupied by a data set and delete catalog entry.
MODIFY	Insert, delete, or replace records in a data set.
PUNCH	Initiate punching of a data set onto cards.
PRINT	Initiate printing of a data set on the system printer.
WRITE TAPE	Initiate writing of a data set onto magnetic tape.

TABLE 10.3   USER SERVICE COMMANDS

Command	Function
LOAD	Load a program into memory without initiating execution.
UNLOAD	Remove a program from memory.
STATUS	Obtain information about data sets from the catalog.
DISPLAY	Display a message on the operator's console.

User Services

User services are generally available through the command language subsystem and with system macro instructions, processed by the assembler system. Features for loading and unloading programs, for communicating with the operator, and for requesting information from the system were considered previously. Two other services, usually available through macros alone, have not been presented.

Many operating systems have facilities for *allocating storage* on a dynamic basis. The user, through a macro like GETMAIN, can request that a specified amount of storage be allocated to his job. This permits the amount of storage required by a job to vary, depending upon input conditions. If most programs utilize storage in this fashion, overall system effectiveness can be increased. A companion macro, such as FREEMAIN, is also provided to release dynamic storage when appropriate.

Through the use of *timer* macros, the user is given access to the system's real time clock and to receive timer *interrupts* when specified conditions are met. Other macros permit program interrupts of various kinds to be enabled or disabled upon demand.

10.3   CONTROL PROGRAM STRUCTURE

Clearly, the control programs of the operating system are responsible for the overall functioning of the computer system and have well-defined objectives, i.e.,

1. To maximize the use of the system's resources;
2. To provide for the continuous operation of the system;
3. To establish and maintain job priorities; and
4. To insure the integrity of individual jobs.

The control programs which satisfy these needs are classed into three categories—System Management, Job Management, and Data Management —and are depicted in Fig. 10.6. The three types also have structural properties, which, perhaps, are as significant as their functions. *System Management* routines provide a logical interface between the hardware and the remainder of the software system. *Job Management* routines provide a logical interface between processing problems and control programs. *Data Management* routines provide a software interface between processing programs and external storage.

The computing system is assumed to operate in two states: the supervisor state and the problem state. These two states exist whether they have hardware equivalents or are implemented in programmed logic. The

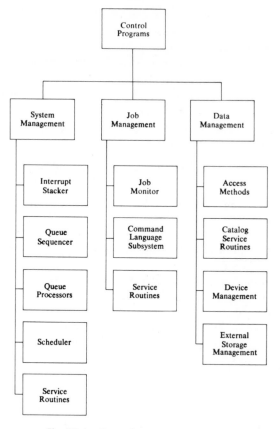

Fig. 10.6   Control program structure.

supervisor state is restricted to System Management routines which have access to all of computer storage and may issue input/output and other restricted instructions, which are not available to processing programs. Programs running in the *problem state* may be privileged or nonprivileged. *Privileged programs* may have access to system facilities such as the catalog and reside in the memory space of all jobs. They may be entered from nonprivileged programs only via System Management routines.   Privileged system programs are usually shared in operating systems with that capability.   Processing programs such as language processors and problem programs normally run as nonprivileged programs.

Most operating systems are *interrupt driven* in the sense that the computing system processes a given unit of work until one of two events occurs: 1. it requires a System Management function; or 2. a System Management function is required for some other reason on a demand basis. In either case, the unit of work is interrupted, and control is passed to a System Management routine to interrogate the interrupt. These interrupts are termed *hardware interrupts* in that they are initiated from an I/O device, the central processing unit,* a machine instruction, or an external electronic device such as a timer or the computer console. For this discussion, interrupts are categorized into five types, recognizing that the classification scheme could easily be modified. The types of interrupts are described as they are listed:

1. *Supervisor call interrupts* (SVCs) result from an appropriate machine instruction and are a means of requesting System Management services when in the problem state;
2. *Program interrupts* result from a programming fault or an unusual condition while executing a machine instruction;
3. *Machine check* interrupts result from actual hardware errors which are detected by the circuitry;
4. *I/O interrupts* are returned by the I/O system to indicate that certain conditions, regarding the actual transmission of data or the status of I/O devices, exist; and
5. *External interrupts* are initiated by the timer, the computer console, or other electronic equipment external to the computer.

System Management

System Management's basic function is to respond to hardware interrupts of the types previously described by classifying them as to type and by initiating appropriate routines to process each. In so doing, System Management maintains control over system facilities. The system facilities include the central processing unit(s), main storage, and input/output devices. System Management routines have several important characteristics which enable them to effectively perform the functions listed above:

1. They reside permanently in main storage;
2. They are not directly addressable by processing programs;
3. They execute in the supervisor state; and
4. Only one active copy of each exists in the system.

Another basic function performed by System Management is that of *job initialization*. More specifically, job initialization is the process of establishing a job as a unit of work to the system and of creating an initial program structure for it. In general, the initial program structure contains

---

*The *central processing unit* (CPU) is often referred to as the *arithmetic and logical unit* (ALU).

Job Management and Data Management routines. The unit of work is identified to the system by a *job control block* (JCB), which contains the following information:

1. Job identification;
2. Job priority and privilege class;
3. Device address of the input job stream;
4. Device address of the output data set;
5. Flags indicating job status, i.e., in execution, ready for execution, or I/O delay;
6. Type of job interruption;
7. Register save areas;-
8. Accounting information;
9. Pointers to preceding and succeeding JCBs in the JCB chain; and
10. Flags for pending job interrupts.

The job control block is maintained by System Management and is not addressable by the job itself. A job control block exists for each job in the system, and it is the mechanism by which the system keeps track of the work it has to do.

Most of the work performed by System Management is handled by a few important routines: 1. the interrupt stacker, 2. the queue sequencer, 3. the queue processors, 4. the scheduler, and 5. the System Management service routines. The function of the *interrupt stacker* is to classify interruptions and enter them into queues as a queue entry. A *queue entry* (QE) is a fixed size block of storage and contains a description of work to be done by a device or one of the *queue processors*. A queue entry contains various kinds of information that are pertinent to the types of interrupts. Three fields are of particular importance. They are a pointer to the job control block and forward and backward pointers to other queue entries for the same queue. The various System Management routines may now be described in more detail.

As mentioned previously, the function of the interrupt stacker is to classify interrupts and to place them on appropriate queues. The queues themselves are processed later on a priority basis. After an interrupt is queued, the interrupt stacker takes the following action: 1. If the interrupt occurred when the system was in the problem state, the complete status of the active job is saved in its job control block, and the interrupt stacker exits to the queue sequencer. 2. If the system was executing in the supervisor state when the interrupt occurred, the interrupt stacker returns to the point of interrupt so that the System Management routines can complete their work in an orderly manner. Fig. 10.7 presents a state diagram of interrupt processing.

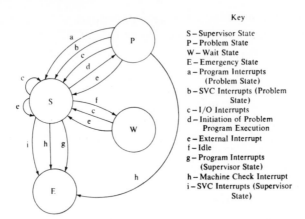

Key

S — Supervisor State
P — Problem State
W — Wait State
E — Emergency State
a — Program Interrupts
        (Problem State)
b — SVC Interrupts (Problem
        State)
c — I/O Interrupts
d — Initiation of Problem
        Program Execution
e — External Interrupt
f — Idle
g — Program Interrupts
        (Supervisor State)
h — Machine Check Interrupt
i — SVC Interrupts (Supervisor
        State)

Fig. 10.7   State diagram of interrupt processing.

In the diagram, two additional states exist: the wait state and the emergency state. They are nonoperative in the sense that they do no physical work for the computing system. Although the *wait state* is now a physical internal state in most machines, it represents a logical situation where there is no work to perform and the hardware/software system goes into an idle mode awaiting an interrupt, which will give it some work to perform. The *emergency state* reflects the deletion of a major system error by either the hardware or software; appropriate error processing routines are usually included as part of the System Management control program.

The *queue sequencer* (QS) provides a sequencing mechanism for deciding which queue processors are to be executed. The queue sequencer contains a *sequence table*, whose entries are in priority order. There is a sequence table entry and a corresponding queue for each of the queue processors. The I/O queue processor may have additional entries depending upon the I/O devices in the system. Fig. 10.8 describes the sequence table and some of its queues. If available work is found, the queue sequencer passes control to the appropriate queue processor. If the queue sequencer determines that there is no available System Management work to be done, then control is transferred to the *scheduler* to select and dispatch a processing program for execution.

The purpose of the *scheduler* is to select a job for execution, to pass interrupts to Job Management routines, and to dispatch a job for execution. A job is selected for execution on either a priority, a first-come-first-served, or a time-sharing basis. In order for a job to be eligible for execution, the status flags in its job control block must indicate one of the following: *in execution* or *ready for execution*. The job is then dispatched

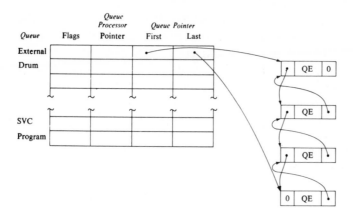

Fig. 10.8   Sequence table.

for execution by passing program control to the point in the program of last interrupt. If, however, a program interrupt has occurred, then information on the particular interrupt conditions, as well as program control, is passed to appropriate Job Management routines, which reside in the memory space of that job.

The purpose of each *queue processor* is to process the queue entries which are on its queue. Normally, a queue entry is processed, and then the queue processor returns to the queue sequencer. This logic enables the interrupts to be processed strictly on a priority basis. If the processing requires the services of more than one queue processor, then the queue entry is transferred to the next queue in order. During the processing of a queue entry, queue processors modify the contents of job control blocks, initiate and post the completion of I/O operations, and call subprocessors. The latter case is particularly true of the *supervisor call queue processor* which calls several system service routines to perform System Management services for jobs in the system. Several typical subprocessors are listed and described as follows:

1. *User Storage Allocation.* Allocates main storage to a job.
2. *I/O Initiation.* Causes I/O to be initiated for a particular job.
3. *Control.* Transfers control from privileged to nonprivileged routines and vice versa.
4. *Timer.* Set and read the system's timer for a job.
5. *Extract.* Extracts information from a job's job control block (available only to a privileged program).
6. *Priority.* Sets and changes the priority of a job (available only to a privileged program).

In general, System Management functioning should be reviewed. The interrupt stacker handles all hardware interrupts, thereby giving the System Management routines complete control over the computer system. Interrupts are classified, queued, and processed by appropriate routines. Only when System Management can do no more work is system control turned over to processing programs. Two important System Management functions still remain and must be mentioned in passing: system reliability and job integrity. *System reliability* pertains to the ability of the system to continue processing under adverse conditions. System Management routines are activated when hardware error conditions exist, regardless if they are in main frame components or peripheral components. The problem(s) can often be resolved by *unhooking* the bad hardware component(s) and continuing with system processing. The unhooking of a component or a subsystem of components is a hardware feature which has implications for maintenance as well as for system error resolution. That is, a portion of the system can be *partitioned out* for preventative maintenance, while the remainder continues to function in a useful manner. This is analogous, in a sense, to the common practice of taking a magnetic tape unit off-line and servicing it. The function of partitioning out a storage bank, an I/O device, or an extra central processing unit, and to continue system operation, is given the name *configuration control*. In operating systems where more than one job resides in computer storage at the same time, precaution must be taken to protect storage areas from access by other users. This is usually referred to as *job integrity* and is accomplished by providing hardware storage keys for blocks of core storage or by providing relocation registers, which can be accessed only by control programs. Regardless of the method of implementation, job integrity is a basic problem which must be faced early in the design cycle.

Job Management

Job Management's prime function is to monitor the execution of a job. Job Management routines reside in the memory space of a job and run in the privileged state. When System Management gives control to a job, it normally returns where execution was last terminated. If a program interrupt is pending, however, control is passed to a subsystem of Job Management called the *job monitor*. This is what is generally meant by a *software interrupt*. The job monitor interrogates the program interrupt condition and passes control to one of its own diagnostic routines or a routine provided by the user. The method of passing control from Job Management, which runs in the privileged state, to a processing program, which runs in the nonprivileged state, is of interest. As was mentioned previously, Job Management routines have access to many system facilities; in fact, they are considered a logical extension of System Management. Therefore, to pass from a privileged to a nonprivileged state requires the changing of critical fields in the job control block, which can only be done by System Management routines. The supervisor call interrupt is used for this purpose as pictured in the following diagram:

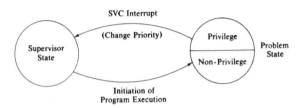

Clearly, the reverse is true when the user, running in the nonprivileged state, requires a service of Job or Data Management.

A major portion of Job Management is concerned with the *command language subsystem*. The command language subsystem contains a *command language director*, which reads the input job stream, interprets commands, and calls appropriate routines to process them. Generally, a processing routine exists for each command, although in many cases, Data Management routines are used to perform the major portion of the requested operation. Job Management also contains several service routines, e.g., GETMAIN,* which are available through macro instructions and are implemented through the supervisor call interrupt mechanism.

The last major function of Job Management is to handle job terminations. Job terminations may result from an actual command, i.e., ENDJOB, or may result from abnormal conditions within the job itself. In either case, a supervisor call interrupt is issued to System Management to delete the job's job control block and release all main storage and I/O devices allocated to it.

Data Management

Four classes of privileged service routines provide Data Management support for both privileged and nonprivileged processing programs. In so doing, these Data Management routines utilize services of System Management and have access to tables which are maintained on a system-wide basis.

The *access method* routines manage the transfer of data between I/O devices and main storage. More specifically, the user requests an input or

---
*That is, obtain a block of main storage.

output operation, and program control is passed to a privileged access routine. Clearly, the access methods use information on data set organization and record types provided by the user. On input, the access routine initially requests that a physical block of data is read by System Management and thereafter unblocks records upon input requests by the user. When a block is empty, another is automatically requested from System Management by the access method. On output, the access method saves logical records until a block is full and then requests that it be written by System Management. The access method routines actually perform no input/output but request that it be performed for them by routines in the System Management control program.

The *catalog service* routine manages the system catalog and, in so doing, has access to a central system facility shared by all users. The catalog is a hierarchical structure of indexes residing in a data set on a direct-access volume. Each index is identified by a symbolic name with the lowest level containing a *data set descriptor block*. The data set descriptor block is of interest because it is the mechanism by which data sets are accessed by name alone. The information contained in a data set descriptor block is included in the following fields:

1. Backward and forward pointers to other index levels;
2. Data set name;
3. Pointers to list of sharers, if any;
4. Location of physical data;
5. Accounting and frequency of use of data;
6. Data set label information;
7. Privilege, access, and shareability flags; and
8. Data set organization.

During actual use, this information is maintained by the catalog service routines and referenced by the access methods.

Device management and *external storage management* are two other Data Management services that access tables which are maintained on a system-wide basis. Both support commands in the command language and allocate devices and space on direct-access devices, respectively.

Although Job Management and Data Management routines are executed in the problem state, they are considered to be extensions of the System Management function. Collectively, they are termed control programs. Although, control programs differ from operating system to operating system, the major components, as presented here, are found in most systems. This model of an operating system is also amenable to a description of time sharing. Clearly, a time-sharing system is an operating system with extended facilities for job scheduling, for main storage allocation, and for the sharing of system resources.

Several additional topics are of importance in the examination of operating systems but are beyond the scope of this treatment. They are simply listed for further study:

1. System startup and shutdown;
2. Static and dynamic updating of the operating system;
3. Microprogramming as an extension of operating system concepts;
4. System usage accounting; and
5. Static and dynamic program loading.

PROBLEMS

10.1 Compare the command language given in this chapter to one with which you are familiar. In what way must either language be extended, or what operations must be performed so that a maximum set of functions is obtained?

10.2 Consider a typical set of hardware interrupts. Using the concepts contained in the state diagram of Fig. 10.7, draw a flow diagram of an *interrupt stacker.*

10.3 A queued access input/output system capable of processing blocked records can be simulated by using a basic access system capable of processing only unblocked records. Develop the logic for a processing program which could perform this function, indicating what control information is required and how it might be stored in memory.

REFERENCES

1. Mealy, G. H., "Operating Systems," Rosen, ed., *Programming Systems and Languages*, New York, McGraw-Hill Book Co., 1967. Gives the basic principles of operating systems design, differentiating between and describing *input-output systems, processors*, and *supervisory systems.*
2. Wood, T. C., "A Generalized Supervisor for a Time-Shared Operating System," *Proceedings FJCC, 1967*, Washington, D.C., Thompson Book Co., 1967. Presents a formalized description of the major components of the supervisor of a time-shared operating system.
3. "IBM Operating System/360 Concepts and Facilities," Rosen, ed., *Programming Systems and Languages*, New York, McGraw-Hill Book Co., 1967. Introduces the OS/360 operating system and describes the data management, task management, and job management facilities which are available therein.
4. IBM System/360 Time-Sharing System Concepts and Facilities, Form C28-2003, IBM Corporation, Yorktown Heights, N.Y., 1967. Although written as an introduction to TSS/360, contains a comprehensive description of data management concepts and program preparation in a complex operating environment.
5. IBM System/360 Time-Sharing System, System Logic Summary, Program Logic Manual, Y28-2009, IBM Corporation, Yorktown Heights, N.Y., 1967. Describes the control program structure of a sophisticated operating system.

11 | TIME-SHARING SYSTEMS

The primary purpose of time-sharing is to provide many users with simultaneous access* to a central computing facility. Although time-sharing systems are usually characterized by remote terminals and a conversational mode of operation, the concept is more general and applies to a variety of operating systems as well. The notion of a time-sharing system is nothing more than a comprehensive operating system† with extended features to cover storage allocation, program relocation, program segmentation, job scheduling, and the sharing of system resources. The CTSS system[2] at M.I.T. is credited with being the forerunner of what could be known as the *utility* type of time-sharing system, where users with diverse applications can be serviced at the same time. On the other hand, special purpose systems, such as airline reservation systems or those associated with many military applications, have existed for many years.

11.1 BASIC PHILOSOPHY

Time-shared operation of a computer system permits the allocation of both space and time on a temporary and dynamically changing basis. Several user programs can reside in computer storage at one time, while many others reside temporarily on auxiliary storage, such as disc or drum. Computer control is turned over to a resident program for a scheduled

*That is, as it is perceived by the user.
†Chapter 10 should be reviewed at this time.

time interval or until the program reaches a delay point (such as an I/O operation), depending upon the priority structure and control algorithm. At this time, CPU* control is turned over to another program. A non-active program may continue to reside in computer storage or may be moved to auxiliary storage to make room for other programs and subsequently be reloaded when its next turn for machine use occurs.

Management of a complex operating environment such as this requires a sophisticated set of control programs of the types covered in chapter 10. Obviously, sophisticated control programs require a sizeable investment for development and use overhead computer time during execution as well. The widespread acceptance of time-shared systems would indicate that ample justification exists. Nevertheless, the reasons for time-sharing are worth considering as a means of introducing the subject.

Reasons for Time Sharing

Time sharing exists for many reasons, and these reasons differ from system to system. Basically, these reasons fall into the following categories:†

1. To maximize the use of the system's facilities;
2. To reduce the turnaround time for small jobs;
3. To give the remote user the operational advantages of having a machine to himself by using his *think, reaction,* or *I/O time* to run other programs in the CPU;
4. To enable remote users to enter data into and receive data from the system via communications facilities;
5. To provide an environment for real time or *"demand"* *type processing*; and
6. To reduce problem set-up and operational times and to minimize the complexities involved with these functions.

Category 1 implies the maximum utilization of hardware resources by allocating these resources to other jobs during *"wait" periods* in the primary job. Category 2 refers to the technique of giving a job a slice of CPU time periodically. Given a time slice of t time units with n jobs in the system, then each job would get approximately t units of CPU time every $n \times t$ time units (discounting overhead), implying that a user would have to wait approximately 20 minutes for a 2-minute job if 10 jobs were in the system at once. With a sequential system, the user might have to

---

*Central Processing Unit.

†Objectively, the categories overlap, although for any given class of users, this may not be the case. In other words, a facility or set of facilities in a utility-class time-sharing system may satisfy several of these needs. The degree to which the needs of users with diverse requirements can be satisfied is a measure of the effectiveness of a time-sharing system.

wait hours, depending on the work load and priority structure. Category 3 implies remote terminals with users operating in the conversational mode with the system. In this case, the speed of the computer is such that many remote terminals can be serviced simultaneously by utilizing their *"think"* and *"I/O" times* to do other work. Category 4 provides the capability for entering information into the system concurrently with the processing of other jobs. Category 5 allows low-priority jobs to be interrupted for the processing of high-priority jobs on a demand basis. In many applications of this type, very little computer time is required; but when it is needed, high data rates must be accommodated. Category 6 is an operational consideration, allowing jobs to be stacked up by the system and executed on a priority basis instead of having the assignment of priorities implicitly done by computer operations personnel.

Although these categories vary in intent, the philosophy of sharing system resources is basic to the method of operation. The answer to the questions of "What system resources are shared?" and "How are the resources shared?" differentiate between the various types of time-sharing systems.

Allocation of CPU Time

The most important resource in a time-sharing system is CPU time, without which no job could be serviced. Because of its importance, time-sharing systems tend to be classified on the basis of how this valuable commodity is allocated. Five relevant concepts or conditions for scheduling and CPU allocation are recognized: 1. sequential; 2. natural wait; 3. time slicing; 4. priority; and 5. demand. The concepts, obviously, are not mutually exclusive and are used in various combinations in the different types of time-sharing systems. The techniques are defined in the following paragraphs; the ideas developed therein are used throughout the chapter:

1. *Sequential.* The system initiates units of work depending upon their time of arrival in the input stream. Once initiated, a unit of work ties up the entire resources of the system (even though it does not use them all) and runs until completed.
2. *Natural Wait.* A natural wait is a condition which causes a particular unit of work to be unable to use the CPU for a period of time (e.g., an input/output operation). Most units of work have natural waits imbedded in them. When this condition occurs, the unit of work that is next in sequence is given CPU time.
3. *Time Slicing.* A time-slicing algorithm recognizes that a certain (dynamic) number of programs must be serviced within a reasonable period of time. To this end, the system maintains a cumulative log

of its resources (such as time) used by each program. When a threshold level is exceeded, the program, being executed, is forced to stop and wait while other programs have a chance to use the CPU.

4. *Priority.* As a unit of work enters the system, it is assigned a priority. The program with the highest priority is given use of the CPU. If it is unable to use the CPU, CPU control is given to a program with lesser priority. If at any time, the program with highest priority needs the CPU, it is immediately given this service.

5. *Demand.* A unit of work is initiated immediately upon request.

From these definitions, an obvious conclusion can be drawn. Time slicing is more restrictive than the natural wait concept; thus, time slicing could be imbedded in a system which uses a natural wait scheduling algorithm, while the reverse is not generally true.

11.2   TYPES OF TIME-SHARING SYSTEMS

The manner in which time-shared operating systems are used, together with methods for allocating system resources, provides a means of differentiating between various types of time-sharing systems. The uses of time-shared operating systems can usually be divided into two general categories: 1. batch computing; and 2. remote computing. *Batch computing* techniques are well-defined (for example, see reference[8]). Jobs are stacked up to be run so as to meet planned objectives, which usually involve turn-around time for small jobs, priority runs, and system effectiveness. *Remote computing* enables the user in a remote location to effectively use a computer system, without having to physically transport his materials to a central location. The philosophy of remote computing relies upon remote devices and data transmission facilities. Because of its great generality, the remote computing concept can be used with any of the above concepts for scheduling and CPU allocation (i.e., natural wait, time slicing, demand, and even sequential). Thus, most major applications of remote computing can be classed into the following three categories:

1. *Remote Job Entry* (RJE). RJE permits units of work to be submitted in the same manner as they are submitted at the installation site. There are no response considerations. Input is usually stored on an external device until run time; output may be transmitted directly from a processing program or indirectly from external storage.

2. *Conversational.* Conversational remote computing is normally associated with time slicing or multiprogramming, i.e., systems in which remote devices can be attached as input/output units. Under these types of systems, the remote user responds as if he had the machine himself.

3. *Real Time.* Real-time processing usually involves obtaining access to the computing facility on a demand basis within given time limits. In fact, the effectiveness of a real-time system is often based on the response of the system to needs for computation.

Time-sharing systems can be further classified as to whether they are *open* or whether they are *closed.* Open systems such as CTSS at M.I.T.[2], Kinslow's system at IBM[11], TSS/360[1,7], and MULTICS[3,4,14] give the user access to all of the facilities of the operating system. Closed systems such as QUIKTRAN[5,9], the JOSS system at RAND[13], BASIC[10], or APL[6] limit the user to a specific language or system. Closed systems are usually limited to the *conversational* mode of operation, whereas open systems tend to be more general in nature.

The five basic types of time-sharing systems can now be presented. Collectively, they encompass the applications given above, utilize each of the concepts for scheduling and CPU allocation, and satisfy all of the reasons which were listed earlier. The basic types are listed as follows:

Type I.   Sequential scheduling systems with peripheral support.
Type II.   Multiprogramming systems with a fixed or variable number of jobs and priority scheduling.
Type III. Closed conversational programming systems using time-slicing methods for scheduling and CPU allocation.
Type IV.   Multiprogramming systems with a high priority job or *foreground partition* for running a conversational system of type III.
Type V.   General purpose time-sharing systems supporting open conversational programming and a batch environment, as well as peripheral support.

A *Type I* system is the null case of a time-sharing system which supports one batch job in addition to peripheral support.* Clearly, some of the more sophisticated systems look like Type I systems when only one job is in the system. *Type II* systems, normally called *multiprogramming systems*†, use the natural wait, priority, demand, and sequential methods of CPU allocation to maximize system efficiency. An internal priority, which is a function of external priority and arrival sequence, is developed. This internal priority is used for CPU scheduling. During multiprogramming

---

*Peripheral support pertains to the practice of reading the input job stream and stacking the information on direct-access storage and of printing and punching of information stored on direct-access devices. Since the amount of CPU time required to perform this type of input/output is minimal, it can be interspersed with the execution of a processing program.

†Related to multiprogramming is the concept of *multiprocessing,* which is defined as the simultaneous use of two or more CPU's in the same computing system. Clearly, each of the CPU's in a multiprocessing system may be executing in a multiprogramming mode of operation.

operation, the program, in the job mix, with highest internal priority runs until a natural wait is encountered. While this wait is being serviced, CPU control is turned over to the program with the next highest priority until the first program's wait is satisfied, at which time, CPU control is returned to the high priority program, regardless of whether the second job can still make use of the system. The first job, in a sense, has demanded the CPU. This concept is extended to as many levels as necessary.   With this method, CPU time is allocated to the highest priority program that can effectively use it.   A *Type III* system uses a time-slicing scheduling algorithm for servicing many users in a conversational programming environment. Users are normally limited as to the available programming system but usually enjoy favorable response time, since the systems in this category, by definition, are dedicated to the service they render.   A variation of Type III contains several programming systems within the operating environment but limits the user to a specific system in any one terminal session.* A *Type IV* system maintains the throughput of a Type II system, while providing the conversational programming capability of a Type III system. Basically, a Type IV system is a multiprogramming system, i.e., Type II, with a very high priority foreground job to provide the conversational support. Because of the generalized environment in which it is imbedded, the conversational programming system can be extended from a *closed* to an *open* system.   Obviously, the motivation behind Type IV systems is that a multiprogramming system of Type II can support a conversational programming facility without loss of generality. The most general and comprehensive variety of time-sharing system is *Type V*, which could be considered the utility class.† Three important functions are provided in a Type V system:

1. An *open* conversational programming environment with resources allocated on the basis of a time slicing scheduling algorithm but recognizing natural wait and demand conditions, as well;
2. A generalized batch capability for executing programs which do not require user intervention; and
3. A high-priority peripheral support capability for running on-line I/O devices at high speeds.

A Type V system is further characterized by providing the following services to users:

1. Communication between the user and an executing program, when in the conversational mode;

---

*A terminal session is generally considered to be the period of time during which the user is engaged in dialogue with a time-sharing system.

†CTSS[2], MULTICS[3,4,14], and TSS/360[1,7] are representative of this type of system.

2. Ability to share information (programs and data);
3. Several procedure-oriented languages for ease of program definition;
4. Facilities for storing programs and data within the system and for accessing this data during program execution;
5. Methods of communicating with the system operator to advise him of I/O requirements and to receive system messages;
6. Execution-time debugging aids;
7. Access by many users to a large data base; and
8. Methods of entering jobs from a remote location into the batch input stream.

Overall, *batch computing* requirements are met by Types I, II, IV, and V systems. *Remote job entry* is provided by Types II and IV, only if an appropriate job resides in the system to perform the required tasks; it is available in a Type V system as a basic function. Similarly, *real-time processing* is feasible with all Types, except I and III, but only if a high-priority program exists to satisfy requirements on a demand basis. *Conversational programming* needs are met, possibly with Type III and IV systems. Type III systems may be limited because of the available programming systems, while Type IV systems may not meet conversational response criteria. Type V systems, which are designed for general purpose conversational programming, meet these needs but require system overhead to support the time-slicing mode of operation.

The principle advantages and disadvantages of multiprogramming and time-slicing are summarized as follows:

1. *Multiprogramming.*

   Advantages. (a) Only those interrupts that would occur in the normal execution of the units of work being processed would be serviced. (b) The number of times the CPU changes units of work for the amount of time the CPU is utilized is minimized.

   Disadvantages. There is no guarantee that a particular unit of work will be activated within a stated time interval.

2. *Time Slicing.*

   Advantage. In every interval of processing program time T with N programs in the system, each program will be given CPU time of approximately T/N, providing a form of guaranteed service.

   Disadvantages. (a) At the end of every T/N units of time, the system is forced to service the interrupt caused by the expiration of a time slice. (b) The forced removal of a unit of work from the CPU, even though it may still be able to use it effectively, increases the number of times the CPU changes units of work, and perhaps dumps them onto external storage and relocates them later for the actual time the CPU is being utilized in the actual processing of programs.

11.3   VIRTUAL MEMORY AND PAGING

Two recurring problems were manifested by the popularization of time sharing. The first involves the concept of a single-level store,* as compared to a planned overlay† scheme for large programs. The second involves the relocation of programs on a dynamic basis so that other users may be serviced.

In a Type I system, the user's storage space is essentially that of the computer system. When a program overflows this space, it is segmented and overlaid. In a dynamic time-sharing environment, however, each user's work space is either limited or handled on a dynamic basis. Furthermore, planning a program to handle the worst case hinders system performance by limiting the number of programs that can coexist with it. Program relocation is a similar problem. It often becomes necessary to move a program out of computer storage before it has finished executing to make room for another job which must be serviced. The moving of an entire program is prohibitive from a performance standpoint, as is its relocation in the original place in memory. These problems are resolved by the concepts of virtual storage, dynamic address translation, and paging.

Virtual Storage Concept

In a standard programming environment, the programmer utilizes a computer with a fixed addressing capacity. Usually, the programmer is not allowed this full capacity because of actual storage limitations or because of other programs which must reside in main computer storage at the same time. In a *virtual storage* system,‡ the user is permitted the full addressing capacity of the hardware, regardless of the actual size of his addressable storage.

The basic element of a virtual storage system is a fixed unit of storage called a *page*.§ Thus, programs, data, and all of virtual storage, as well, are divided into pages, referred to conceptually as *logical pages*. It follows

---

*Single-level storage is a technique that treats all on-line storage as though it were main storage.

†Overlay is the technique of repeatedly using the same blocks of main storage during different stages of a program. When one routine is no longer needed in storage, another routine can replace all or part of it.

‡Sometimes referred to as a *single-level* store.

§In TSS/360[1,7] pages are fixed at 4096 bytes. In MULTICS[3,4,14], pages can either be 64 or 1024 computer words.

that any address in virtual storage is composed of two parts: a *page reference number* and a location within that page (often called a *byte number*). When a logical address is represented numerically, the page reference number occupies the high-order bits, and the byte number occupies the low-order bits. Main storage may then be allocated in page increments without requiring that contiguous logical pages occupy contiguous physical pages. Obviously, a means of mapping virtual addresses into physical addresses is required, and this is discussed later. During execution of a program, it is necessary that only the active pages be kept in main storage. Whenever a program references a page that is not in main storage, the condition is recognized by the hardware which generates an interrupt. The interrupt is processed by the operating system, which brings the page in from auxiliary* storage and relocates it. The program may then continue from the point of interruption. The concept of bringing pages in as they are needed and locating them in a useful manner is a sophisticated and costly (in terms of execution time) process. It is made economically feasible by a development termed dynamic address translation.

Dynamic Address Translation

The virtual storage concept is implemented through a hardware development called *dynamic address translation*. During the execution of a program that resides in virtual storage, the system translates each *virtual storage address* (i.e., logical address) into a corresponding *real address*, which designates an actual location in main storage. The translation is accomplished by means of a table-lookup procedure implemented in hardware. Conceptually, a translation table is of the form:†

(<page reference number>, <real page address>)

and enables a page reference number to be replaced by the real address of that page.

Although the idea of simply dividing a virtual storage space into pages is straightforward from an overall point of view, it causes operational problems in implementing the automatic address translation in hardware. The major problem is the length of the translation table (called a *page table*) required for the table lookup, since in a single table system a page table entry must exist for each page, regardless if it has been allocated or not. Several schemes for obviating this problem have been developed.

*The term *auxiliary* storage is often used for storage external to the computer which is used for the paging operation. The term *external* storage is used for storage external to the computer which is used for data and program libraries.
†See chapter 2.

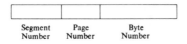

Fig. 11.1   Logical address.

One method which incorporates both simplicity and efficiency is used in TSS/360[1,7] and is presented here.

Automatic translation of logical addresses is made possible by dividing a user's virtual storage space into segments and sectioning these segments into pages. The segment-page structure is inherent in every logical address, as shown in Fig. 11.1. Segmentation is implemented by making the table lookup (of address translation) a two-step process. Instead of one page table for each job, there exists a page table for each segment and a segment table for each job. The high-order bits of the page reference number are interpreted as a segment number, and a segment table entry is referenced to fetch the address of the page table to be used in the second step of address translation, which substitutes a physical page address for the segment-page portion of the logical address.

In line with the above discussion, each job in the system requires for its operation one segment table and a page table for each segment used. These tables are developed in computer storage by the System Management control program,* as the job is initiated and as new page requirements are made by the user. When a needed page is brought into main storage by the paging routines in the operating system, the physical location of the logical page is entered into the appropriate page table.

During program execution, the hardware automatically performs a table lookup on each address as it is referenced by the user, and the corresponding physical address is selected for each logical address reference. If the required physical page is not in main storage,† then the hardware generates an automatic interrupt which is fielded by the operating system. A *page-turning routine* is then requested to fetch the needed page, while the CPU is assigned to another job. The waiting program is then placed in a wait status until its page has been retrieved and assigned an actual storage location, and the specific page table is updated accordingly. The entire dynamic translation process is depicted in Fig. 11.2. The automatic table-lookup procedure can be speeded up by a small associative memory, which contains the logical and physical addresses for the pages last referenced. If a logical address is not contained in the associative memory,

*See chapter 10.
†If a physical page is not in main storage, then the page table entry for that page is marked accordingly. Thus, an appropriate hardware interrupt can be generated.

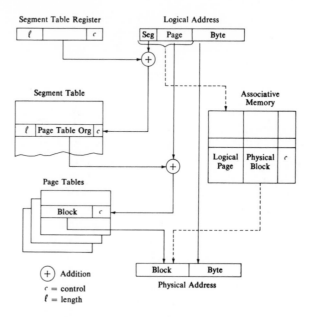

Fig. 11.2   Dynamic address translation.

the lookup of the segment and page tables follows, and an associative register is updated accordingly. This process is also depicted in Fig. 11.2.

Paging

The paging process is queue-driven in that requests to have pages written from auxiliary storage or written to auxiliary storage are queued for processing by the paging routine, which attempts to satisfy paging needs with minimal I/O activity. If an unchanged* page is queued for *page-out*, and a copy already exists on auxiliary storage, then the page is not written. Similarly, pages may be reclaimed. If a page is needed which exists on the page-out queue, then the page is reclaimed, taken off the page-out queue, and no input or output is required.

Because of the dynamic address translation feature and the segmentation tables, pages need not be relocated in their original slot. Not only is page relocation efficient and straightforward, but also this philosophy facilitates storage allocation by preventing unnecessary fragmentation. The paging procedure is pictured in Fig. 11.3.

---

*Obviously, indications of whether or not a page has been changed must be implemented in hardware. If this facility does exist, the potential benefits are very great.

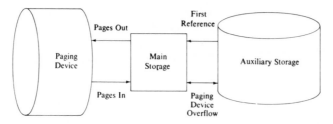

Fig. 11.3 Paging procedure.

11.4 SHARING OF PROGRAMS AND DATA

The efficiency of a time-sharing system is related to the extent to which both programs and data can be shared. Clearly, if two programs can share a common page, then the paging load is reduced accordingly. Dynamic address translation makes page sharing feasible. Clearly, a given physical page can exist at two different logical addresses, i.e., in the virtual storage of two different jobs. During address translation, the different logical addresses are mapped into the same physical address. Programs which are used by many jobs are candidates for sharing; Job Management and Data Management routines, as well as language processors, fall into this category.

Shared pages are fragments of programs (or modules) that may be shared. Shared programs must be written so that the coding does not modify itself; that is, the program and data parts must exist as distinct entities. Consider Fig. 11.4. The module to be shared must be a *read-*

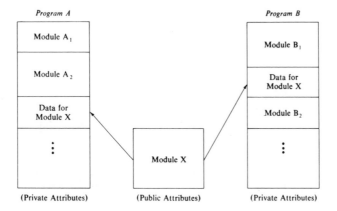

Fig. 11.4 Sharing a module.

only* and possess public attributes.† Only one copy will exist in main storage. The data portion of the shared module must possess private attributes; and a data part will exist for each sharer.

As described in chapter 10, access to a cataloged data set is possible only with the correct authorization.‡ Therefore, the owner of a data set must *permit* his data to be shared before another user can address it, and the sharer must inform the system of his intentions to *share* it. Although data set sharing facilities vary widely from system to system, the various *levels of access* tend to be the same and are of interest here. Three levels are defined:

1. *Read-only access.* The sharer may read the data set but may not change it in any way.
2. *Read-and-write access.* The sharer may read and write (i.e., update) the data set but may not erase it or delete its catalog entry.
3. *Unlimited access.* The sharer may treat the data set as his own. He may even erase it or delete its catalog entry.

The need for data set sharing is most apparent in a Type V or utility-class time-sharing system which uses the concept of a *public storage*. In a system which relies primarily on public storage, most of the direct-access volumes§ are considered to be part of (or an extension to) the system. Thus, the user is allocated space on these volumes for his data sets, and many users have data sets on the same physical unit. Access to these data sets is available only through the system, so that the user may not physically remove and save his own files. Therefore, the act of sharing a data set requires that the system be informed of both user's intentions, so that the privacy of a user's data can be assured.

11.5 SUMMARY

Unlike batch computing systems where throughput is of prime consideration, the goal of time-sharing systems is to make it easier to prepare programs while maintaining a high degree of resource utilization. This is

---

*A *read-only* procedure is one that does not modify itself during execution.

†In a sophisticated time-sharing system, program modules must have attributes so that loader routines will know what to do with them. Two of these attributes are *read-only* or *not read-only* and *public* or *private*. Read-only has been discussed. A *public* module may be used by several users. A *private* module may be used only by a user with an appropriate identification. Clearly, a module could be read-only and private and thus not be a candidate for sharing.

‡That is, with an appropriate user ID, which is used as the highest level of qualification in the data set name.

§Units of disc or drum storage.

accomplished through the following features in an operating system:

1. Remote computing facilities;
2. Virtual storage concepts;
3. Program relocation and dynamic address translation; and
4. Resource sharing.

Accordingly, time-sharing can be described as the concurrent use of the facilities of a general purpose computing system by a number of users.

PROBLEMS

11.1   Develop a catalog structure and organization which would permit the sharing of data sets.
11.2   Discuss why it might be feasible to imbed a time-slicing scheduling algorithm in a multiprogramming system.
11.3   Consider a multiprocessing system (more than one CPU) attached to the same memory and sharing the same copy of the system control programs. Two general methods are used to prevent conflicts:

1. Interlocks are programmed to prevent more than one CPU from executing in the system control programs at any one time.
2. Appropriate tables and queues are interlocked separately (by programming) so that they may be referenced by only one CPU) at any one time.

Give the advantages and disadvantages of each method and attempt to define a decision function which would determine the optimum method under given conditions. Remember, under ordinary circumstances, a given CPU would execute both control and processing programs, on a demand basis, depending upon the work to be done.

REFERENCES

1. Comfort, W. T., "A Computing System Design for User Service," *Proceedings, FJCC,* 1965.   Gives a user's overview of the TSS/360 time-sharing system.
2. Corbato, F. J., *et al., The Compatible Time-Sharing System,* Cambridge, Mass., The M.I.T. Press, 1963. Although primarily a user's manual for the CTSS system, contains basic information on the design and use of time-sharing systems.
3. Corbato, F. J., and V. A. Vyssotsky, "Introduction and Overview of the MULTICS System," *Proceedings, FJCC,* 1965. Describes the design features, software considerations, and the hardware requirements of the MULTICS system.
4. Daley, R. C., and J. B. Dennis, "Virtual Memory, Processes, and Sharing in MULTICS," *Comm. ACM,* Vol. **11,** No. 5 (May, 1968). Contains a technical description of how virtual memory is implemented, how processes are represented, and how programs, and data are shared in MULTICS.

5. Dunn, T. M., and J. H. Morrisey, "Remote Computing—An Experimental System, Part 1: External Specifications," *Proceedings, SJCC*, 1964. Presents the external specifications (command language, programming language, etc.) and requirements of the QUIKTRAN conversational time-sharing system.

6. Falkoff, A. D., and K. E. Iverson, *APL/360 User's Manual*, IBM Thomas J. Watson Research Center, Yorktown Heights, N.Y., 1968. Covers use of the APL conversational system patterned after Iverson's language (*A Programming Language*, Wiley, 1962).

7. Gibson, C. T., "Time-Sharing in the IBM System/360: Model 67," *Proceedings, SJCC*, 1966. Describes the hardware design of the TSS/360 time-sharing system.

8. Irons, E. T., "A Rapid Turnaround Multi-Programming System," *Comm. ACM*, Vol. 8, No. 3, (March, 1965). Describes a time-sharing system for a small machine which uses a time-sharing algorithm for scheduling, protects against excessive supervisor overhead, and does not utilize remote terminals.

9. Keller, J. M., *et al.*, "Remote Computing—An Experimental System, Part 2: Internal Design," *Proceedings, SJCC*, 1964. Presents the internal design of the QUIKTRAN system including a description of the internal form used to represent FORTRAN programs.

10. Kemeny, J. G., and T. E. Kurtz, *BASIC*, Dartmouth College Computation Center, Hanover, N.H., 1965. Contains a description of the BASIC language used with the Dartmouth time-sharing system.

11. Kinslow, H. A., "The Time-Sharing Monitor System," *Proceedings FJCC*, 1964. Describes a large experimental time-sharing system for the IBM 7090. As the primary predecessor to the TSS/360 system, contains a discussion of many basic design problems.

12. Randell, B., and C. J. Kuchner, "Dynamic Storage Allocation Systems, *Comm. ACM*, Vol. **11**, No. 5 (May, 1968). Includes a survey of methods of implementing virtual memory and discusses methods of mapping virtual addresses into physical addresses.

13. Shaw, J. C., "JOSS: A Designer's View of an Experimental On-Line Computing System," *Proceedings, FJCC*, 1964. Contains an early description of the JOSS language implemented on the Johnniac computer at the RAND Corporation.

14. Vyssotsky, V. A., *et al.*, "Structure of the MULTICS Supervisor," *Proceedings, FJCC*, 1965. Covers software writing policies, the concept of a process, and internal software features of the MULTICS system.

INTRODUCTION TO
THE APPENDICES

The appendices provide an introductory description of each of the programming languages, ALGOL, COBOL, FORTRAN, and PL/I. The descriptions adhere to a standard outline, allowing the languages to be compared to some degree.

The remainder of this introduction presents the outline and supplies descriptive information as required.

The *introduction* relates the purposes of the language and gives a brief history of its development. Outstanding facilities and major differences are also noted. These items are followed by an overview of the language, emphasizing points of general interest to its intended audience.

Basic Program Structure is the section which includes information basic to an understanding of the language. "Program Elements" describes the constituent parts of a statement, and "Programs" contains the manner in which statements can be grouped to form larger structures and finally programs. In all but trivial languages, data may be organized in several ways, may be named, and may be of various types. Moreover, it may possess other attributes necessary for effective programming. This information is given in the subdivision entitled "Data," which also describes the ways in which data can be declared, whether it be explicitly, implicitly, or contextually. The last category in "Basic Program Structure" is named "Operations" and describes the procedural operations which are available to the programmer.

Statements of the Language describes the statements of the language and gives the function of each. The description includes skeleton entries and appropriate definitions. The statements are classified into five groups: Data Manipulation Statements," "Control Statements," "Specification Statements," "Input/Output Statements," and "Program Structure Statements." No attempt is made to describe all of the implications of each statement or the interrelationships between statements; for this purpose, at lease one appropriate reference is given.

The remaining three sections consider *Built-in Functions*, *Special Topics*, and *References*. "Special Topics" describes unique or unusual features which are available in the language being examined.

A comprehensive outline is presented as follows:

1. INTRODUCTION

2. BASIC PROGRAM STRUCTURE

2.1 Program Elements
      2.1.1 Characters
      2.1.2 Operators
      2.1.3 Delimiters
      2.1.4 Identifiers
      2.1.5 Keywords
      2.1.6 Statements
      2.1.7 Comments

2.2 Programs
      2.2.1 Simple Statements
      2.2.2 Prefixes
      2.2.3 Loops
      2.2.4 Compound Statements
      2.2.5 Blocks
      2.2.6 Procedures
      2.2.7 Programs

2.3 Data
      2.3.1 Data Organization
      2.3.2 Naming
      2.3.3 Data Types
      2.3.4 Data Description

2.4 Operations
      2.4.1 Arithmetic Expressions
      2.4.2 Relational Expressions
      2.4.3 Logical Expressions
      2.4.4 Operations on Strings
      2.4.5 Operations on Structured Operands
      2.4.6 File Manipulation
      2.4.7 Sequence Control

3. STATEMENTS OF THE LANGUAGE
3.1 Data Manipulation Statements
3.2 Control Statements
3.3 Specification Statements
3.4 Input/Output Statements
3.5 Program Structure Statements

4. BUILT-IN FUNCTIONS

5. SPECIAL TOPICS
5.1 Format and Picture Specifications
5.2 Error Control Statements
5.3 Abbreviations
5.4 Other topics as required.

6. REFERENCES

A syntactical notation is required at various places in the appendices. Inverted notation is used for COBOL, FORTRAN, and PL/I. Backus normal form is used for ALGOL. The following conventions are defined:

1. *Backus Normal Form.*

    The symbol ":: =" stands for "is defined to be"; " | " stands for "or" and is used to separate alternate forms of the definition. The angular brackets "<" and ">" are used to enclose the name of a phrase type, distinguishing it as a name rather than as a thing named. All other symbols are literals which represent themselves.

2. *Inverted Notation.*

    { }—The braces are used to denote grouping. The vertical stacking of syntactical units or the vertical stroke character | indicates that a choice is to be made.

    [ ]—The square brackets denote options. Anything enclosed in brackets may appear one time or may not appear at all.

    . . .—Three dots denote the occurrence of the immediately preceding syntactical unit one or more times in succession.

Upper case letters represent keywords in the language and must be supplied by the programmer.

A short note on the use of the outline is necessary. Obviously, not all of the languages will have subject material for each entry in the outline. Absence of information on a topic implies that the particular facility does not exist in the language.

APPENDIX A
ALGOL

1. INTRODUCTION

As stated in the Revised ALGOL 60 Report, the purpose of the algorithmic language is to describe computational processes. The basic constituent is the well-known arithmetic expression from which arithmetic statements, iterative processes, and control statements are formed. Executable statements are supported by declarations and a block structure from which programs are formed.

The objective of developing ALGOL was the establishment of an international language for the description of computing procedures. The cooperative effort was supported by computer scientists from the United States and Europe, and the language which resulted overcame many of the limitations of FORTRAN and was free from the influence of IBM which completely dominated the computer market at that time.*

The syntax of ALGOL is conveniently described with a metalanguage, developed specifically for ALGOL, and called Backus normal form in honor of its principle designer.† This appendix utilizes metalinguistic formulae written in this metalanguage by including them in the standard outline whenever appropriate. Metalinguistic statements are derived from the Revised ALGOL Report. Metalinguistic expressions are used when introductory material is needed.

---

*Saul Rosen in his book entitled, *Programming Systems and Languages*, New York, McGraw-Hill Book Co., 1967, gives an excellent historical introduction to the development of ALGOL.

†See chapter 5.

2. BASIC PROGRAM STRUCTURE

ALGOL statements are composed of the following basic symbols:

<basic symbol>:: = <letter> | <digit> | <logical value> | <delimiter>

A key concept is that some of the symbols are English words like **if, for, real**, etc. These symbols should be interpreted in a manner similar to letters and digits and are in no way related to their apparent equivalents composed of distinct letters.

2.1.1 Characters

$$<\text{letter}>:: = a\,|\,b\,|\,c\,|\,d\,|\,e\,|\,f\,|\,g\,|\,h\,|\,i\,|\,j\,|\,k\,|\,l\,|\,m\,|\,n\,|\,o\,|\,p\,|\,q\,|\,r\,|\,s\,|$$
$$t\,|\,u\,|\,v\,|\,w\,|\,x\,|\,y\,|\,z\,|$$
$$A\,|\,B\,|\,C\,|\,D\,|\,E\,|\,F\,|\,G\,|\,H\,|\,I\,|\,J\,|\,K\,|\,L\,|\,M\,|\,N\,|\,O\,|\,P\,|$$
$$Q\,|\,R\,|\,S\,|\,T\,|\,U\,|\,V\,|\,W\,|\,X\,|\,Y\,|\,Z$$
$$<\text{digit}>:: = 0\,|\,1\,|\,2\,|\,3\,|\,4\,|\,5\,|\,6\,|\,7\,|\,8\,|\,9$$
$$<\text{logical value}>:: = \textbf{true}\,|\,\textbf{false}$$

2.1.2 Operators

ALGOL operators are considered a form of delimiter and are defined in the following section. Three basic types are provided: arithmetic operators, relational operators, and logical operators. A fourth type, namely the sequential operator, is also presented. They are analogous to the keywords in most other programming languages.

2.1.3 Delimiters

<delimiter>:: = <operator> | <separator> | <bracket> | <declarator> |
<specificator>
<operator>:: = <arithmetic operator> | <relational operator> |
<logical operator> | <sequential operator>
<arithmetic operator>:: = $+\,|\,-\,|\,\times\,|\,/\,|\,\div\,|\,\uparrow$
<relational operator>:: = $<\,|\,\leq\,|\,=\,|\,\geq\,|\,>\,|\,\neq$
<logical operator>:: = $\equiv\,|\,\supset\,|\,\vee\,|\,\wedge\,|\,\neg$
<sequential operator>:: = **go to** | **if** | **then** | **else** | **for** | **do**
<separator>:: = $,\,|\,.\,|\,_{10}\,|\,:\,|\,;\,|\,:=\,|\,\sqcup\,|$ **step** | **until** | **while** | **comment**
<bracket>:: = $(\,|\,)\,|\,[\,|\,]\,|\,`\,|\,'\,|$ **begin** | **end**

Most delimiters are components of other constructs and are described in that context.

2.1.4 Identifiers

Identifiers serve to identify scalar variables, arrays, labels, switches, and procedures and are defined as follows:

<identifier>:: = <letter> | <identifier><letter> | <identifier><digit>

2.1.5   Keywords

ALGOL has no keywords, per se, but the <sequential operator>, <declarator>, and <specificator> symbols serve the same purpose. A recommended list of standard functions has been included with the language specification and is covered in a later section.

2.1.6   Statements

The concept of a statement in ALGOL is considered in detail in sections 2.2.1–2.2.5. From an introductory point of view, however, it is a sequence of symbols from the language optionally preceded by a statement label and followed by a semicolon; i.e., a sequence of symbols of the form:

<statement label>:<statement body>;

The representation of an ALGOL statement is considered to be independent of the medium in which it is encoded. Thus, more than one statement may be written on a line, and statements may be continued to other lines, as required.

2.1.7   Comments

Comments are permitted so that descriptive text may be included among the symbols of a program. The following conventions hold:

Form	Equivalent to
; **comment** <any sequence not containing;>;	;
begin comment <any sequence not containing;>;	**begin**
end <any sequence not containing **end** or; or **else** >	**end**

2.2   Programs

2.2.1   Simple Statements

The basic unit of operation within the language is a statement. Statements are executed consecutively until the sequence is broken by an appropriate keyword such as **goto** or **if**. The syntax of a basic or simple statement in ALGOL is defined as follows:

<basic statement>:: = <unlabelled basic statement> | <label>:

<basic statement>

where:

<unlabelled basic statement>:: = <assignment statement> |
       <goto statement> | <dummy statement> | <procedure statement>

These metalinguistic formulae are used in sections 2.2.4 and 2.2.5 in the definitions of compound statements and blocks. Obvious omissions here are conditional and looping statements. They are considered to be compound statements.

2.2.2   Prefixes

The statement label is permitted in ALGOL as a statement prefix. It is separated from the body of the statement by a colon and has the following form:

$$<label>:: = <identifier> \mid <unsigned\ integer>$$

Section 2.3.3 contains a description of an unsigned integer.

2.2.3   Loops

The **for** statement in ALGOL provides the facility for program looping and has the following form:

$$\textbf{for} <variable>: = <for\ list> \textbf{ do } <statement>$$

Clearly, <variable> is the induction variable, and the <for list> controls the number of iterations. The <for list> is defined in section 3. Example:

for I: = 1 **step** 1 **until** 10 **do** A[I]: = B[I+3] − 13.2;

2.2.4   Compound Statements

Generally, a compound statement is one which contains more than one program element. Thus, the **for** and **if** statements can be logically placed in this category, although formally, ALGOL restricts the definition to sequences of the form:

L:L:...**begin** S; S;...S; S **end**

where the L's denote labels and the S's denote statements. An ALGOL compound statement can be used anywhere that a simple statement is used and is defined, formally, in the section 3.5. Informally, the **if** statement is presented as follows:

if <boolean expression> **then** <statement> **else** <statement>

where the **else** clause may be omitted. Example:

if X>Y **then** A: = B+C **else goto** LOOP;

2.2.5   Blocks

A block is a compound statement in which one or more declarations precede the first statement. A block may be used anywhere that a statement is used. Several points should be noted concerning blocks:

1. The statement parenthesis **begin** and **end** are treated as any other parenthesis where rules of formation must be observed. Nevertheless, nesting is permitted so that blocks may have subblocks, etc.
2. An identifier declared in a block has meaning *only* in that block.
3. An identifier declared in an outer block retains its definition throughout the block except in subblocks in which the same identifier is declared.

A block is pictured informally as follows:

L:L:... **begin** D;D; ... D;S;S; ... S;S **end**

where the L's denote labels, the D's denote declarations, and the S's denote statements. The block is defined formally in section 3.5. Example:*

```
Q:  begin integer I,K; real W;
        for I: = 1 step 1 until M do
        for K: = I + 1 step 1 until M do
        begin W: = A[I,K]; A[I,K]: = A[K,I];
          A[K,I]; = W
        end for I and K
        end block Q
```

2.2.6   Procedures

Three types of procedures are available in ALGOL: *standard functions,*[†] *internal functions*, and *internal procedures*. Standard functions are those commonly used in analysis and are provided with the language. Internal functions are defined with the *procedure* symbol and referenced with a function designator. Procedures are also defined with the *procedure* symbol and are envoked by a procedure statement.

A *procedure declaration* is a procedure head followed by a procedure body. A *procedure head* is the procedure statement followed by a declaration of parameters. The *procedure body* always acts like a block, although it need only be a statement of the language (see section 3).

2.2.7   Programs

An ALGOL program is a block or compound statement which is not contained within another block or compound statement and which makes no use of other statements not contained within it.

2.3   Data

2.3.1   Data Organization

Data can be organized as scalars, arrays, or a list of statement labels termed a *switch list*. A scalar item may be a constant item or a scalar variable. A constant is a number which stands for itself, a logical value, or a string written as a literal enclosed in quotation marks. A scalar variable names a data item but may assume different values during the course of a program. Data items may also be organized as n-dimensional arrays for which upper and lower bounds may be declared.

2.3.2   Naming

A variable is a designation given to a single value; it may refer to a scalar or an element of a multidimensional array. A variable is defined as follows:

<variable identifier> :: = <identifier>
<simple variable> :: = <variable identifier>

*Taken from the ALGOL Report.
†Which includes the transfer functions.

<subscript expression> :: = <arithmetic expression>
<subscript list> :: = <subscript expression> |
                    <subscript list>, <subscript expression>
<array identifier> :: = <identifier>
<subscripted variable> :: = <array identifier> [<subscript list>]
<variable> :: = <simple variable> | <subscripted variable>

Each subscript position is equivalent to the assignment of the subscript expression to a variable of type integer. The value of a subscripted variable is defined only if the subscript expression(s) is within designated bounds. Examples:

$$\text{DELTA}$$
$$A[1,2]$$
$$X3[\textbf{sin}\,(PI/2), B[16,I]]$$

2.3.3   Data Types

Five types of data are permitted in ALGOL: integer, real, boolean, string, and label. String data may only be used as actual parameters of procedures. Label data may be used in a switch list. Boolean data may assume the values **true** and **false**. Number and string data are defined as follows:

<unsigned integer> :: = <digit> | <unsigned integer> <digit>
<integer> :: = <unsigned integer> | + <unsigned integer> |
                                   − <unsigned integer>
<decimal fraction> :: = .<unsigned integer>
<exponent part> :: = $_{10}$<integer>
<decimal number> :: = <unsigned integer> | <decimal fraction> |
                         <unsigned integer> <decimal fraction>
<unsigned number> :: = <decimal number> | <exponent part> |
                         <decimal number> <exponent part>
<number> :: = <unsigned number> | + <unsigned number> |
                                 − <unsigned number>
<proper string> :: = <any sequence of basic symbols not
                      containing ' or ' > | <empty>
<open string> :: = <proper string> | '<open string>' |
                         <open string> <open string>
<string> :: = '<open string>'

Examples:

$$135$$
$$10^{9}$$
$$-17.1_{10}{}^{+7}$$
$$\text{'5T16.} \quad /=:\text{'}$$

2.3.4   Data Description

Declarations are used to define the attributes* of data and to associate them with identifiers. Four types of declarations are recognized: 1. a type declaration;

*Properties.

2. an array declaration; 3. a switch declaration; and 4. a procedure declaration. The procedure declaration is discussed in section 3.5. The *type declaration* gives the type and attributes of scalar variables. The *array declaration* gives the type, the subscript bounds, and the storage requirements for array variables.   The *switch declaration* defines a list of statement labels. All variables must be declared in ALGOL.

2.4   Operations

2.4.1   Arithmetic Expressions*

An arithmetic expression is a combination of arithmetic operators, operands, and parenthesis. Parentheses are used for grouping, as required. An operand is a constant, a scalar variable, an element of an array, an arithmetic expression enclosed in parentheses, or a string of symbols of the form

if <boolean expression> **then** <arithmetic expression> **else**

<arithmetic expression>

enclosed in parentheses. Example:

$$A+B+(\textbf{if } X<0 \textbf{ then } 0 \textbf{ else } X \uparrow 2)$$

An arithmetic expression is defined formally as follows:

<adding operator> :: = + | −
<multiplying operator> :: = × | / | ÷
<primary> :: = <unsigned number> | <variable> | <function designator> |

(<arithmetic expression>)

<factor> :: = <primary>| <factor> ↑ <primary>
<term> :: = <factor> | <term> <multiplying operator> <factor>
<simple arithmetic expression> :: = <term> | <adding operator>

<term> | <simple arithmetic expression> <adding operator> <term>
<if clause> :: = **if** <Boolean expression> **then**
<arithmetic expression> :: = <simple arithmetic expression> | <if clause>

<simple arithmetic expression> **else** <arithmetic expression>

A necessary definition is that of a function designator, which is the method by which standard or internal functions are envoked. It is defined as follows:

<procedure identifier> :: = <identifier>
<actual parameter> :: = <string> | <expression> | <array identifier> |

<switch identifier> | <procedure identifier>
<letter string> :: = <letter> | <letter string> <letter>
:: = , |) <letter string> :(
<actual parameter list> :: = <actual parameter> | <actual parameter list>

<actual parameter>
<actual parameter part> :: = <empty> | (<actual parameter list>)
<function designator> :: = <procedure identifier> <actual parameter part>

*Table A.1 gives the hierarchy of arithmetic, relational, and logical operators.

Examples:

$$\textbf{abs } (X-Y)$$
$$\textbf{root } (A, B, C, EPS)$$

2.4.2 Relational Expression

A relational expression, which can only have either of the values **true** or **false**, is permitted only in the context of a boolean expression, as described in section 2.4.3.

2.4.3 Logical Expressions

A logical expression is defined as a boolean expression in ALGOL and may assume either a **true** value or a **false** value. It is defined as follows:

```
<relational operator> :: = < | ≤ | = | ≥ | > | ≠
<relation> :: = <simple arithmetic expression> <relational operator>
                                    <simple arithmetic expression>
<boolean primary> :: = <logical value> | <variable> |
                <function designator> | <relation> | (<boolean expression>)
<boolean secondary> :: = <boolean primary> | ¬ <boolean primary>
<boolean factor> :: = <boolean secondary> | <boolean factor> ∧
                                    <boolean secondary>
<boolean term> :: = <boolean factor> | <boolean term> ∨ <boolean factor>
<implication> :: = <boolean term> | <implication> ⊃ <boolean term>
<simple boolean> :: = <implication> | <simple boolean> ≡ <implication>
<boolean expression> :: = <simple boolean> | <if clause>
                            <simple boolean> else <boolean expression>
```

Examples:

$$A > B$$
$$X1 > X2 \land Y1 < Y2$$

2.4.4 Operations on Strings

2.4.5 Operations on Structure Operands

Operations on entire arrays is limited to passing array names between procedures.

TABLE A.1 HIERARCHY OF ALGOL OPERATORS

Operation	Hierarchy
Exponentiation ($\uparrow$)	1st
Multiplication and division ($\times / \div$)	2nd
Addition and Subtraction ($+\ -$)	3rd
$<, \leq, =, \geq, >, \neq$	4th
$\neg$	5th
$\land$	6th
$\lor$	7th
$\supset$	8th
$\equiv$	9th

2.4.6   File Manipulation

File operations are not defined in ALGOL.

2.4.7   Sequence Control

Three sequence control statements are available in ALGOL. The three types are: 1. the goto statement; 2. the conditional statement; and 3. the for statement.

The *goto statement* provides an unconditional and computed branch facility. The *conditional statement* provides a means of making logical decisions within a program. The *for statement* provides a looping facility, as discussed in section 2.2.3.

3.   STATEMENTS OF THE LANGUAGE

The functions performed by the various statements of the ALGOL language are summarized in Table A.2. The following sections contain formal definitions of the statements.

TABLE A.2   STATEMENTS OF THE ALGOL LANGUAGE

array declaration	Declares the type, subscript bounds, and storage requirements for array variables.
Assignment statement	Evaluates arithmetic and boolean expressions and assigns values to variables.
for statement	Provides controlled looping facilities.
goto statement	Causes control to be transferred to a designated statement.
if statement	Provides for conditional execution of program elements.
procedure declaration	Identifies the beginning of a procedure definition and gives its name and arguments.
Procedure statement	Invokes a designated procedure and gives actual parameters (if any).
switch declaration	Defines a list of statement labels.
Type declaration	Declares the type and attributes of scalar variables.

3.1   Data Manipulation Statements

1. *The Assignment Statement.*

    <left part> :: = <variable> : = | <procedure identifier> : =
    <left part list> :: = <left part> | <left part list> <left part>
    <assignment statement> :: = <left part list> <arithmetic expression> |
                            <left part list> <boolean expression>

2. *The Procedure Statement.*

<actual parameter> :: = <string> | <expression>[1] | <array identifier> |
                            <switch identifier> | <procedure identifier>
<letter string> :: = <letter> | <letter string> <letter>
:: = , |) <letter string> :(
<actual parameter list> :: = <actual parameter> |
            <actual parameter list> <parameter delimiter> <actual parameter>
<actual parameter part> :: = <empty> | (<actual parameter list>)
<procedure statement> :: = <procedure identifier> <actual
                                                    parameter part>

[1] An expression is defined as an arithmetic expression, a Boolean expression, or a designational expression.

3.2   Control Statements

1. The Designational Expression.

<label> :: = <identifier> | <unsigned integer>
<switch identifier> :: = <identifier>
<switch designator> :: = <switch identifier>[<subscript expression>]
<simple designational expression> :: = <label> |
                        <switch designator> | (<designational expression>)
<designational expression> :: = <simple designational expression> |
            <if clause> <simple designational expression> **else**
                                        <designational expression>

2. *The Goto Statement.*

            <goto statement> :: = **goto** <designational expression>

3. *The Conditional Statement.*

<if clause> :: = **if** <boolean expression> **then**
<unconditional statement> :: = <basic statement> |
                                <compound statement> | <block>
<if statement> :: = <if clause> <unconditional statement>
<conditional statement> :: = <if statement> |
        <if statement> **else** <statement> | <if clause> <for statement> |
                                <label> : <conditional statement>

4. *The For Statement.*

<for list element> :: = <arithmetic expression> |
                        <arithmetic expression> **step** <arithmetic expression>
                        until <arithmetic expression> |
                        <arithmetic expression> **while** <Boolean expression>
<for list> :: = <for list element> | <for list>, <for list element>

<for clause> :: = **for** <variable> : = <for list> **do**
<for statement> :: = <for clause> <statement> |
: <for statement>

3.3   Specification Statements

1. *The Type Declaration.*

<type list> :: = <simple variable> | <simple variable>, <type list>
<type> :: = **real** | **integer** | **boolean**
<local or own type> :: = <type> | **own** <type>
<type declaration> :: = <local or own type> <type list>

2. *The Array Declaration.*

<lower bound> :: = <arithmetic expression>
<upper bound> :: = <arithmetic expression>
<bound pair> :: = <lower bound> : <upper bound>
<bound pair list> :: = <bound pair> | <bound pair list>, <bound pair>
<array segment> :: = <array identifier>[<bound pair list>] |
<array identifier>, <array segment>
<array list> :: = <array segment> | <array list>, <array segment>
<array declaration> :: = **array** <array list> |
<local or own type> **array** <array list>

3. *The Switch Declaration.*

<switch list> :: = <designational expression> | <switch list>,
<designational expression>
<switch declaration> :: = **switch** <switch identifier> : = <switch list>

3.4   Input/Output Statements

3.5   Program Structure Statements

1. *Compound Statements and Blocks.*

<unlabelled basic statement> :: = <assignment statement> |
<goto statement> | <dummy statement> | <procedure statement>
<basic statement> :: = <unlabelled basic statement> | <label> :
<basic statement>
<unconditional statement> :: = <basic statement> |
<compound statement> | <block>
<statement> :: = <unconditional statement> | <conditional statement> |
<for statement>
<compound tail> :: = <statement> **end** | <statement>;<compound tail>

<block head> :: = **begin** <declaration> | <block head>;<declaration>[2]
<unlabelled compound> :: = **begin** <compound tail>
<unlabelled block> :: = <block head>;<compound tail>
<compound statement> :: = <unlabelled compound> | <label> :
                                                    <compound statement>
<block> :: = <unlabelled block> | <label> : <block>
<program> :: = <block> | <compound statement>

[2] A declaration is defined as a type declaration, an array declaration, a switch declaration, or a procedure declaration.

2. *The Procedure Declaration.*

<formal parameter> :: = <identifier>
<formal parameter list> :: = <formal parameter> |
        <formal parameter list> <parameter delimiter> <formal parameter>
<formal parameter part> :: = <empty> | (<formal parameter list>)
<identifier list> :: = <identifier> | <identifier list>, <identifier>
<value part> :: = **value** <identifier list>;| <empty>
<specifier> :: = **string** | <type> | **array** | <type> **array** | **label** |
                           switch | **procedure** | <type> **procedure**
<specification part> :: = <empty> | <specifier> <identifier list>; |
                      <specification part> <specifier> <identifier list>;
<procedure heading> :: = <procedure identifier>
              <formal parameter part>;<value part> <specification part>
<procedure body> :: = <statement> | <code>[3]
<procedure declaration> :: = **procedure** <procedure heading>
        <procedure body> | <type> **procedure** <procedure heading>
                                                    <procedure body>

[3] Code is a procedure body that is expressed in non-ALGOL language.

4.   BUILT-IN FUNCTIONS

Built-in functions include standard functions and transfer functions, as specified in the Revised ALGOL Report. They are included as Table A.3.

5.   SPECIAL TOPICS

5.1   The Own Attribute

Variables and arrays declared in a block head are normally defined upon entry to a block and discarded upon exit. The **own** attribute, as defined in section 3.3, provides the facility for a block to retain values between different invocations.

TABLE A.3   ALGOL FUNCTIONS

Function	Definition
abs (E)	Absolute value of the value of the expression E.
sign (E)	The sign of the value of E (+1 if E>0, 0 if E=0, −1 if E<0).
sqrt (E)	Square root of the value of E.
sin (E)	Sine of the value of E.
cos (E)	Cosine of the value of E.
arctan (E)	Principle value of the arctangent of the value of E.
ln (E)	Natural logarithm of the value of E.
exp (E)	Exponential function of the value of E (i.e., e^E).
entier (E)	Largest integer not greater than the value of E.

5.2   The Value Declaration

In the declaration of a procedure, a **value** declaration is permitted. Parameters* listed in a **value** declaration are computed once at the point of entry to the procedure. Parameters not listed in a **value** declaration are assumed to be computed (i.e., the expressions which replace the parameters are computed) each time the parameter is referenced in the procedure.

6.   REFERENCES

Naur, P., ed., "Revised Report on the Algorithmic Language Algol 60," *Comm. ACM*, Vol. **6,** No. 1 (January, 1963).

Rosen, S., "The Algol Programming Language," *Programming Systems and Languages*, New York, McGraw-Hill Book Co., 1967.

*During a procedure call, parameters may be replaced by expressions or arrays.

APPENDIX B

COBOL

1. INTRODUCTION

COBOL (Common Business Oriented Language) is a procedure-oriented programming language designed to be used for the programming of business applications. The objectives in designing COBOL were to provide a language with the following characteristics: 1. machine independence; 2. easily understood in format and notation; 3. provides good program documentation; and 4. lends itself to compilation into efficient object code. As a result, COBOL is a subset of normal English with any program being divided into four natural divisions: The Identification Division, the Environment Division, the Data Division, and the Procedure Division. The various divisions are the mechanism by which independence, clarity, simplicity, efficiency, and readability are achieved.

The COBOL effort was initiated in a meeting held in the Pentagon in May of 1959 for the purpose of considering the desirability and feasibility of establishing a common language for the programming of digital computers for business type applications. Computer users, computer manufacturers, and interested parties were represented, and it was generally agreed that the project should be undertaken. The first comprehensive COBOL report was issued in August of 1961 with the language evolving, in a constructive sense, ever since. Throughout its history, COBOL has been strongly supported by business and industry.

The four divisions of a COBOL program are presented here, so that the reader can establish a correspondence between them and the elements of basic program structure.

1. *Identification Division.* The Identification Division identifies the source program and the output of a compilation.

2. *Environment Division.* The Environment Division specifies the computer equipment being used for both compilation and execution of a program.
3. *Data Division.* The Data Division describes the data that the object program will accept as input, will produce as output, and that which it will use to perform any data manipulations that are required.
4. *Procedure Division.* The Procedure Division describes the data manipulation, control, and input/output steps that the user wants the computer to execute.

COBOL is described using inverted notation with the following additions:

1. All upper case words which are underlined are required when the functions of which they are a part are used.
2. All upper case words which are not underlined may be included for readability. They may or may not be present in the source program.
3. When two or more nouns are written in a series, commas are shown as connectives (i.e., punctuation). Where a comma is shown, it may be omitted or replaced by either "AND" or " AND".

2.   BASIC PROGRAM STRUCTURE

2.1   Program Elements

2.1.1   Characters

The basic program constituent in COBOL is the *word* composed of characters from the COBOL character set given in Table B.1.

2.1.2   Operators

COBOL permits arithmetic, relational, and logical operators, as shown in Table B.2.

2.1.3   Delimiters

The basic delimiter is the *space* which separates words in the COBOL language. *Commas* may be used to separate clauses, and the *period* is used to end paragraph names, section headings, and sentences. Other delimiters are required but are dependent upon a program constituent of which they are a part.

2.1.4   Identifiers

An identifier in COBOL is termed a name (i.e., *data name, condition name,* or *procedure name*), a verb, or a reserved word. They are placed in a category known as *words*, which is structured as follows:

```
                    1.  Words
                    1.1  Nouns
                         1.1.1   Data Names
                         1.1.2   Condition Names
                         1.1.3   Procedure Names
```

TABLE B.1   COBOL CHARACTER SET AND
EDITING CHARACTERS

Letters

A, B, C, D, E, F, G, H, I, J, K, L, M, N, O, P,
Q, R, S, T, U, V, W, X, Y, Z

Digits

0, 1, 2, 3, 4, 5, 6, 7, 8, 9

Special Characters

	space (blank)
+	plus sign
−	minus sign
*	asterisk
/	stroke (virgule, slash)
=	equal sign
$	currency sign
,	comma
;	semicolon
.	period
'	quotation mark
(	left parenthesis
)	right parenthesis
>	greater than symbol
<	less than symbol

Editing Characters

B	space
0	zero
+	plus
−	minus
CR	credit
DB	debit
Z	zero suppress
*	check protect
$	currency sign
,	comma
.	period

    1.1.4   Literals
    1.1.5   Figurative Constants
  1.2   Verbs
  1.3   Reserved Words

A word may be composed of up to 30 digits, letters, or the character hyphen, which must not be first or last. A word is always terminated with a delimiter (i.e., punctuation character). The following conventions exist with respect to COBOL

TABLE B.2   COBOL OPERATORS

1. Arithmetic:

Character	Substitutable English Equivalent	Meaning
+	PLUS	Addition
−	MINUS	Subtraction
*	MULTIPLIED BY or TIMES	Multiplication
/	DIVIDED BY	Division
**	EXPONENTIATED BY	Exponentiation

2. Relational:

Operator	Meaning
IS [NOT] GREATER THAN	Greater than or not greater than
IS [NOT] >	
IS [NOT] LESS THAN	Less than or not less than
IS [NOT] <	
IS [NOT] EQUAL TO	Equal to or not equal to
IS [NOT] =	
IS UNEQUAL TO	Not equal to
EQUALS	Equal to
EXCEEDS	Greater than

3. Logical:

Operator	Meaning
AND	Conjunction
OR	Disjunction
NOT	Negation

words:

1. A *data-name* must contain at least one alphabetic character.
2. A *condition-name* must contain at least one alphabetic character.
3. A *procedure-name* is either a section-name or a paragraph-name and may be composed of all digits. Two procedure-names are equivalent if they have the same value and the same number of digits.
4. A literal is a value which stands for itself. A nonnumeric literal is enclosed in quotation marks. A numeric literal must contain at least one digit.
5. A figurative constant is a commonly used value which has been assigned a data-name. For example, the words

ZERO
SPACE
QUOTE

are all figurative constants.

2.1.5 Keywords

A keyword is the *verb* in COBOL; it denotes an action and is the first word of a statement in the Procedure Division. For example,

MOVE A TO B.

The *reserved word* is a special case of the keyword condition. A reserved word may not be used as a noun or verb and is used for connectives (AND, OR, etc.) or to improve the readability of a program.

2.1.6 Statements

The reference format for a line in COBOL is represented as follows:

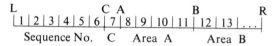

where

L denotes the leftmost character position of a line;
C denotes the 7th character position relative to L;
A denotes the 8th character position relative to L;
B denotes the 12th character position relative to L;
R denotes the rightmost character position in a line.

Four areas are designated: sequence number, continuation, area A, and area B. The areas are used as follows:

1. Sequence numbers (6 digits) are placed in the sequence number area;
2. Division, section, or paragraph names begin in area A;
3. Sentences begin in area B;
4. Continuation lines are indicated by placing a hyphen in the continuation area (column 7).

2.1.7 Comments

The programmer may insert comments into the Procedure Division of his program by using the NOTE verb (see section 3).

2.2 Programs

2.2.1 Simple Statement

A statement is a syntactically valid combination of words and symbols beginning with a COBOL verb.

2.2.2 Prefixes

COBOL does not provide a single statement identifier. It does provide a paragraph-name, which can be used with control statements; a paragraph is defined below (section 2.2.5).

2.2.3 Loops

A looping facility is provided whereby a paragraph or series of paragraphs may be executed in a controlled manner (see the PERFORM verb).

2.2.4 Compound Statements

Two types of compound statements exist: sentences and conditional statements. A *sentence* consists of one or more statements and is terminated by a period followed by a space. A *conditional statement* is a statement which contains other program elements and has the following format:

$$\underline{\text{IF}} \quad \text{condition} \quad [\text{THEN}] \left\{ \begin{array}{l} \text{statement} - 1 \\ \underline{\text{NEXT SENTENCE}} \end{array} \right\}$$

$$\left[\left\{ \begin{array}{l} \underline{\text{ELSE}} \\ \underline{\text{OTHERWISE}} \end{array} \right\} \right] \quad [\underline{\text{THEN}}] \left\{ \begin{array}{l} \text{statement} - 2 \\ \underline{\text{NEXT SENTENCE}} \end{array} \right\}$$

2.2.5 Blocks

A *paragraph* consists of a paragraph-name followed by one or more sentences. A paragraph ends with the next *paragraph-name, section-name*, or the end of the Procedure Division. Paragraphs may be grouped to form a SECTION, which is a section header followed by one or more paragraphs. Paragraph and section-names are termed *procedure-names* in COBOL.

2.2.6 Procedures

Procedures (i.e., subroutines) may be written in COBOL by using the ENTER verb to enter a mode such that entry points and parameters may be declared. Moreover, the ENTER verb must also be used to establish return linkage and to invoke a subroutine.

2.2.7 Programs

A program is composed of an Identification Division, an Environment Division, a Data Division, and a Procedure Division. They must be presented to the compiler in the given order.

2.3   Data

2.3.1 Data Organization

Data may be organized as scalars, arrays, or structures. Scalars and arrays may be part of a structure which is the basic method of data definition. *Scalars* may be literals (numeric or nonnumeric) or variables. *Arrays* may have one, two, or three dimensions and must be declared with the OCCURS clause. It follows that records are formed from structures, and files are formed from records.

A *file* is the largest set of related information and consists of any number of *records*, which in turn are made up of subrecords of smaller sizes. A piece of data which is never subdivided is called an *elementary item*. *Level numbers* are used to show how data items are related to each other.

2.3.2   Naming

A *simple name* is a data-name used to reference a scalar value or a structure. A *subscripted name* is a means of referring to an element of an array. A subscript is an integer constant or a scalar variable having an integer value. A subscripted variable is a data-name followed by the required number of subscripts separated by commas and enclosed in parentheses. Nonunique paragraph-names may exist in different sections. Similarly, nonunique data-names may exist in different structures. A *qualified name* is a means of referring to nonunique names within different hierarchies. Examples of qualified names are given as follows:

A OF B

TOM IN JONES

A *condition-name** is a name given to a value that a variable may assume. For example, the condition-name MARRIED might be given to the condition where the value of the variable MARITAL-STATUS is 'MARRIED', i.e., instead of writing

IF MARITAL-STATUS = 'MARRIED' . . .

the following abbreviated form could be used:

IF MARRIED . . .

2.3.3   Data Types

COBOL permits data to be represented internally in the following ways: COMPUTATIONAL (i.e., the data is to be used for computations and may be coded in an internal form), DISPLAY (i.e., the data is stored in a BCD form), and INDEX (i.e., the data is to be used to index tables). In addition, the user may specify the precision of his data. The implementor is given considerable freedom in implementing data types depending upon the object computer. As a result, several manufacturers have implemented floating point and extended precision.

When declaring data in the Data Division, the user is permitted two attributes which affect data type. The USAGE clause specifies whether the data is computational, display, or index. The CLASS clause specifies the nature of the data as to whether it is alphabetic, numeric, or alphanumeric.

2.3.4   Data Description

The DATA DIVISION describes the input and output files; constants, data and temporary storage; and the formats and descriptions of reports. It consists of four sections: FILE, WORKING-STORAGE, CONSTANT, and REPORT.

The File Section describes standard input/output files, sort files, and random-access files. The description of a standard file includes the recording mode, the grouping of logical records, identification information, keys, and the names of data records. The description of a sort file includes the name, size, and number of records in the file. A random-access file description is used to define a saved area for use with random processing. Record descriptions for records contained in a

---

*The condition-name is represented by having a level number of 88.

file follow their respective file declarations. A record description consists of a set of related data entries, grouped into a hierarchy indicated by means of level numbers. For example,

```
01  EMPLOYEE-IDENTIFICATION
    04  NAME
        05  LAST-NAME
        05  FIRST-NAME
        05  MIDDLE-INITIAL
    04  ID-NUMBER
    04  ADDRESS
        06  STREET
        06  CITY-STATE
            08  CITY
            08  ZONE
            08  STATE
```

The Working-Storage Section contains data description entries for noncontiguous working-storage items and record description entries in that order. Noncontiguous working-storage items are given a level number of 77.

The Constant Section sets aside parts of computer storage for named constants. Entries are similar to those for the Working-Storage Section.

The Report Section describes the overall format of a report named in the File Section. The characteristics of a report are provided by describing the lines per page, headings, footings, and details within the page structure. Each report named in a File Description entry must have a Report Description.

Outlines and skeleton formats of the constituents of the Data Division are presented in the following pages instead of section 3.3, which is limited to Procedure Division declaratives.*

Data Division Outline

```
DATA DIVISION.
FILE SECTION.
    File Description entries
        Record Description entries
    Sort Description entries
        Record Description entries
    Saved Area Entries
        Record Description entries
WORKING-STORAGE SECTION.
    Record Description entries
CONSTANT SECTION.
    Record Description entries
```

---

*Obviously, not all attributes and implications are contained here. For this type of information, the COBOL reference manual from any computer manufacturer should be consulted.

REPORT SECTION.
   Report Description entries
     Report Group Description entries
     Report Element Description entries

File Description Entry

FD   file-name

$$\underline{\text{LABEL}} \quad \begin{Bmatrix} \underline{\text{RECORD}} & \text{IS} \\ \underline{\text{RECORDS}} & \text{ARE} \end{Bmatrix} \begin{Bmatrix} \underline{\text{STANDARD}} \\ \underline{\text{OMITTED}} \\ \text{data-name} \end{Bmatrix}$$

[$\underline{\text{RECORDING}}$ MODE IS mode]

$$\left[\underline{\text{BLOCK}} \quad \text{CONTAINS} \quad \text{integer} \begin{Bmatrix} \underline{\text{CHARACTERS}} \\ \underline{\text{RECORDS}} \end{Bmatrix} \right]$$

[$\underline{\text{RECORD}}$ CONTAINS [integer-1 $\underline{\text{TO}}$]
    integer-2 CHARACTERS]

$$\underline{\text{DATA}} \quad \begin{Bmatrix} \underline{\text{RECORD}} & \text{IS} \\ \underline{\text{RECORDS}} & \text{ARE} \end{Bmatrix} \text{record-name} \ldots$$

$$\left[\begin{Bmatrix} \underline{\text{REPORT}} & \text{IS} \\ \underline{\text{REPORTS}} & \text{ARE} \end{Bmatrix} \text{report-name} \ldots \right].$$

Sort Description Entry

SD   sort-file description-name

$$\underline{\text{DATA}} \quad \begin{Bmatrix} \underline{\text{RECORD}} & \text{IS} \\ \underline{\text{RECORDS}} & \text{ARE} \end{Bmatrix} \text{record-name} \ldots$$

[$\underline{\text{RECORDING}}$ MODE IS mode]

[$\underline{\text{RECORD}}$ CONTAINS [integer-1 $\underline{\text{TO}}$]
    integer-2 CHARACTERS].

Saved Area Description Entry

SA   saved-area-name

[$\underline{\text{RECORD}}$ $\underline{\text{CONTAINS}}$ [integer-1 $\underline{\text{TO}}$]
    integer-2 CHARACTERS].

Working-Storage Section Outline

WORKING-STORAGE SECTION.
   77-Level entries
   Record Description entries

Constant Section Outline

CONSTANT SECTION.
   77-Level entries
   Record Description entries

Report Description Entry

> RD   report-name
>   [CODE-clause]   [CONTROL-clause]
>   [PAGE-clause].

Record Description Entry

The skeleton of a record description entry contains provisions for the following specifications:

1. Level number,
2. Data-name,
3. Size of data (length),
4. Usage,
5. Occurrences (number) of the element,
6. Class or type of data,
7. Editing symbols,
8. Value of the data,
9. Synchronization of the data,
10. A picture of the data.

The skeleton entries are presented as a description of the group item and a series of elementary items.

Group Item

level-number   {data-name / FILLER}   [OCCURS...]   [USAGE...]   [CLASS...].

Alphanumeric Item

level-number   {data-name / FILLER}   [OCCURS...]   [SIZE...]   [SYNCHRONIZED...]

[PICTURE...]   [USAGE IS DISPLAY,]
                [VALUE IS non-numeric-literal]

[CLASS IS {ALPHANUMERIC / ALPHABETIC}]

Report Item

level-number   {data-name / FILLER}   [OCCURS...]

[SYNCHRONIZED...]   [editing clauses...]
[SIZE...]   [CLASS IS ALPHANUMERIC]
[USAGE IS DISPLAY]   [PICTURE IS...]
[VALUE IS numeric-literal].

External Decimal Item

$$\text{level-number} \quad \begin{Bmatrix} \text{data-name} \\ \underline{\text{FILLER}} \end{Bmatrix} \quad [\underline{\text{OCCURS}} \ldots] \quad [\underline{\text{SYNCHRONIZED}} \ldots]$$

[SIZE...]   [USAGE IS DISPLAY]   [PICTURE...]
[VALUE IS numeric-literal]
[CLASS IS NUMERIC].

Internal Decimal Item

$$\text{level-number} \quad \begin{Bmatrix} \text{data-name} \\ \underline{\text{FILLER}} \end{Bmatrix} \quad [\underline{\text{OCCURS}} \ldots]$$

[SIZE...]   [USAGE IS COMPUTATIONAL]
[PICTURE...]   [VALUE IS numeric-literal]
[CLASS IS NUMERIC]   [SYNCHRONIZED RIGHT].

The elements of Record Description entries are summarized in Table B.3.

TABLE B.3   FUNCTIONS OF ELEMENTS OF RECORD DESCRIPTION ENTRIES

Element	Function
CLASS	To indicate the type of data being described.
data-name	To specify the name of the data being described, or to specify a portion of the logical record to which reference is made.
Editing-clauses	To specify suppression of nonsignificant zeros and commas, or to specify floating dollar signs or check protection.
JUSTIFIED	To specify nonstandard positioning of data within a recurring data item.
level-number	To show the hierarchy of data within a logical record.
OCCURS	To describe a sequence of data items with the same format and to supply information required in the application of subscripts.
PICTURE	To describe the general characteristics and editing requirements of an elementary item.
REDEFINES	To allow the same computer storage area to contain different data items.
SIGN	To specify the operational sign of an elementary item.
SIZE	To specify the size of an item in terms of the number of characters or digits.
SYNCHRONIZED	To specify positioning of an elementary item within a computer word or words.
USAGE	To specify the format of a data item in computer storage.
VALUE	To define the value of constants, the initial value of working-storage items, or the values associated with a condition-name.

2.4   Operations

2.4.1   Arithmetic Expressions

Arithmetic expressions are permitted with the COMPUTE verb, utilizing the arithmetic operators (Table B.2), numeric operands, and the left and right parentheses for grouping. Arithmetic operators may be replaced by word equivalents as required.

2.4.2   Relational Expressions

Relational expressions are called *conditions* in COBOL and are permitted in the IF statement. A condition is one of the following:

Type	*Example*
Relation-condition	A > B
Class condition	VALU IS NUMERIC
Condition-name condition	MARRIED
Switch-status condition*	
Sign condition	VALU IS POSITIVE
NOT condition	NOT (A < B)
Logical condition	MALE AND AGE > 32

2.4.3   Logical Expressions

Conditions, as described in section 2.4.2, may be combined with the logical operators to form other conditions.

2.4.4   Operations on Strings

Two verbs permit operations on strings of characters. The EXAMINE verb replaces or counts the number of occurrences of a given character in a data item. The MOVE verb permits strings to be moved from one area to another.

2.4.5   Operations on Structured Operands

Operations on structures are permitted in two ways: 1. the movement of group items; and 2. the MOVE CORRESPONDING verb shown in the following example:

MOVE CORRESPONDING NAME-1 TO NAME-2.

2.4.6   File Manipulation

One method is defined for transmitting data to and from external devices; it is defined by a particular implementation. Data conversion and editing is performed during the course of computation.

*The *switch-status condition* refers to a hardware switch defined in the Environment Division.

2.4.7   Sequence Control

Four types of sequence control statements are permitted in COBOL. The four types are: unconditional branches, computed branches, conditional statements, and the facility to PERFORM a paragraph or sequence of paragraphs under loop control.

The GOTO statement provides the unconditional branch. The GOTO.... DEPENDING ON... statement provides the computed branch. The IF statement provides the conditional facility and the PERFORM verb provides the controlled looping facility.

3.   STATEMENTS OF THE LANGUAGE

This section describes the statements which may be used in the Procedure Division of a COBOL program. The general format of the Procedure Division is as follows:

```
PROCEDURE DIVISION.
DECLARATIVES.
⎡{section-name  SECTION.  declarative-sentence.⎤
⎢{paragraph-name.  {sentence}...}...}...           ⎥
⎢ END DECLARATIVES.                                 ⎥
⎣{[section-name  SECTION.  [priority]. ]            ⎦
 {paragraph-name.  {sentence}...}...}...
```

The functions performed by each of the statements are summarized in Table B.4. Statements may be informally classified as imperative statements, conditional statements, and compiler-directing statements. These classifications are used in the skeleton entries which follow.

The official definition of the COBOL language contains several verbs which are optional to the implementor and may be termed *extended*. Skeleton entries for all of these verbs is beyond the scope of this appendix. These extended verbs are listed in their respective section.

Some statement types have several formats of which only the most common skeleton entry is given. These statements are marked with the †.

3.1   Data Manipulation Statements

$$
\dagger \underline{\text{ADD}} \quad \left\{ \begin{matrix} \text{data-name-1} \\ \text{numeric-literal-1} \end{matrix} \right\} \left[\begin{matrix} \text{, data-name-2} \\ \text{, numeric-literal-2} \end{matrix} \right] \dots \left\{ \begin{matrix} \underline{\text{TO}} \\ \underline{\text{GIVING}} \end{matrix} \right\}
$$

data-name-3 [ROUNDED] [, data-name-4 [ROUNDED]] ...

[ON SIZE ERROR imperative statement]

COMPUTE data-name-1 [ROUNDED] [, data-name-2 [ROUNDED]] ...

$$
\left\{ \begin{matrix} \underline{\text{FROM}} \\ = \\ \underline{\text{EQUALS}} \end{matrix} \right\} \quad \text{arithmetic-expression [ON } \underline{\text{SIZE}} \ \underline{\text{ERROR}} \text{ imperative-statement]}
$$

$$
\dagger \underline{\text{DIVIDE}} \quad \left\{ \begin{matrix} \text{data-name-1} \\ \text{numeric-literal-1} \end{matrix} \right\} \quad \underline{\text{INTO}} \quad \left\{ \begin{matrix} \text{data-name-2} \\ \quad \underline{\text{GIVING}} \text{ data-name-3]} \\ \text{numeric-literal-2} \\ \quad \underline{\text{GIVING}} \text{ data-name-3} \end{matrix} \right\}
$$

[ROUNDED]   [ON SIZE ERROR imperative-statement]

TABLE B.4   STATEMENTS OF THE COBOL LANGUAGE

ACCEPT	Causes low volume data to be read from an input device.
ADD	Causes numeric operands to be summed and the result stored.
ALTER	Modifies an unconditional GO TO statement thus changing the sequence of control.
CLOSE	Terminates the processing of input and output files.
COMPUTE	Assigns the value of an arithmetic expression to a data item.
DEFINE	Allows new statements to be defined in terms of standard COBOL statements.
DISPLAY	Causes low volume data to be written on an output device.
DIVIDE	Divides one data item into another and sets the value of an item equal to the quotient.
ENTER	Allows the use of more than one programming language in the same program.
EXAMINE	Replaces or counts the number of occurrences of a given character in a data item.
EXIT	Provides an end point for a procedure.
GENERATE	Links the Procedure Division to the report writer.
GO TO	Transfers control from one part of a program to another.
HOLD	Provides a delay point in an asynchronous environment.
IF	Provides for the execution of statements on a conditional basis.
INCLUDE	Incorporates library routines into the Procedure Division.
INITIATE	Begins processing of a report.
MOVE	Transfers data from one area of main storage to another and performs editing and/or conversion of the data moved.
MULTIPLY	Causes numeric operands to be multiplied and the result stored.
NOTE	Allows comments in a program.
OPEN	Initiates the processing of input and output files.
PERFORM	Provides controlled looping facilities.
PROCESS	Initiates a set of asynchronous procedures.
READ	Makes available the next logical record from an input file.
RELEASE	Transfers records to the initial phase of a SORT operation.
RETURN	Obtains sorted records from the final phase of SORT operation.
SEARCH	Searches a table for a specified element.
SEEK	Initiates the accessing of a data record on a direct-access device.
SET	Establishes reference points for table handling by setting index values.
SORT	Creates a sort file, sorts it, and makes the sorted records available for further processing.

STOP	Halts the execution of an object program.
SUBTRACT	Subtracts one or more data items from a given item and sets a data item equal to the difference.
TERMINATE	Terminates the processing of a report.
TRANSFORM	Alters characters according to a transformation rule.
USE	Identifies a Procedure Division declarative.
WRITE	Releases a logical record for an output file.

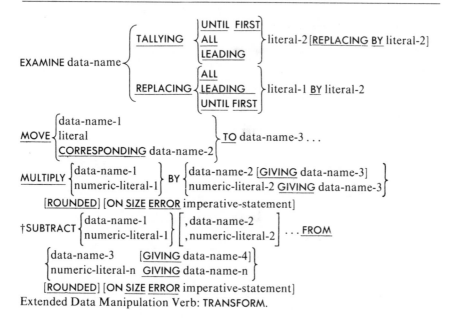

EXAMINE data-name $\begin{cases} \text{TALLYING} \begin{cases} \text{UNTIL FIRST} \\ \text{ALL} \\ \text{LEADING} \end{cases} \text{literal-2} [\underline{\text{REPLACING}} \ \underline{\text{BY}} \ \text{literal-2}] \\ \underline{\text{REPLACING}} \begin{cases} \text{ALL} \\ \underline{\text{LEADING}} \\ \text{UNTIL FIRST} \end{cases} \text{literal-1} \ \underline{\text{BY}} \ \text{literal-2} \end{cases}$

$\underline{\text{MOVE}} \begin{cases} \text{data-name-1} \\ \text{literal} \\ \underline{\text{CORRESPONDING}} \ \text{data-name-2} \end{cases} \underline{\text{TO}} \ \text{data-name-3} \ldots$

$\underline{\text{MULTIPLY}} \begin{cases} \text{data-name-1} \\ \text{numeric-literal-1} \end{cases} \underline{\text{BY}} \begin{cases} \text{data-name-2} [\underline{\text{GIVING}} \ \text{data-name-3}] \\ \text{numeric-literal-2} \ \underline{\text{GIVING}} \ \text{data-name-3} \end{cases}$

[$\underline{\text{ROUNDED}}$] [ON $\underline{\text{SIZE}}$ $\underline{\text{ERROR}}$ imperative-statement]

†$\underline{\text{SUBTRACT}} \begin{cases} \text{data-name-1} \\ \text{numeric-literal-1} \end{cases} \begin{bmatrix} , \text{data-name-2} \\ , \text{numeric-literal-2} \end{bmatrix} \ldots \underline{\text{FROM}}$

$\begin{cases} \text{data-name-3} \quad [\underline{\text{GIVING}} \ \text{data-name-4}] \\ \text{numeric-literal-n} \ \underline{\text{GIVING}} \ \text{data-name-n} \end{cases}$

[$\underline{\text{ROUNDED}}$] [ON $\underline{\text{SIZE}}$ $\underline{\text{ERROR}}$ imperative-statement]

Extended Data Manipulation Verb: TRANSFORM.

3.2 Control Statements

$\underline{\text{ALTER}}$ procedure-name-1 $\underline{\text{TO}}$ $\underline{\text{PROCEED}}$ $\underline{\text{TO}}$ procedure-name-2
    [, procedure-name-3 $\underline{\text{TO}}$ $\underline{\text{PROCEED}}$ $\underline{\text{TO}}$ procedure-name-4] ....

$\underline{\text{GO}}$ $\underline{\text{TO}}$ [procedure-name]

$\underline{\text{GO}}$ $\underline{\text{TO}}$ procedure-name-1 [, procedure-name-2] ...
    $\underline{\text{DEPENDING}}$ $\underline{\text{ON}}$ data-name

$\underline{\text{IF}}$ condition [$\underline{\text{THEN}}$] $\begin{cases} \text{statement-1} \\ \underline{\text{NEXT}} \ \underline{\text{SENTENCE}} \end{cases}$

$\begin{cases} \underline{\text{OTHERWISE}} \\ \underline{\text{ELSE}} \end{cases} \begin{cases} \text{statement-2} \\ \underline{\text{NEXT}} \ \underline{\text{SENTENCE}} \end{cases}$

$\underline{\text{PERFORM}}$ procedure-name-1 [$\underline{\text{THRU}}$ procedure-name-2]

$\underline{\text{PERFORM}}$ procedure-name-1 [$\underline{\text{THRU}}$ procedure-name-2] $\underline{\text{UNTIL}}$ condition-1

$\underline{\text{PERFORM}}$ procedure-name-1 [$\underline{\text{THRU}}$ procedure-name-2] $\begin{cases} \text{data-name-1} \\ \text{integer-1} \end{cases}$ $\underline{\text{TIMES}}$

†<u>PERFORM</u> procedure-name-1 [<u>THRU</u> procedure-name-2] <u>VARYING</u> data-name-2

    <u>FROM</u> $\begin{Bmatrix} \text{data-name-3} \\ \text{literal-1} \end{Bmatrix}$ <u>BY</u> $\begin{Bmatrix} \text{data-name-4} \\ \text{literal-2} \end{Bmatrix}$ <u>UNTIL</u> condition-1

<u>STOP</u> $\begin{Bmatrix} \text{literal} \\ \underline{\text{RUN}} \end{Bmatrix}$

Extended Control Verbs: HOLD, PROCESS, SEARCH, SET.

3.3   Specification Statements

Specification statements ordinarily relate to data and its attributes, which are specified in section 2.3.4. Specification statements in the Procedure Division are termed declaratives and must be included in the declaratives section.

†<u>USE</u> <u>AFTER</u> STANDARD <u>ERROR</u> <u>PROCEDURE</u> ON

$$\begin{Bmatrix} \text{file-name-1 } [\,, \text{file-name-2}] \dots \\ \underline{\text{INPUT}} \\ \underline{\text{OUTPUT}} \\ \underline{\text{INPUT-OUTPUT}} \\ \underline{\text{I-O}} \end{Bmatrix}$$

Extended Specification Verb: DEFINE.

3.4   Input/Output Statements

<u>ACCEPT</u> data-name [<u>FROM</u> mnemonic-name]

<u>CLOSE</u> $\left\{ \text{file-name-1} \begin{bmatrix} \underline{\text{REEL}} \\ \underline{\text{UNIT}} \end{bmatrix} \begin{bmatrix} \text{WITH} \begin{Bmatrix} \underline{\text{NO REWIND}} \\ \underline{\text{LOCK}} \end{Bmatrix} \end{bmatrix} \right\} \dots$

<u>DISPLAY</u> $\begin{Bmatrix} \text{literal-1} \\ \text{data-name-1} \end{Bmatrix} \begin{bmatrix} , \text{literal-2} \\ , \text{data-name-2} \end{bmatrix} \dots$ [<u>UPON</u> mnemonic-name]

<u>OPEN</u> [<u>INPUT</u> $\left\{ \text{file-name} \begin{matrix} \underline{\text{REVERSED}} \\ \text{WITH} \underline{\text{NO}} \text{ REWIND} \end{matrix} \right\} \dots$]

    [<u>OUTPUT</u> {file-name [WITH <u>NO</u> REWIND]} . . .]

    $\begin{bmatrix} \underline{\text{I-O}} \\ \underline{\text{INPUT-OUTPUT}} \end{bmatrix}$ {file-name} . . .

†<u>READ</u> file-name RECORD [<u>INTO</u> data-name]

    AT <u>END</u> imperative-statement

<u>WRITE</u> record-name [<u>FROM</u> data-name]

    [<u>INVALID KEY</u> imperative-statement]

Extended Input/Output Verbs: GENERATE, INITIATE, RELEASE, RETURN, SEEK, SORT, TERMINATE.

3.5   Program Structure Statements

        <u>ENTER</u> language-name [routine-name].

        paragraph-name.   <u>EXIT.</u>

$$\left\{\begin{array}{l}\text{paragraph-name,}\\ \text{section-name } \underline{\text{SECTION.}}\end{array}\right\} \quad \underline{\text{INCLUDE}} \text{ library-name.}$$

$$\underline{\text{NOTE}} \text{ character-string.}$$

4. BUILT-IN FUNCTIONS

No functions are provided in the reference language.

5. SPECIAL TOPICS

5.1 Picture Specifications

5.1.1 Basic Facts

Function: To describe the general characteristics and editing requirements of an elementary item.

Format:

$$\underline{\text{PICTURE}} \text{ IS } \left\{\begin{array}{l}\text{alpha-form}\\ \text{an-form}\\ \text{numeric-form}\\ \text{report-form}\end{array}\right\}$$

Picture characters:

    B—insertion character in the report-form.
    0—insertion character in the report-form.
    .—insertion character in the report-form.
    ,—insertion character in the report-form.
    +—sign control character in the report-form.
    - —sign control character in the report-form.
  CR—sign control character in the report-form.
  DB—sign control character in the report-form.
    *—suppression character in the report-form.
    $—suppression character in the report-form.
    Z—zero suppress character in the report-form.
    9—digit position character in the report-form or the numeric-form.
    V—character indicating the position of the assumed decimal point in the report-form or the numeric-form.
    P—precision character in the report-form or the numeric-form.
    S—operational sign character in the numeric-form.
    A—the only permitted character in the alpha-form.
    X—the only permitted character in the an-form.

5.1.2 Alphabetic Form (alpha-form)

Characters permitted: A
Example: PICTURE IS A (13).

5.1.3 Alphanumeric Form (an-form)

Characters permitted: X
Example: PICTURE IS XXX.

5.1.4   Numeric Form (numeric form)

Characters permitted: 9 V P S
Example: PICTURE IS S9 (4)PPV.

5.1.5   Report Form (report-form)

Characters permitted: 9 V P . Z * CR DB , 0 B S + −.
Example: PICTURE IS $$,$$$.99DB.

5.2   Identification Division Skeleton

     IDENTIFICATION DIVISION.
     PROGRAM-ID.   program-name.
     [AUTHOR.   comment-paragraph.]
     [INSTALLATION.   comment-paragraph.]
     [DATE-WRITTEN.   comment-paragraph.]
     [DATE-COMPILED.   comment-paragraph.]
     [SECURITY.   comment paragraph.]
     [REMARKS.   comment paragraph.]

5.3   Environment Division Skeleton

     ENVIRONMENT DIVISION.
     CONFIGURATION SECTION.
     SOURCE-COMPUTER.   source-computer entry
     OBJECT-COMPUTER.   object-computer entry
     [SPECIAL-NAMES.   special-names entry]
     INPUT-OUTPUT SECTION.
     FILE-CONTROL.   file-control entry
     [I-O-CONTROL.   input-output-control entry]

6.   REFERENCES

COBOL, Edition 1965, Department of Defense, U.S. Government Printing Office, Washington, D.C.

APPENDIX C
FORTRAN

1. INTRODUCTION

The purpose of FORTRAN is to provide a programming language with which the scientific community can prepare programs for execution on a digital computer with a minimum of involvement. The language closely resembles the notation of ordinary mathematics, and built-in functions are available for executing most basic mathematical functions, such as the square root and the trigonometric functions. Additional facilities are available which permit the programmer to define his own functions and subroutines as well. Because of its mathematical nature, the language is computation oriented, deals with words of data, and possesses a limited number of data types. As a result, FORTRAN is not generally amenable to applications that involve character or file operations.

The first FORTRAN compiler was developed by the IBM Corporation for their Type 704 computer and released to customers in 1957. The language satisfied an obvious void in programming and has achieved tremendous success. In fact, the language has eveolved from a limited subset to a comprehensive programming language recognized by the American Standards Association.

2. BASIC PROGRAM STRUCTURE

2.1   Program Elements

2.1.1   Characters

A program unit composed of letters, digits, and special characters are described in Table C.1.

239

TABLE C.1   FORTRAN CHARACTER SET

Letters
A,B,C,D,E,F,G,H,I,J,K,L,M,N,O,P,
Q,R,S,T,U,V,W,X,Y,Z

Digits
0,1,2,3,4,5,6,7,8,9,

Special Characters

	Blank
=	Equals
+	Plus
−	Minus
*	Asterisk
/	Slash
(	Left Parenthesis
)	Right Parenthesis
,	Comma
.	Decimal Point (Period)
$	Dollar Sign

2.1.2   Operators

FORTRAN operators may be of three types: arithmetic operators, relational operators, and logical operators. As listed in Table C.2, FORTRAN operators may consist of special characters or a series of letters enclosed in periods.

2.1.3   Delimiters

FORTRAN requires no delimiter characters other than those required by a particular statement itself. The blank character is not significant and may be included anywhere, except in hollerith literals and FORMAT statements, to improve the appearance of the program.

2.1.4   Identifiers

An identifier consists of from one to six letters or digits, the first of which must be alphabetic. Identifiers can be used to name the following items:

1. Scalar variable names
2. Array names
3. Names of common blocks
4. Subprogram names
5. Keywords

2.1.5   Keywords

A keyword is an identifier which is part of the language, although they are *not* reserved words. They are classified as: statement identifiers, and built-in function names. A *statement identifier* is a sequence of one or more keywords used to

TABLE C.2   FORTRAN OPERATORS

1. Arithmetic	
Operator	*Meaning*
+	Addition or positive value (zero + element)
−	Subtraction or negative value (zero − element)
*	Multiplication
/	Division
**	Exponentiation
2. Relational	
Operator	*Meaning*
.LT.	Less than
.LE.	Less than or equal to
.EQ.	Equal to
.NE.	Not equal to
.GT.	Greater than
.GE.	Greater than or equal to
3. Logical	
Operator	*Meaning*
.OR.	Logical disjunction
.AND.	Logical conjunction
.NOT.	Logical negation

indicate a specific type of statement. Examples:

DO
WRITE
GOTO

A *built-in function name* is a keyword which represents a subroutine supplied by the compiler; the function is referenced by using its name in an arithmetic or logical expression with appropriate arguments. Examples:

SQRT
INT

2.1.6   Statements

A line in FORTRAN is a string of 72 characters, numbered consecutively. Columns one through five are reserved for the statement number, and column six is reserved for the continuation indicator. An initial line contains a statement number or blanks in columns one through five and a zero or blank in column six. A continuation line contains blanks in columns one through five and a character other than a zero or blank in column six. A FORTRAN statement is then an initial line followed optionally by from one to nineteen continuation lines.

2.1.7   Comments

The letter C in column one of a line designates that line as a comments line. Commentary information may be placed in columns two through seventy-two.

2.2   Programs

2.2.1   Simple Statements

A *simple statement* is a statement composed of a statement number (optionally), a statement identifier (also optional), and a statement body. If the statement identifier does not appear, then the statement is an assignment statement. Examples:

$$DO \ 50 \ I = 1,10$$
$$192 \ A = B + C$$

In the first statement DO is the keyword. The second statement contains a statement number but no keyword.

2.2.2   Statement Prefixes

FORTRAN contains one type of statement prefix, which is the statement number. A statement number consists of from one to five digits and may be placed anywhere in columns one through five of the initial line of a statement. Leading zeros are not significant.

2.2.3   Loops

The DO statement in FORTRAN provides the facility for program looping. The components of a DO loop are the DO statement, the range of the DO (i.e., those executable statements from and including the first executable statement following the DO), to and including the terminal statement associated with the DO), and the control variable* which is used to control the number of times the loop is executed. The DO statement is described in section 3.2. Example:

$$DO \ 50 \ I = 1,10$$
$$50 \ A(I) = B(I+3) - 13.2$$

2.2.4   Compound Statements

A *compound statement* is a statement which contains other program elements. FORTRAN contains one compound statement which is the logical IF statement described in section 3.2. Example:

$$IF(A + 34.2 \ .GT.E) \ A = (DELTA + 1.0) ** 2$$

2.2.5   Blocks

FORTRAN contains no procedure blocks but allows blocks of data to be allocated in COMMON storage. See section 2.3.4.

2.2.6   Procedures

There are four categories of procedures: statement functions, built-in functions, external functions, and external subroutines. *Statement functions* are one-statement functions defined by the programmer. *Built-in functions* are basic algorith-

*Often called an induction variable.

mic processes provided by the compiler. An *external function* is defined externally to the program that references it. It is defined by a set of FORTRAN statements and headed by a FUNCTION statement. All functions are referenced by their appearance in an arithmetic or logical statement. Similarly, an *external subroutine* is also defined externally to the program which references it and is defined by a set of FORTRAN statements, which are headed by the SUBROUTINE statement. An external subroutine is referenced with the CALL statement. External functions and external subroutines are both terminated with the END statement.

2.2.7   Programs

A FORTRAN program is a main program plus any number of external subprograms. A *main program* is a collection of statements and comments lines terminated with an END statement, while a *subprogram* is either an external FUNCTION or an external SUBROUTINE. A main program must contain at least one executable statement.

2.3   Data

2.3.1   Data Organization

Data may be organized as scalars or arrays. A scalar item may be either a *constant* or a *scalar variable*. A constant is a data item which stands for itself. As described in section 2.3.3, a constant is defined for each type of problem data. A scalar variable also denotes a data item but may assume different values during the execution of a program. Data items may also be organized as one-, two-, or three-dimensional arrays. All items in an array must be of the same data type. One-origin indexing is assumed in arrays, and the upper bound for each dimension must be declared in an appropriate specification statement.

2.3.2   Naming

A *simple name* is an identifier that is used to refer to a scalar variable or an entire array. A *subscripted name* is used to refer to an element of an array and is written as an identifier followed by an appropriate number of subscripts separated by commas and enclosed in parentheses. A subscript is one of the following constructs:

$$c * v + k$$
$$c * v - k$$
$$c * v$$
$$v + k$$
$$v - k$$
$$v$$
$$k$$

where c and k are integer constants, and v is a reference to an integer variable.

2.3.3 Data Types

Six types of data are permitted in FORTRAN: integer, real, double precision, complex, logical, or hollerith. Hollerith data may only appear as an argument in the CALL statement or in the DATA initialization statement. All other types of data may be formed from constants, through computations, or be read in from external input devices. Table C.3 describes the permissable constants.

TABLE C.3 FORTRAN CONSTANTS

Type	Description
INTEGER	A whole number, with or without a sign, written without a decimal point. Example: 87, −1362
REAL	A sign or unsigned number with a decimal point optionally followed by the letter E followed by an integer constant termed an exponent. The exponent is a base ten exponential multiplier. The decimal point may be omitted if the exponent is written. Example: 25.1, 13E + 17
DOUBLE PRECISION	A real constant with the E replaced by a D. Example: −.13684000163D4
COMPLEX	An ordered pair of optionally signed real constants separated by commas and enclosed in parentheses. Example: (13., −4.) meaning $13 - 4i$
LOGICAL	The logical constants true and false are written .TRUE. and .FALSE., respectively.
HOLLERITH	An integer constant n followed by an H followed by the n characters comprising the literal. Example: 6H + . */A

2.3.4 Data Description

Specification statements are used to declare the attributes of data and its arrangement in storage. Six types of specification statements are provided: 1. the DIMENSION statement; 2. the COMMON statement; 3. the EQUIVALENCE statement; 4. the EXTERNAL statement; 5. type statements; and 6. the DATA statement. The DIMENSION statement is used to specify the size and dimensions of arrays in storage. The COMMON statement is used to specify that variables or arrays in a main program or subprogram are to share the same storage locations with variables or arrays in other subprograms. The EQUIVALENCE statement provides the capability for controlling the allocation of storage for variables or arrays in a single main program or subprogram. The EXTERNAL statement is used to declare an identifier as an external procedure name. The *type statements* are used to declare the type of variables and arrays and to supply dimension information for arrays. The DATA initialization statement is used to define initial values of variables and arrays. All specification statements are listed in section 3.3.

An identifier that names a scalar variable, an array, or a function may have its type declared in a specification statement. In the absence of an explicit declaration, the type is implied by the first character of the name: I, J, K, L, M, and N imply type INTEGER; any other letter implies type REAL.

2.4   Operations*

2.4.1   Arithmetic Expressions

An arithmetic expression is a combination of arithmetic operators, operands, and parentheses. Parentheses may be used for grouping as required. Operands

TABLE C.4   HIERARCHY OF FORTRAN OPERATORS

Operation	Hierarchy
Evaluation of Functions	1st (highest)
Exponentiation (**)	2nd
Multiplication and Division (* and /)	3rd
Addition and Subtraction (+ and −)	4th
.LT.,.LE.,.EQ.,.NE.,.GE.,.GT.	5th
.NOT.	6th
.AND.	7th
.OR.	8th

may be constants, scalar variables, elements of arrays, and function references. Except for exponentiation, as described below, any operand may be combined with an operand of the same type, and the resultant is of the same type.† In addition, a real operand may be combined with a double precision or complex operand, and the result is of type double precision or complex, respectively.

2.4.2   Relational Expressions

A relational expression is permitted only in the context of a logical expression and consists of two arithmetic expressions separated by a relational operator. A relational expression will have the value true or false as the relation is true or

TABLE C.5   VALID TYPE COMBINATIONS FOR THE EXPONENTIATION
(**)

Base	Exponent	Result
Integer	Integer	Integer
Real	Integer, Real	Real
Real	Double Precision	Double Precision
Double Precision	Real, Double Precision	Double Precision

*Table C.4 gives the hierarchy of arithmetic, relational, and logical operators.
†Table C.5 gives the valid type combinations for the exponentiation operator.

false, respectively. One arithmetic expression may be of type real or double precision, and the other may be either real or double precision, or both may be of type integer.

2.4.3   Logical Expressions

A logical expression has the value true or false and is formed with logical operators and logical elements. A logical element may be a logical expression, a logical constant, or a relational expression.

2.4.4   Operations on Strings

2.4.5   Operations on Structured Operands

Operations on entire arrays is limited to their input and output and the passing of the location of an array from a main program or subprogram to another subprogram.

2.4.6   File Manipulation

Two types of file manipulation are provided in FORTRAN; they are distinguished by the way in which the data is transmitted. The two methods are: 1. FORMAT directed input/output; and 2. unformatted input/output. In the first case, the data is converted, as specified by a given format statement. In the latter case, data is transmitted to and from an external device in an internal form.

2.4.7   Sequence Control

Four types of sequence control statements are permitted in FORTRAN. The four types are: 1. unconditional branches; 2. computed branches; 3. conditional statements; and 4. loop control.

The *unconditional* GOTO statement provides the unconditional branch. Two computed branches are permitted: the *computed* GOTO and the *assigned* GOTO. Two conditional statements are available: the *arithmetic* IF and the *logical* IF. Loop control is available through the DO *statement* (see section 2.2.3).

3.   STATEMENTS OF THE LANGUAGE

The functions performed by the statements of the FORTRAN language are summarized in Table C.6. The following sections list the skeleton entries for each of the statements. Necessary definitions are given at the end of each section.

3.1   Data Manipulation Statements

> *arithmetic-variable = arithmetic-expression*
> *logical-variable = logical-expression*
> ASSIGN *statement-number* TO *integer-scalar-variable*

TABLE C.6   STATEMENTS OF THE FORTRAN LANGUAGE

ASSIGN	Assigns a statement number to an integer variable for use with the assigned GOTO statement.
Assignment	Evaluates expressions and assigns values to variables.
BACKSPACE	Backspaces an input/output unit one record.
BLOCK DATA	Enters initial values into elements of labeled common-blocks.
CALL	Invokes a designated subroutine and gives actual parameters (if any).
COMMON	Designates common areas of storage between main program or subprogram and another subprogram.
CONTINUE	A dummy statement not affecting the sequence of execution.
DATA	Initializes variables at compile time.
DIMENSION	Declares size of arrays.
DO	Provides controlled looping facilities.
END	Designates end of main program or subprogram.
END FILE	Writes an end-of-data marker.
EQUIVALENCE	Provides for controlling the allocation of storage within a single main program or subprogram.
EXTERNAL	Declares an identifier as an external procedure name.
FORMAT	Specifies form of data to be transmitted.
FUNCTION	Signifies the beginning of an external function, gives its name, and identifies its arguments.
GOTO	Causes control to be transferred to a given statement.
IF	Provides for control to be transferred conditionally or for conditional execution of another statement.
PAUSE	Provides temporary halt in execution.
READ	Causes data to be transmitted from an input device.
RETURN	Ends execution of subprograms and returns control to invoking program.
REWIND	Repositions an input/output unit at the beginning of a set of data.
Statement Function	Provides a one-statement arithmetic or logical function.
STOP	Terminates program execution.
SUBROUTINE	Signifies the beginning of an external subroutine and gives its name and arguments.
Type Statements	Declares the type of scalar variables, arrays, and functions and gives the dimension of arrays.
WRITE	Causes data to be transmitted to an output device.

3.2 Control Statements

GOTO *statement-number*
GOTO (*statement-number* [, *statement-number*] ...), *integer-scalar-variable*
GOTO *integer-scalar-variable*, (*statement-number* [, *statement-number*] ...)
IF (*arithmetic-expression*) *statement-number, statement-number, statement-number*
IF (*logical-expression*) *executable-statement*[1]
DO *statement-number integer-scalar-variable* = *initial-value, test-value*
    [, *increment*][2]
PAUSE [*integer-constant*]
STOP [*integer-constant*]
CONTINUE

[1] Any executable statement other than a DO or another logical IF statement is permitted.

[2] The *initial-value, test-value,* and *increment* must be unsigned integer constants greater than zero or *integer-scalar-variables* with unsigned values greater than zero. If the *increment* is omitted it is assumed to be one.

3.3 Specification Statements

COMMON [/*block-name*/] $\begin{Bmatrix} scalar\text{-}variable \\ array\text{-}declarator \end{Bmatrix}$ $\begin{bmatrix} , scalar\text{-}variable \\ , array\text{-}declarator \end{bmatrix}$ ...

　　[, [/*block-name*/] $\begin{Bmatrix} scalar\text{-}variable \\ array\text{-}declarator \end{Bmatrix}$ $\begin{bmatrix} , scalar\text{-}variable \\ , array\text{-}declarator \end{bmatrix}$ ...] ...

DATA *variable*[4] [, *variable*] ... /[*integer-constant* *] *value*[5]
　　[, [*integer-constant* *] *value*] ... / [, *variable* [, *variable*] ... /
　　[*integer-constant* *] *value* [, [*integer-constant* *] *value*] ... /] ...

DIMENSION *array-declarator* [, *array-declarator*] ...
EQUIVALENCE (*variable*[3], *variable* [, *variable*] ...)
　　[, (*variable, variable* [, *variable*] ...)] ...
EXTERNAL *subprogram-name* [, *subprogram-name*] ...

$\begin{Bmatrix} INTEGER \\ REAL \\ DOUBLE\ PRECISION \\ COMPLEX \\ LOGICAL \end{Bmatrix}$ $\begin{Bmatrix} scalar\text{-}variable \\ array\text{-}declarator \\ function\text{-}name \end{Bmatrix}$ $\begin{bmatrix} , scalar\text{-}variable \\ , array\text{-}declarator \\ , function\text{-}name \end{bmatrix}$ ...

[3] *Variable* is a scalar or subscripted variable. A position within a 2-or 3-dimensional array may be denoted with one subscript.

[4] *Variable* is a *scalar-variable* or an element of an array.

[5] Values may be integer, real, double precision, complex, logical, or hollerith constants.

3.4 Input/Output Statements

READ (*unit-number*[, *format-statement-number*]) [*list*][6]
WRITE (*unit-number*[, *format-statement-number*]) [*list*]
REWIND *unit-number*
BACKSPACE *unit-number*
ENDFILE *unit-number*
statement-number FORMAT (*format-specification*)[7]

[6]A *list* is a simple list, a simple list enclosed in parentheses, a DO-implied list, or two lists separated by commas. A simple list is a *scalar-variable*, an array element, an array name, or two simple lists separated by a comma. A DO-implied list is a list followed by a comma and a DO specification of the form: *integer-scalar-variable* = *initial-value, test-value* [, *increment*], all enclosed in parentheses.

[7]Format specifications are described in section 5.1.

3.5 Program Structure Statements

$$\left\lceil \left\{ \begin{matrix} \text{INTEGER} \\ \text{REAL} \\ \text{DOUBLE PRECISION} \\ \text{COMPLEX} \\ \text{LOGICAL} \end{matrix} \right\} \right\rceil \text{FUNCTION } function\text{-}name\,(argument^8\,[\,,argument\,]\dots)$$

SUBROUTINE *subroutine-name* [(*argument*[8] [, *argument*] ...)]
RETURN
END
statement-function-name (*argument*[9] [, *argument*] ...) = *arithmetic-expression*
statement-function-name (*argument* [, *argument*] ...) = *logical-expression*
BLOCK DATA[10]
CALL *subroutine-name* [(*argument*[11] [, *argument*] ...)]

[8]*Arguments* in FUNCTION or SUBROUTINE statements are dummy arguments and represent scalar-variables, arrays, or external procedure names.

[9]*Arguments* in a statement-function statement must represent distinct variable identifiers.

[10]A BLOCK DATA subprogram is a type of subprogram which may contain only specification statements. It is used to initialize area of labeled COMMON.

[11]*Arguments* in a CALL statement may be one of the following: 1. a Hollerith constant; 2. an arithmetic or logical expression; 3. an array name; and 4. the name of an external procedure.

4. BUILT-IN FUNCTIONS

Built-in functions is a general category which refers to intrinsic functions and basic external functions. The FORTRAN functions are summarized in Table C.7. They

TABLE C.7   FORTRAN FUNCTIONS

Function	Definition	Symbolic Names
Absolute value	$\lvert a \rvert$	ABS, IABS, or DABS
Truncation	Sign of a times largest integer $\leq a$	AINT, INT, or IDINT
Remaindering	$a_1 \pmod{a_2}$	AMOD, MOD, or DMOD
Largest Value	$\max(a_1, a_2, \dots)$	AMAX0, AMAX1, MAX0, MAX1, or DMAX1
Smallest Value	$\min(a_1, a_2, \dots)$	AMIN0, AMIN1, MIN0, MIN1, or DMIN1
Float	Conversion from integer to real	FLOAT
Fix	Conversion from real to integer	IFIX
Transfer of Sign	Sign of a_2 times $\lvert a_1 \rvert$	SIGN, ISIGN, or DSIGN
Positive Difference	$a_1 - \min(a_1, a_2)$	DIM or IDIM
Obtain Most Significant Part of Double Precision Argument		SNGL
Obtain Real Part of Complex Argument		REAL
Obtain Imaginary Part of Complex Argument		AIMAG
Express Single Precision Argument in Double Precision Form		DBLE
Express Two Real Arguments in Complex Form	$a_1 + a_2 i$	CMPLX
Obtain Conjugate of a Complex Argument		CONJG
Exponential	e^a	EXP, DEXP, or CEXP
Natural Logarithm	$\log_e(a)$	ALOG, DLOG, or **CLOG**
Common Logarithm	$\log_{10}(a)$	ALOG10 or DLOG10
Trigonometric Sine	$\sin(a)$	SIN, DSIN, or CSIN
Trigonometric Cosine	$\cos(a)$	COS, DCOS, or CCOS
Hyperbolic Tangent	$\tanh(a)$	TANH
Square Root	$(a)^{1/2}$	SQRT, DSQRT, or CSQRT
Arctangent	$\arctan(a)$	ATAN or DATAN
Arctangent	$\arctan(a_1/a_2)$	ATAN2 or DATAN2
Modulus		CABS

can be regarded, perhaps, as a minimum set to be provided with any compiler or operating system.

5.   SPECIAL TOPICS

5.1   Format Specifications

The FORMAT statement is used with the READ and WRITE statements to specify the desired form of data to be transmitted. The statement is of the form:

$$\text{FORMAT } (q_1 t_1 z_1 t_2 z_2 \ldots t_n z_n q_2)$$

where:

1. $(q_1 t_1 z_1 t_2 z_2 \ldots t_n z_n q_2)$ is the format specification.
2. Each q is a series of slashes or is empty.
3. Each t is a field descriptor or group of field descriptors.
4. Each z is a field separator (comma, slash, series of slashes, or parentheses).
5. n may be zero.

The format field descriptors are of the forms:

$$srFw.d$$
$$srEw.d$$
$$srGw.d$$
$$srDw.d$$
$$rIw$$
$$rLw$$
$$rAw$$
$$nHc_1 c_2 \ldots c_n$$
$$nX$$

where:

1. The letters F, E, G, D, I, L, A, H, and X indicate the manner of conversion and editing between the internal and external representations and are called the *conversion codes*. They may be used as follows:

   F —to transfer real data without an exponent;
   E — to transfer real data with an E exponent;
   G—to transfer integer, real, complex, or logical data;
   D—to transfer real data with a D exponent;
   I —to transfer integer data;
   L —to transfer logical data;
   A—to transfer alphanumeric data;
   H—to transfer Hollerith (literal) data;
   X —to either skip data when reading or insert blanks when writing;

2. w and n are nonzero integer constants representing the width of the field in the external character string.

3. *d* is an integer constant representing the number of digits in the fractional part of the external character string (except for G conversion code).
4. *r*, the repeat count, is an optional nonzero integer constant indicating the number of times to repeat the succeeding field descriptor.
5. *s* is optional and represents a scale factor designator.
6. Each *c* is one of the characters in the FORTRAN character set.

Field designators or *field separators* may be grouped by enclosing them in parentheses. Repetition of a group is accomplished by preceding the left parenthesis by an integer constant representing the repeat count.

A *scale factor designator* is defined for use with the F, E, G, and D conversions and is of the form:

$$nP$$

where *n*, the scale factor, is an integer constant or minus followed by an integer constant.

6.   REFERENCES

"FORTRAN vs. Basic FORTRAN," *Comm. ACM*, Vol. 7, No. 10 (Oct., 1964).
American Standard FORTRAN, American Standards Association, Inc., March, 1966.

APPENDIX D
PL/I

1. INTRODUCTION

PL/I is a higher-level programming language designed jointly by IBM and the SHARE organization. It is intended for use in scientific and commercial applications and for the great many additional applications which possess features of both. One of the major objectives of the language is modularity, enabling users with different applications and at different experience levels to utilize its facilities effectively. A programmer in one category need not know of unused features which apply to another category.

Some of the outstanding features of PL/I are listed as follows:

1. Versatile I/O,
2. Wide variety of data formats and operand types,
3. Dynamic storage allocation,
4. Asynchronous processing,
5. Compile-time facilities,
6. Block structure, and
7. List processing facilities.

The first PL/I compiler was delivered to the field by IBM in September, 1966. Although its history has been short, PL/I has attracted considerable attention from government, business, and the academic world.

253

2. BASIC PROGRAM STRUCTURE

2.1   Program Elements

2.1.1   Characters

The reference version of PL/I uses the 60-character set shown in Table D.1. As an extended feature of the language, a 48-character set is defined, which utilizes character sequences to represent those that have been omitted.

TABLE D.1   PL/I CHARACTERS

---

1. *Alphabetic characters:* A through Z, currency symbol ($), commercial AT-sign (@), number sign (#).
2. *Digits:* decimal digits (0 through 9), binary digits (0 and 1).
3. *Alphameric characters:* alphabetic character or a digit.
4. *Special characters:*

Name	Graphic
Blank	
Equal or assignment symbol	=
Plus	+
Minus	−
Asterisk or multiply symbol	*
Slash or divide symbol	/
Left parenthesis	(
Right parenthesis	)
Comma	,
Decimal point or period	.
Quotation mark	'
Percent symbol	%
Semicolon	;
Colon	:
Not symbol	¬
And symbol	&
Or symbol	|
Greater than symbol	>
Less than symbol	<
Break—character	—
Question mark	?

2.1.2   Operators

Four types of operators are used in PL/I: arithmetic operators, relational operators, logical operators, and string operators. Logical operators are termed *bit string* operators, since true and false values are represented by 1 and 0, respectively. The PL/I operators are summarized in Table D.2.

TABLE D.2   PL/I OPERATORS

Arithmetic Operator	Meaning
+	infix addition or prefix plus
−	infix subtraction or prefix minus
*	multiplication
/	division
**	exponentiation

Comparison Operator	Meaning
>	greater than
¬>	not greater than
>=	greater than or equal to
=	equal to
¬=	not equal to
<=	less than or equal to
<	less than
¬<	not less than

Bit-String Operator (logical)	Meaning
¬	not
&	and
|	or
||	concatenation

2.1.3   Delimiters

Delimiters are used to separate statements, words, names, and expressions, and to denote labels, assignment statements, compile-time statements, picture specifications, string constants, and pointers. Delimiters are summarized in Table D.3.

2.1.4   Identifiers

An *identifier* is a string of not more than 31 characters formed from the alphameric characters and the break character; the first character of an identifier must be alphabetic. Identifiers may be used for:

1. Scalar variable names,
2. Array names,
3. Structure names,
4. Statement labels,
5. Entry names,
6. File names,
7. Keywords.

TABLE D.3   PL/I DELIMITERS

Name	Graphic	Use
parentheses	(and)	grouping in expressions; enclosing lists
comma	,	separates elements of a list
semicolon	;	terminates statements
assignment symbol	=	used in assignment statement and DO statement
colon	:	follows labels and condition prefixes; also used with dimension specifications
blank		used as a separator
quotation mark	'	encloses string constants and picture specifications
period	.	separates items in qualified names; used as a decimal or binary point in constants
percent	%	precedes macro statement
pointer qualification symbol	->	qualifies a reference to a based variable

2.1.5   Keywords

A *keyword* is an identifier which is part of the language, although they are *not* reserved words. They are classified as:

1. Statement identifiers,
2. Attributes,
3. Separating keywords,
4. Built-in function names,
5. Option names,
6. Conditions.

A *statement identifier* indicates a type of statement; e.g.,

PUT
DECLARE
DO

An *attribute* specifies the properties of a program element, e.g.,

FIXED
RECURSIVE

Separating keywords separate parts of the IF and DO statements; e.g.,

ELSE
TO

Built-in function names represent subprograms supplied by the compiler; e.g.,

SUBSTR
CEIL

An *option* affects the execution of a statement; e.g.,

BY NAME

A *condition* specifies an event for which special action must be taken; e.g.,

OVERFLOW

2.1.6 Statements

The input stream to the PL/I compiler is considered to be a continuous string of characters. Thus, statements may be continued to succeeding logical records, as required (see section 2.2.1).

2.1.7 Comments

A comment is permitted in PL/I wherever a blank may be used and is of the form:

/*   character string   */

2.2 Programs

2.2.1 Simple Statements

A simple statement is a sequence of the form:

[*statement identifier*] *statement-body*;

If the statement identifier is omitted, then the statement is an assignment statement; e.g.,

```
DO I = 1 TO 10;        (DO is the statement identifier)
X = Y + 1;             (statement identifier omitted)
```

A null statement is permitted for which the programmer need only include the semicolon.

2.2.2 Prefixes

Two types of prefixes are permitted: label prefixes and condition prefixes. The label prefix is a statement label written as follows:

identifier: [*identifier*:] ... *statement*

Statement labels permit statements to be named (for branching, etc.) and also name procedures and entry points. Condition prefixes specify the conditions under which a program interrupt will occur and are of the form:

(*condition-name*[, *condition name*] ...): [*label*:] ... *statement*

2.2.3 Loops

The DO group in PL/I provides a controlled looping facility. A *group* is a collection of one or more statements used for control purposes. The DO group (or simply the DO loop) is written as follows:

[*label*:] . . . DO-*statement*
statement-1
statement-2
.
.
END [*label*];

For example,

LOOPA: DO I = 1 TO 10;
A (I) = B (I) + C (I);
END LOOPA;

2.2.4 Compound Statements

A compound statement contains other program elements. The IF and ON statements are used in this manner; e.g.,

IF X < 0 THEN Y = 0; ELSE Y = X * * Z;
ON SIZE GOTO BOMB__OUT;

2.2.5 Blocks

A block defines a program region for purposes of combining statements or for denoting the scope of variables. Blocks are delimited by the keywords BEGIN and END and permit internal declarations. Two types of block exist: the begin block and the procedure block. The begin block is defined as follows:

[*label*:] . . . BEGIN;
statement-1
statement-2
.
.
END [*label*];

The procedure block is defined similarly:

label: [*label*:] . . . PROCEDURE-*statement*
statement-1
statement-2
.
.
END [*label*];

The PROCEDURE statement is defined in section 3.5.

2.2.6 Procedures

The procedure block is defined in section 2.2.5. Two types of procedure are permitted: function procedures and subroutine procedures. Function procedures are evoked by their presence in an expression. Subroutine procedures are evoked with the CALL statement. Moreover, procedures may be written internal to a program unit (program or external procedure) or external to it. Standard conventions with respect to local and global variables apply to internal procedures.

2.2.7 Programs

A program is a collection of one or more external procedures, one of which must be given the attribute MAIN.

2.3   Data

2.3.1 Data Organization

Data may be organized as scalars, arrays, or structures. Scalar data may be constants or scalar variables. Arrays may be n-dimensional, and all elements must have the same attributes. Moreover, upper and lower bounds for subscript values may be declared. A structure is a hierarchical collection of scalar variables, arrays, and other structures; i.e., structures may contain other structures. An example of a structure is:

$$\text{DECLARE 1 A, 2 B, 2 C, 3 D(2), 2 E;}$$

which has the form:

```
                A
                    B
                    C
                        D(1)
                        D(2)
                    E
```

An array of structures may be declared by giving a dimension attribute to a structure; using the preceding example, it would be transformed to an array of structures as follows:

$$\text{DECLARE 1 A(3), 2 B, \ldots}$$

2.3.2 Naming

Data may be named in 3 ways: by simple names, by subscripted names, and by qualified names. A *simple name* is an identifier and names a scalar item. A *subscripted name* is used to refer to an element of an array; e.g.,

$$\text{X(2)}$$
$$\text{VALUE(I}+2*\text{J, B)}$$

The cross section of an array may be denoted by replacing the appropriate subscript with an asterisk; e.g.,

$$XDOT(I,*)$$

which denotes the Ith row of array XDOT.

Unique data items with the same name may be declared in different structures. A valid reference requires a *qualified name* defined as follows:

$$identifier . identifier [. identifier] . . .$$

For example,

NAME.OLD MASTER

Qualified names may also be subscripted as required.

Any expression may be used as a subscript. At execution-time, it is evaluated and converted to an integer.

2.3.3 Data Types

Data is classified as problem data or program control data. Problem data is further classified as arithmetic data and string data.

The following characteristics of arithmetic data may be specified: BASE (decimal or binary), SCALE (fixed point or floating point), MODE (real or complex), and PRECISION (number of digits of accuracy). Table D.4 lists the arithmetic data types.

TABLE D.4   PL/I ARITHMETIC DATA

Type	Definition
Decimal fixed point constant	Decimal digits with an optional decimal point; e.g., 123.45.
Binary fixed point constant	Binary digits with an optional binary point followed by a B; e.g., 1101B or 101.1011B.
Sterling fixed point constant	Decimal integer, decimal point, decimal integer less than 20, decimal point, decimal integer less than 12, an L; e.g., 20.13.8L.
Decimal floating point constant	Decimal digits with an optional decimal point, the letter E, an optionally signed integer; e.g., 15E-2, .418E19.
Binary floating point constant	Binary digits with an optional binary point, the letter E, decimal exponent, the letter B; e.g., 1.101E-8B.
Imaginary constant	Real arithmetic constant followed by the letter I; e.g., 21.3I.

String data may be of type character string or bit string. A character string is written as follows:

$$[(replication\text{-}factor)]\ `character\text{-}sequence\text{'}$$

For example,

'ABC /2, 1Z'
(5) 'AB'

Bit string data consists of binary digits enclosed in quotation marks, followed by the letter **B**, and optionally preceded by a replication factor; i.e.,

$$[(replication\text{-}factor)]\ `binary\text{-}digits\text{'}\ B$$

For example,

'10101'B
(6)'1'B

Program control data is data that can be classified as type label, task, event, pointer, area, or cell. These types of data are summarized in Table D.5.

TABLE D.5   PL/I PROGRAM CONTROL DATA

Type	Definition
Label	Identifier that appears as a statement label.
Task	Name of a task; assigned a value with the PRIORITY pseudo-variable.
Event	Name of an event has the value "not completed" or "completed"; assigned with the EVENT pseudo-variable.
Pointer	Used to identify a based variable.
Area	Name of an area in storage and used with based variables and the ALLOCATE statement.
Cell	A unit of storage which may contain a number of alternative declarations.

2.3.4   Data Description

An identifier is established as a named data type, explicitly with the DECLARE statement or implicitly through implicit or contextual* declarations.

The general form of a DECLARE statement is as follows:

DECLARE [level] name [attribute] ...
[, [level] name [attribute] ...] ...;

Attributes common to more than one name declaration may be factored to eliminate repeated specifications; e.g.,

DECLARE (A, B, C, D) FLOAT;

*Such as a file name or a statement label.

TABLE D.6   PL/I DATA ATTRIBUTES

Attribute	Function	Format
Base	Specifies the internal form of data	BINARY | DECIMAL
Scale	Specifies fixed or floating point representation	FIXED | FLOAT
Mode	Specifies real or complex data	REAL | COMPLEX
Precision	Specifies the number of significant digits (must follow base, scale, or mode attributes)	(*number-of-digits* [, *scale-factor*])
Picture	Specifies internal and external data formats and the editing of data	PICTURE '*picture-specifications*'
String	Specifies the form of string data	$\left\{ \begin{array}{l} \text{BIT} \\ \text{CHARACTER} \end{array} \right\}$ (*length*) [VARYING]
Label	Specifies a variable that will have labels as values	LABEL [(*statement-label* [, *statement-label*] ...)]
Task	Specifies a task name	TASK
Event	Specifies an event name	EVENT
Dimension	Specifies the bounds of an array	(*bound* [, *bound*] ...) where bound is: [*lower-bound*:] *upper-bound*
Secondary	Specifies that data does not need efficient storage	SECONDARY
Abnormal/ Normal	Specifies that a variable may be altered at an unpredictable time (ABNORMAL)	ABNORMAL | NORMAL
Reducible/ Irreducible	Specifies the properties of entry points to enable program optimization	REDUCIBLE | IRREDUCIBLE
Uses/Sets	Specifies the nature of the irreducibility for an entry name	USES (*item* [, *item*] ...) SETS (*item* [, *item*] ...)
Entry	Declares entry points to procedures	ENTRY [(*parameter-attribute-list* [, *parameter-attribute-list*] ...)]
Generic	Declares a family of entry names	GENERIC (*entry-name-declaration* [, *entry-name-declaration*] ...)

Built-in	Declares an identifier as a reference to a built-in function	BUILTIN
Returns	Specifies the attributes of a data value returned by a procedure	RETURNS (*attribute*...)
Scope	Specifies scope of declared variables	EXTERNAL	INTERNAL
Storage Class	Specifies type of storage desired for a variable	STATIC	AUTOMATIC	CONTROLLED	CONTROLLED (*pointer-variable*)
Aligned/Packed	Specific arrangement of data in storage	ALIGNED	PACKED
Defined	Specifies that data is to occupy storage assigned to other data	DEFINED *base-identifier* (*subscript list*)
Position	Specifies the position in a data field for use with the DEFINED attribute	POSITION (*decimal-integer-constant*)
Cell	Establishes an identifier as naming cell data	CELL *alternative-list*
Initial	Specifies initial values or a procedure to be evoked at allocation	$\left\{\begin{array}{l}\text{INITIAL (}item\text{[},item\text{]}...\text{)} \\ \text{INITIAL CALL }entry\text{-}name \\ \quad\text{[}argument\text{-}list\text{]}\end{array}\right\}$
Like	Specifies a name as having a given structure	LIKE *structure-name*
Pointer	Specifies that an identifier may be used to locate data values	POINTER
Area	Defines an area of storage for collecting and referring to based data items	AREA AREA (*d* [,*d*]...) where *d* is a data declaration without identifiers

TABLE D.7 PL/I FILE ATTRIBUTES

Attribute	Function	Format
File	Specifies a file name	FILE
File Usage	Specifies manner in which a file is to be processed	STREAM | RECORD
Function	Specifies the function of a file	INPUT | OUTPUT | UPDATE
Print	Denotes that the ultimate disposition of data is the printed page	PRINT
Access	Specifies the manner in which records are to be accessed	SEQUENTIAL | DIRECT
Buffering	Specifies if input/output buffering is desired (sequential file)	BUFFERED | UNBUFFERED
Backwards	Specifies that a sequential file is to be accessed in reverse order	BACKWARDS
Exclusive	Specifies that only one task may reference a DIRECT UPDATE file at any one time	EXCLUSIVE
Environment	Specifies implementation dependent characteristics of a file	ENVIRONMENT (*option-list*)
Keyed	Specifies that "key" options may be used to reference a file	KEYED

Arithmetic data have default attributes. If the identifier starts with any of the letters I-N, then the default attributes are FIXED BINARY; otherwise, the default attributes are FLOAT DECIMAL.

Data attributes are summarized in Table D.6. File attributes are listed in Table D.7.

2.4 Operations

2.4.1 Arithmetic Expressions

Arithmic operations are permitted on all data types, except for statement label designators, area data, task data, event data, and pointer data. Conversion to an appropriate internal form is made when necessary. Section 5.5 contains a description of arithmetic and type conversions. The form of an elementary arithmetic operation is as follows:

$$\{\{+ \mid -\}\, operand\,\} \mid \{operand\,\{+ \mid - \mid * \mid / \mid **\}\, operand\,\}$$

Parentheses may be used for grouping. Bit string (logical) and comparison (relational) expressions are permitted in arithmetic expressions; the conversion of intermediate values to arithmetic data is automatically made, utilizing the hierarchy table (Table D.8) and the type conversion conventions (section 5.5).

TABLE D.8 HIERARCHY OF PL/I OPERATORS

Operator	Hierarchy
¬, **, prefix +, prefix −	1st
*; /	2nd
infix +, infix −	3rd
> =, >, ¬>, ¬=, <, ¬<, <=, =	4th
&	5th
|	6th
||	7th

2.4.2 Relational Expressions

Relational (comparison) operators are given in Table D.2. Three types of comparison operations are defined:

1. *Algebraic.* Signed numeric values in coded form are compared. Conversion of data is performed when required.
2. *Character.* Character strings are compared, using the collating sequence, from left-to-right on a character-by-character basis. Shorter operands are extended to the right with blanks.
3. *Bit.* Binary strings are compared from left-to-right on a bit-by-bit basis. Shorter operands are extended to the right with binary zeros.

The result of a comparison operation is a bit string of length one. If the relationship is true, the value is '1'B; otherwise, the value is '0'B.

2.4.3   Logical Expressions

Logical (bit-string) operations have the following form:

$$\neg \; operand$$
$$operand \mid operand$$
$$operand \; \& \; operand$$

The operations are performed on a bit-by-bit basis; shorter operands are extended to the right with binary zeros.

2.4.4   Operations on Strings

Concatenation is the only operation performed on strings and has the form:

$$operand \mid\mid operand$$

If both operands are of bit-string type, the result is bit-string. Otherwise, the operands are converted to type character, when necessary, and the result is of that type. The length of the result is the sum of the lengths of the two operands.

2.4.5   Operations on Structured Operands

Operations are permitted on arrays and on structures. Prefix and infix operators are extended to arrays on an element-by-element basis. With infix operators, one operand may also be a scalar data item.

Prefix and infix operations are also extended to structures with the same structuring, but not necessarily of the same data types. Operations are performed on an element-by-element basis, as with arrays, and one operand may be a scalar data item.

2.4.6   File Manipulation

Two basic methods of input/output are provided in PL/I: stream I/O and record I/O.

1. *Stream I/O.* The data set is regarded as a stream of characters.   The GET and PUT statements are used.
2. *Record I/O.* The data set consists of discrete records.   The READ and WRITE statements are used.

Stream I/O is further classified into list-directed transmission, data-directed transmission, and edit-directed transmission.

1. *List-Directed Transmission.* The user specifies storage area to which data is assigned or from which data is transmitted, without specifying format.
2. *Data-Directed Transmission.* The user is permitted to GET or PUT self-identifying data.
3. *Edit-Directed Transmission.* The user specifies storage areas and format lists for input and output operations.

Table D.9 summarizes the data transmission capabilities.

TABLE D.9 TYPES OF DATA TRANSMISSION

STREAM	DATA *directed*		INPUT			
	LIST *directed*		OUTPUT	[PRINT]		
	EDIT *directed*					
RECORD	*Not keyed*	SEQUENTIAL	BUFFERED	INPUT	*Forwards*	
	KEYED		UNBUFFERED	INPUT	BACKWARDS	
				OUTPUT		
				UPDATE	[REWRITE]	
	KEYED	DIRECT	INPUT			
			OUTPUT			
			UPDATE	[EXCLUSIVE] [UNLOCK] [REWRITE] [DELETE]		

2.4.7   Sequence Control

PL/I provides the capability for unconditional branches, computed branches, conditional statement execution, and controlled looping.

The GOTO statement, where the operand may be a statement-label constant, a scalar variable of type label, or an array variable of type label provides the unconditional and computed branches.

The IF statement of the form:

$$\text{IF } scalar\text{-}expression \text{ THEN } unit\text{-}1 \text{ [ELSE } unit\text{-}2]$$

e.g.,

$$\text{IF A} > \text{B THEN GOTO ERR; ELSE A} = \text{A} + \text{B:}$$

provides conditional statement execution.

Controlled looping is provided with the DO statement discussed in section 2.2.3.

3.   STATEMENTS OF THE LANGUAGE

The functions performed by the statements of PL/I are summarized in Table D.10; skeleton entries are given in this section. Statements marked with the character (†) have additional forms for which the given reference should be consulted.

3.1   Data Manipulation Statements

†*scalar-variable* [, *scalar-variable*] . . . = *scalar-expression*;
†*array* [, *array*] . . . = {*array-expression* | *scalar-expression*};
†*structure* [, *structure*] . . . = *structure-expression* [, BY NAME];
scalar-label-variable [, *scalar-label-variable*] . . . = {*label-constant* |
    scalar-label-variable};
array-label-variable [, *array-label-variable*] . . . = {*label-constant* |
    scalar-label-variable | *array-label-variable*};
pointer-variable [, *pointer-variable*] . . . = *pointer-expression*
array-pointer-variable [, *array-pointer-variable*] . . . = { *pointer-expression* |
    array-pointer-variable};

3.2   Control Statements

DELAY (*scalar-expression*);
DO;
DO WHILE (*scalar-expression*);
†DO *variable* = *specification* [, *specification*] . . .;
    where a "specification" has the format:

$$expression\text{-}1 \begin{bmatrix} \text{TO } expression\text{-}2 & \text{[BY } expression\text{-}3] \\ \text{BY } expression\text{-}3 & \text{[TO } expression\text{-}2] \end{bmatrix} \text{[WHILE } (expression\text{-}4)]$$

TABLE D.10   STATEMENTS OF THE PL/I LANGUAGE

ALLOCATE	Causes storage to be allocated for specified controlled data.
Assignment	Evaluates expressions and assigns values to variables.
BEGIN	Serves as the heading statement of the begin block.
CALL	Invokes a procedure and causes control to be transferred to a specified entry point of the procedure.
CLOSE	Terminates processing of a file.
DECLARE	Specifies identifiers and attributes.
DELAY	Suspends execution of the controlling task for a specified period of time.
DELETE	Deletes a record from a DIRECT UPDATE file.
DISPLAY	Causes a message to be displayed to the machine operator.
DO	Specifies the start of a DO group.
END	Terminates blocks and groups.
ENTRY	Specifies a secondary entry point to a procedure.
EXIT	Causes immediate termination of a task.
FORMAT	Specifies a data format for edited-directed I/O.
FREE	Causes storage for controlled variables to be released.
GET	Causes stream data to be transmitted to data variables.
GOTO	Causes program control to be transferred to a specified statement.
IF	Provides conditional statement execution.
LOCATE	Allows a record to be created in an output buffer.
ON	Specifies action to be taken under interrupt conditions.
OPEN	Initiates processing of a file.
PROCEDURE	Defines a procedure head and gives its attributes and parameters.
PUT	Causes stream data to be transmitted from data variables.
READ	Transfers a data record into internal storage.
RETURN	Terminates execution of a procedure.
REVERT	Nullifies the effect of an ON statement.
REWRITE	Replaces an existing record in an update file.
SIGNAL	Simulates the occurrence of an interrupt.
STOP	Causes immediate termination of the major task and all subtasks.
UNLOCK	Makes a specified locked record available.
WAIT	Suspends execution of a task until a specified event occurs.
WRITE	Transfers a data record from internal storage.

$$\begin{Bmatrix} \text{GO TO} \\ \text{GOTO} \end{Bmatrix} \begin{Bmatrix} \textit{label-constant} \\ \textit{label-variable} \end{Bmatrix};$$

IF *scalar-expression* THEN *unit-1* [ELSE *unit-2*]
†ON *condition* [SNAP] *on-unit*
REVERT *condition*;
SIGNAL *condition*;
WAIT (*event-name* [, *event-name*] . . .)
    [(*scalar-expression*)];

3.3   Specification Statements

DECLARE [*level*] *name* [*attribute*] . . .
    [, [*level*] *name* [*attribute*] . . .] . . . ;
label: [*label*] . . . FORMAT *format-list*;

3.4   Input/Output Statements

CLOSE *options-group* [, *option-group*] . . . ;
    where the format of "options-group" is:
    FILE (*filename*) [IDENT (*argument*)]
DELETE *option-list*;
    where the format of "option-list" is:
    FILE (*filename*) KEY (*expression*) [EVENT (*event-variable*)]
†DISPLAY (*scalar-expression*);
GET [FILE (*filename*) | STRING (*character-string-name*)]
    data-specification [COPY];
LOCATE *variable* FILE (*filename*) SET (*pointer-variable*)
    [KEYFROM (*expression*)];
OPEN *options-group* [, *options-group*] . . . ;
    where the format of "options-group" is:
    FILE (*filename*) [IDENT (*argument*)]
    [TITLE (*expression*)]
    [INPUT | OUTPUT | UPDATE] [STREAM | RECORD]
    [DIRECT | SEQUENTIAL] [BUFFERED | UNBUFFERED]
    [EXCLUSIVE] [KEYED]
    [BACKWARDS] [PRINT]
    [LINESIZE (*expression*)]
    [PAGESIZE (*expression*)]
PUT [FILE (*filename*) | STRING (*character-string-name*)]
    [*data-specification*] [PAGE]
    [SKIP [(*expression*)]]
    [LINE (*expression*)]

READ FILE (*filename*)
⎡INTO (*variable*)   ⎤
⎢SET (*pointer-variable*)   ⎥
⎣IGNORE (*expression*)   ⎦
[KEY (*expression*)]
[KEYTO
  (*character-string-variable*)]
[EVENT (*event-variable*)]
  [NOLOCK];
REWRITE FILE (*filename*) [KEY (*expression*)]
  [FROM (*variable*)]
  [EVENT (*event-variable*)];
UNLOCK FILE (*filename*) KEY (*expression*);
WRITE FILE (*filename*) FROM (*variable*)
  [KEYFROM (*expression*)]
  [EVENT (*event-variable*)];

3.5   Program Structure Statements

†ALLOCATE [*level*] *identifier* [*dimension*] [*attribute*] . . .
  [, [*level*] *identifier* [*dimension*] [*attribute*] . . .] . . . ;
BEGIN;
CALL *entry-name* [(*argument* [, *argument*] . . .)]
  [TASK [(*scalar-task-name*)]]
  [EVENT (*scalar-event-name*)]
  [PRIORITY (*expression*)];
END [*label*];
entry-name: [*entry-name*:] . . . ENTRY
  [(*parameter* [, *parameter*] . . .)]
  [*data-attributes*];
EXIT;
†FREE *identifier* [, *identifier*] . . . ;
entry-name: PROCEDURE [(*parameter* [, *parameter*] . . .)]
  [OPTIONS (*option-list*)]
  [RECURSIVE] [*data-attributes*];
RETURN [(*expression*)];
STOP;

4.   BUILT-IN FUNCTIONS

The great number of built-in functions in PL/I prohibit a description of each. They are classified into the following categories and simply listed:

1. Arithmetic generic functions,
2. Float arithmetic generic functions,

3. String generic functions,
4. Array generic functions,
5. Condition built-in functions,
6. List processing built-in functions,
7. Other built-in functions.

4.1   Arithmetic Generic Functions

ABS	FLOOR
ADD	IMAG
BINARY	MAX
CEIL	MIN
COMPLEX	MOD
CONJG	MULTIPLY
DECIMAL	PRECISION
DIVIDE	REAL
FLOAT	SIGN
FIXED	TRUNC

4.2   Float Arithmetic Generic Functions

ATAN	LOG10
ATAND	LOG2
ATANH	SIN
COS	SIND
COSD	SINH
COSH	SQRT
ERF	TAN
ERFC	TAND
EXP	TANH
LOG	

4.3   String Generic Functions

BIT	LENGTH
BOOL	LOW
CHAR	REPEAT
HIGH	SUBSTR
INDEX	UNSPEC

4.4   Array Generic Functions

ALL	LBOUND
ANY	POLY
DIM	PROD
HBOUND	SUM

4.5 Condition Built-In Functions

DATAFIELD	ONKEY
ONCHAR	ONLOC
ONCODE	ONSOURCE
ONFILE	

4.6 List Processing Built-In Functions

ADDR
NULL

4.7 Other Built-In Functions

ALLOCATION	PRIORITY
COUNT	ROUND
DATE	STRING
EVENT	TIME
LINENO	

5. SPECIAL TOPICS

5.1 Format Lists

5.1.1 General Format

Function: To specify data conversions desired under edited-directed transmission.

$$\left(\left\{ \begin{array}{l} item \\ n\ item \\ n\ format\text{-}list \end{array} \right\} \left[\begin{array}{l} ,item \\ ,n\ item \\ ,n\ format\text{-}list \end{array} \right] \ldots \right)$$

where

n represents an iteration factor,
w represents the length of a data field,
d represents the number of positions after the decimal point,
s represents the number of significant digits to appear, and
p represents the scale factor.

5.1.2 Fixed Point-Items

Format:

$$\left\{ \begin{array}{l} F(w) \\ F(w,d) \\ F(w,d,p) \end{array} \right\}$$

5.1.3 Floating-Point Items

Format:

$$E(w,d\,[,s])$$

5.1.4 Picture Format Items
Format: P '*numeric-picture-specification*'

5.1.5 Bit-String Items
Format: B(w)

5.1.6 Character-String Items
Format:

$$\begin{Bmatrix} A(w) \\ P\text{'}character\text{-}picture\text{-}specification\text{'} \end{Bmatrix}$$

5.1.7 Control Items
Format:

$$\begin{Bmatrix} X(w) \\ \text{PAGE} \\ \text{SKIP}[(w)] \\ \text{LINE}(w) \\ \text{COLUMN}(w) \end{Bmatrix}$$

5.1.8 Remote Format Items
Format:

$$R\,(statement\text{-}label\text{-}designator\,)$$

5.2 Picture Specifications

5.2.1 Basic Facts
Function: To define the internal and external formats of numeric and character string data fields and to specify the editing of data.
General format:
PICTURE '*picture-specification*'

5.2.2 Digit Point and Subfield Delimiters

9 specifies decimal digit position;
V specifies decimal point location;
K specifies start of exponent field;
E inserts the letter E for an exponent.

5.2.3 Zero Suppression Characters

Z specifies replacement of leading zeros with a blank;
* specifies replacement of leading zeros with an asterisk;
Y specifies replacement of zeros with a blank.

5.2.4 Drifting Editing Symbols

$$\left.\begin{matrix} S \\ + \\ - \end{matrix}\right\}$$ specify sign characters;

$ specifies the currency symbol.

5.2.5 Editing Characters

B specifies a blank position in the indicated data position;
A specifies alphabetic data;
X specifies that the indicated data position may contain any character;
F specifies a scale factor.

5.2.6 Conditional Editing Characters

$$\left.\begin{matrix} , \\ / \\ . \end{matrix}\right\}$$ specify insertion when an unsuppressed digit appears to the left of the field position;

T specifies a sign digit overpunch;
I specifies a condition + overpunch;
R specifies a conditional-overpunch;

$$\left.\begin{matrix} CR \\ DB \end{matrix}\right\}$$ specify credit/debit insertion to the right of the data field.

5.2.7 Sterling Editing Characters

PL/I additionally permits sterling editing characters for which the reader is referred to the given reference.

5.3 Interrupt Conditions

During the execution of a program, conditions may arise which result in a program interrupt. An interrupt condition causes normal execution to be suspended and special processing to be initiated. After the special processing has been completed, normal program execution may or may not be resumed.

PL/I contains two features which facilitate the resolution of interrupt conditions: the ON statement and the SIGNAL statement.

The ON statement (see section 3.2) specifies the action to be taken when an interrupt occurs for the condition named. The following conditions may be monitored:

1. Computational conditions,
2. Input/output conditions,
3. Program-checkout conditions,
4. List processing conditions,
5. Programmer-named conditions,
6. System action conditions.

The SIGNAL statement enables interrupt conditions to be simulated; thus, program flow under abnormal conditions may be tested.

5.4   Abbreviations

The following abbreviations for keywords are defined:

Keyword	Abbreviation
ABNORMAL	ABNL
ACTIVATE	ACT
AUTOMATIC	AUTO
BINARY	BIN
CHARACTER	CHAR
COMPLEX	CPLX
CONTROLLED	CTL
CONVERSION	CONV
DEACTIVATE	DEACT
DECIMAL	DEC
DECLARE	DCL
DEFINED	DEF
ENVIRONMENT	ENV
EXTERNAL	EXT
FIXEDOVERFLOW	FOFL
INITIAL	INIT
INTERNAL	INT
IRREDUCIBLE	IRRED
OVERFLOW	OFL
PICTURE	PIC
POINTER	PTR
POSITION	POS
PRECISION	PREC
PROCEDURE	PROC
REDUCIBLE	RED
SUBSCRIPTRANGE	SUBRG
UNDERFLOW	UFL
UNDEFINEDFILE	UNDF
VARYING	VAR
ZERODIVIDE	ZDIV

5.5   Arithmetic and Type Conversion

1. *Complex to Real.* The result is the real part of the complex value.
2. *Real to Complex.* The result is a complex value that has the real value as the real part and zero as the imaginary part.
3. *Conversion to Integer.* The precision of the result is implementation defined.

4. *Bit String to Character String.* The bit 1 becomes the character '1'; the bit 0 becomes the character '0'.
5. *Character String to Bit String.* The characters 1 and 0 become the bits 1 and 0; otherwise, the conversion is illegal.
6. *Character String to Arithmetic.* The character string must contain one of the following:
    1. [+ | −] *arithmetic-constant.*
    2. [+ | −] *real-constant* {+ | −} *imaginary-constant.*
    The arithmetic value has the attributes REAL FIXED DECIMAL of default precision.
7. *Bit String to Arithmetic.* The bit string is interpreted as an unsigned binary integer and converted to a real fixed binary value of default precision.
8. *Arithmetic to Character String.* The number is converted to a character string according to the rules of list-directed output (see reference).
9. *Arithmetic to Bit String.* The value is converted to real, then a fixed value, and then a bit string of precision p, where p is the precision of the original value.

5.6 Asynchronous Operations

PL/I contains language facilities for executing parts of a program asychronously and for the testing of status indications. An asychronous task is created with a CALL statement that possesses appropriate attributes. Status may then be tested with the WAIT statement and the EVENT pseudo-variable (see reference).

5.7 Compile-Time Facilities

PL/I contains a compile-time macro facility for performing text editing of program elements. This topic is discussed in chapter 7.

5.8 List Processing

PL/I contains a list processing capability through use of pointer variables and through controlled and based storage. This topic is discussed in chapter 6.

6. REFERENCE

PL/I Language Specifications, IBM Systems Reference Library, Form C28-6571, IBM Corporation, Department D39, 1271 Avenue of the Americas, New York, N.Y., 10020.

INDEX

types of, 193, 194
  utility, 190
Time slicing, 196
T-junction, 56, 57, 58
Token, 33
Translator, *see* Metaprogram
Tree method, 27
Triples, 52, 53

Unhooking, 186
University of Massachusetts, 62
User
  considerations, 169
  functions, 170
  services, 173

Variable
  based, 101

global, 120
head, 89
local, 120
pointer, 100
scope of, 120
tail, 89
Virtual memory and paging, 197–201
  dynamic address translation, 198
  logical page, 197
  page, 197
  page table, 198
  page-turning routine, 199
  real address, 198
  virtual storage address, 198

Wait state, 184
Weakly separating, 51
Well-formed formulas, 69